THE DEVIL IN FRANCE
My Encounter with Him in the Summer of 1940

D1459724

THE DEVIL IN FRANCE
My Encounter with Him in the Summer of 1940

Lion Feuchtwanger

USC LIBRARIES   UNIVERSITY OF SOUTHERN CALIFORNIA

USC LIBRARIES

Published by Figueroa Press
840 Childs Way, 3rd Floor
University of Southern California
Los Angeles, CA 90089-2540

Every reasonable attempt has been made to identify owners of copyright. All historic photographs
are from the collections of USC's Feuchtwanger Memorial Library. Cover illustrations appear
courtesy of USC School of Architecture students Marcos Carrillo, Alex Hagentorn, Lillian Lin,
Nicholas Tedesco, and Kevin Yan.

ISBN-10: 1-932800-66-2
ISBN-13: 978-1-932800-66-1
Library of Congress Control Number: 2010925617

Library of Congress Cataloging-in-Publication Data

Feuchtwanger, Lion.
    The devil in France: my encounter with him in the summer of 1940 / Lion Feuchtwanger.
Translated from the German by Elisabeth Abbott. Edited by Bill Dotson, Marje Schuetze-Coburn,
and Michaela Ullmann.
        p.   cm.
    Includes The escape / Marta Feuchtwanger. Translated from the German by Adrian
Feuchtwanger.
    1. Feuchtwanger, Lion, 1884-1958. 2. World War, 1939-1945—Prisoners and prisons, French.
3. World War, 1939-1945—Personal narratives, German. I. Feuchtwanger, Marta—The escape.
II. Feuchtwanger, Adrian, tr. III. Abbott, Elisabeth, tr.

The first English language edition of *The Devil in France*—which did not include Marta
Feuchtwanger's "The Escape"—was published by the Viking Press, New York, in 1941. Mexico's
El Libro Libre published the first German edition under the title *Unholdes Frankreich* in 1942.

Book and map design by Howard P. Smith

Contents

FOREWORD

CATHERINE QUINLAN

When the USC Libraries published *Against the Eternal Yesterday* in 2009, we took an important step in our commitment to preserving and carrying forward the story and stories of Lion Feuchtwanger. Published in partnership with the International Feuchtwanger Society, that collection of essays explored the cultural, historical, and academic context of Feuchtwanger's work and supported the active community of inquiry that thrives around his legacy.

We are now proud to present a new edition of Feuchtwanger's memoir, *The Devil in France: My Encounter with Him in the Summer of 1940*. This is the first updated, English-language edition since Viking Press issued the original in 1941. We invite the USC community, Feuchtwanger scholars around the world, and new generations of readers to rediscover or explore for the first time this exceptionally personal story set against global upheaval and impending atrocity.

When Feuchtwanger writes in *The Devil in France* that his interest in history lures him "into thinking out loud of how a writer of the year 2000 will...express what a journalist of the year 1940 is saying now," he is expressing curiosity about how we tell and retell stories. He is asking how the evolution of language complicates the documentation of human experience and the comprehension of history. He is wondering—as he does once more when invoking the words of German philosopher Theodor Lessing—how writers in the next century will "give meaning to the meaningless" through acts of creativity.

Great libraries like ours share Feuchtwanger's concern for the continuity of knowledge, and reissuing *The Devil in France* is one of the many ways we are acting on that concern. With this new edition, we are helping readers of 2010 understand what compelled a writer of historical fiction to tell a true story—that of his internment at Les

Milles in 1940. We are protecting a unique articulation of a personal history. We are preserving a valuable intellectual resource that will inform research yet to be conducted and inspire stories yet to be told.

As home to the Feuchtwanger Memorial Library, we have been able to supplement this edition of *The Devil in France* by drawing upon our extensive collections relating to Feuchtwanger and the study of German exiles. We have created a detailed timeline and map to provide more biographical and geographical perspective; we have included as a postscript Marta Feuchtwanger's account of the couple's escape from Europe; and we have consulted the German-language manuscript to refine the original, 1941 English translation.

I am grateful to our partners at Villa Aurora and USC Visions and Voices, with whom we are collaborating to build a series of events around this memoir. Much as we have sought to enrich explorations of this narrative by adding context, our events will encourage members of our community to discover Feuchtwanger's story through diverse and challenging experiences.

Programming such as performances, readings, and inventive online experiences have the potential to inspire meaningful engagement with many aspects of the USC Libraries' collections, and so this publication and related events also serve as a pilot project for introducing a one campus, one book program to USC. Beginning this fall with *The Devil in France*, we will hold annual events that support the perseverance of vital stories like those of Lion Feuchtwanger, and that demonstrate the essential role of libraries in preserving individual voices amid the tumult of history.

Catherine Quinlan
Dean of the USC Libraries

INTRODUCTION

MARJE SCHUETZE-COBURN

Lion Feuchtwanger's memoir *The Devil in France: My Encounter with Him in the Summer of 1940* is unique among the author's extensive writings. With this work, Feuchtwanger shares his personal thoughts and feelings, blending his observations with the chronology of events during his time behind barbed wire. At the time of its publication, Feuchtwanger's fans knew and loved him for his historical fiction—his long, dense novels filled with rich descriptions and details from the past. This work, a dramatic departure written in the first person with Feuchtwanger as the protagonist, recounts the true story of his internment and close escape from capture by Nazi forces.

Lion Feuchtwanger (1884-1958) was an early and outspoken critic of the National Socialist Party. In his novel *Success*, published in 1930, Feuchtwanger exposed Nazi barbarism to the world. His fictional depictions—along with anti-Hitler statements published in European newspapers—secured Feuchtwanger's place among the prominent intellectuals whose German citizenship was revoked in 1933.

As soon as Adolf Hitler was appointed chancellor in early 1933, Feuchtwanger and his wife, Marta, had no choice but to live in exile: first in southern France and later in Pacific Palisades, California. Feuchtwanger's seven years in France were surprisingly productive, and the author developed a false sense of security living in the remote fishing village of Sanary-sur-Mer.

His memoir chronicles Feuchtwanger's experiences during a three-month internment by the French after Germany's invasion of France in May of 1940. Feuchtwanger recounts how he was torn from his beloved home in Sanary, with its view of the Mediterranean and ready supply of books. He had felt completely at ease there, describing how it filled him with a "deep sense of harmony, communion, happiness."

On May 21, 1940, at 5:01 in the afternoon, Feuchtwanger entered the internment camp at Les Milles. From that point onward, he lost his freedom, and his identity became synonymous with his number, 187. In *The Devil in France*, Feuchtwanger depicts the terror and uncertainty he and hundreds of men faced during their captivity by the French. They feared being handed over at any moment to the Nazis, which would have meant certain death in the concentration camps.

Feuchtwanger acknowledged that he like everyone else had no real understanding of what caused the war. Instead of outlining the reasons, he set out to describe what happened to him as sincerely, as personally, and as subjectively as possible with "no pretence of detachment."

Although Feuchtwanger's account of his agonizing internment details the poor conditions, lack of hygiene, and apathy of the French officials, his descriptions lack bitterness, and he remains a rational observer. Feuchtwanger notes the absurd paradox in which he found himself—a well-known anti-Fascist whom the Nazis called their "Enemy Number One"—being held captive by the French because of their fear of Germans and their possible connections to the National Socialists. This meant that Feuchtwanger, along with hundreds of anti-Fascists, was interned alongside Nazi sympathizers and spies.

The physical world of the camp—the thousands of bricks surrounding the internees, the dust from the bricks, harsh sunlight in the day, darkness at night, and lack of space—oppressed and exhausted Feuchtwanger with its relentlessness and constancy.

He observed that while the dust and dirt of the camp made everyone look more and more alike at first glance, each man wore his individual personality as though it was stamped on him. Each person's essential character shone through the grit and grime with every action or word.

During nearly ninety days of internment, Feuchtwanger had time on his hands to observe and contemplate humanity in all its forms. As a respected public figure, he became a magnet for other inmates, who brought him their questions, problems, and fears. He explained that early in life he learned from wise teachers about the art of listening.

Feuchtwanger described himself as a man of contemplation rather than action. He explained that, while he considered himself fearful of physical danger, his fellow internees considered him courageous, since he withstood the hardships and uncertainties with stoicism. Feuchtwanger countered that his moral courage provided his internal strength. He always spoke his mind, even when this put him at risk. His continued public critique of the National Socialists attested to his drive to express his views about the world regardless of the implications of his words.

Feuchtwanger vividly depicted the mental games he played to avoid being consumed by fear and worries. As a writer and scholar, he drew upon his knowledge of languages, poems, and memories of past events to distract himself from the reality of his situation. Feuchtwanger defined memory as the "most singular function of the human spirit." Memory became paramount during this time when Feuchtwanger lacked his books and friends to confirm his recollections.

The devil that Feuchtwanger blamed for his incarceration—the one responsible for the sloppy indifference of the French officials—was not motivated by maliciousness but rather by thoughtlessness. Feuchtwanger explained that the French themselves had a phrase for this type of lackadaisical behavior—*je-m'en-foutisme*—that found expression through a lack of care or attention. While the results were disastrous for many of those interned, the motivation was not to harm or punish. While this may seem a minor distinction, the observation helped Feuchtwanger cope with the dire circumstances and remain optimistic about the outcome of his detention.

Throughout the book, Feuchtwanger discusses his beliefs regarding fate and chance. He observes that we have a fundamental urge to explain why things happen to us by looking for causes one at a time, since we are often unable to comprehend complex networks of causes and effects. Although Feuchtwanger understands the foolishness of this endeavor, he, too, finds himself looking for "a secret law that determines the course of my life."

As a keen observer of life and humanity, Feuchtwanger provided an unusual blend of fact, observation, and insight about a terrifying period of twentieth-century history. Feuchtwanger's wit and optimism were his true strengths, helping him cope with the uncertainty and seeming hopelessness of his plight.

Marje Schuetze-Coburn
Feuchtwanger Librarian and Senior Associate Dean of the USC Libraries

THE DEVIL IN FRANCE

PART ONE

THE BRICKS OF LES MILLES

LION FEUCHTWANGER

And the Egyptians made the children of Israel to serve with rigour: and they made their lives bitter with hard bondage, in mortar, and in brick. And the children of Israel built for Pharaoh treasure cities, Pithom and Raamses.

I have no very clear picture of those treasure cities, and I do not know whether Biblical historians have unearthed any information as to conditions existing at Pithom and Raamses. What I do know is that for me those two exotic, hostile, richly melodious names have acquired a meaning—a meaning that no historical reconstruction, however well documented, will ever be able to change.

It came about in this way. At the outbreak of the present war, political exiles from Germany, Austria, and Czechoslovakia, who were living in southeastern France, were ordered by the French authorities to report for internment at Les Milles, a town near Aix-en-Provence. The internment camp was a huge brickyard that had long been out of use. There were more than a thousand of us, but the number varied: sometimes we were as many as three thousand. Most of us were Jews.

In that brickyard a brick building was our shelter, and bricks were otherwise to become the distinguishing feature of those days in our lives. Brick walls, reinforced with barbed wire, shut off our enclosures from the beautiful green fields beyond. Broken bricks were heaped in piles on every hand. We used them as seats to sit on, as tables for our meals, as partitions to separate our straw piles, one from another. Brick dust filled our lungs and got into our eyes. Brick racks made of laths lined the walls of our building and took away even more of the meagre space and the meagre light. We were often cold, and at such times many of us would have liked to crawl into one of the great kilns, now empty, that had once been used for baking the bricks, in order to enjoy a little of the warmth that the word "kiln" suggested.

Work was given us. We were obliged to move the bricks about, piling them up now here, now there. We trundled them around in wheelbarrows and then, at the command of a sergeant, tossed them from hand to hand and stacked them up in neat rows. The work was not really hard. What irritated and angered us was its utter fatuousness. There was no reasonable purpose behind the order—the authorities intended simply to keep us busy. We knew that the next day or the day after or at the latest on the third day we would be directed to tear down the beautifully ordered pile of bricks and build it up again somewhere else.

Then, all of a sudden, one day while the bricks were flying from hand to hand under the sharp commands of a sergeant, while we professors, lawyers, physicians, agronomists, artisans, instead of busying ourselves with books, legal papers, diagnoses, weather forecasts, machine parts, were making piles of bricks that we would be ordered to unpile the day following, that verse from Exodus came into my mind, the verse in which the children of Israel are forced to bake bricks for Pharaoh of Egypt to build the treasure cities of Pithom and Raamses. My mind ran on into all sorts of disconnected and even incongruous reflections. Our forefathers doubtless had been worse off than we: they had been obliged to labour under the whip of a slave-driver. But no—in another respect they were better off than we: their labour at least had a purpose. Then, too, I mused, the slave who was forced to help build one of those treasure cities for Pharaoh was, in all probability, more or less indifferent as to whether he was performing a useful task or a useless one. After a time I gave the question up. But, mechanically, as I caught my brick and tossed it to my neighbour, the words rang in my head: Pithom—Raamses— Pithom—Raamses.

So, from that day, the verse from Exodus has had for me its definite colouring, its definite undertones. It will always be associated in my mind with the thought of brick dust, blistering sunshine, barbed wire; with the thought of a bored sergeant in a red fez, rhythmically counting in a gruff voice: "Un, deux, un, deux;" with the thought of men in shabby, tattered clothes and with listless, dust-streaked faces, men who were there tossing bricks to one another, but who not so long before had been well-dressed gentlemen working at significant occupations.

Pithom—Raamses—Pithom—Raamses.

As I look out of the window of my hotel in New York over Central Park, with its lines of skyscrapers to right and left, as I look out over this great, throbbing city bustling with the pursuits of peace, I ask myself again and again: Can this be real? Am I really here? And, if so, how?

Nine years ago I was sitting in my house in the Grunewald in Berlin. I had my books around me. From my garden a peaceful little pine-grove sloped gently down to a peaceful little pond. I was content. I had not the remotest idea of ever moving from that house. Six years ago I was sitting in my tranquil, white-stuccoed house in Sanary, in the South of France. I had my books around me. Olive-groves sloped down to a deep, azure sea. I was content. I had not the remotest idea of ever moving from that house.

I could, of course, marshal a hundred sound reasons to show why, from the beginning of the First World War down to now, things had to happen exactly as they have happened; and also why I, too, a victim of that course of events, had to suffer exactly what I have suffered. I could produce a hundred plausible explanations to account for my internment at the beginning of the First World War in a French prison in Tunis; to show why, later on, I was thrust into a German uniform; why I was sucked into the vortices first of the short-lived German revolution, then of the long-lived German counter-revolution; why thenceforward I made up my mind to look at the world as a mere spectator from my study desk in Berlin; why, in spite of that resolve, I was driven into exile in France; and why, finally, I had to spend the earlier portion of the Second World War in an internment camp in France. Of course! There are as many rationally adequate explanations as one may wish for the particular course of my own trifling experiences no less than for the issues of greater moment on which they depended. Ingenious minds stand ready to enumerate those reasons—economic reasons, biological, sociological, psychological reasons, reasons deriving from one or another of the philosophies of the universe. I myself, for that matter, could write a book on the subject, sharpening my wits to find logical concatenations.

Deep down in my heart, however, I know that I have not the slightest understanding of the causes of the barbaric turmoil in which all of us are writhing. I am like a savage from the jungle who suddenly comes upon a line of telephone wires and has no idea at all of why it has been set up, what it is for, or how it works. I know, furthermore, that no one in the world, not even the best-informed statesman, can comprehend the whys, the hows, and the wherefores of this present war. Some day, one may guess, "all the documents" will be available. But what of that? At the most we shall know only a little more about the immediate causes and consequences of this or that particular fact. The judgment we pass on the course of events as a whole will still be a matter solely of the interpreter's temperament and throw light only on him. Thousands of expert historians offer ingenious and persuasive reasons to show why the Roman Empire perished, why Christianity replaced the pagan world, why the French Revolution occurred, and why it all had to happen just so and not in some other way. But the reasons differ in every case. "History is the art of giving meaning to the meaningless," said a brilliant German professor (who was later killed by the Nazis).

When, therefore, I set out to tell in the following pages what befell me in France during the present war at the turn of my fifty-sixth into my fifty-seventh year, I shall not try to force upon the reader any interpretation of the ultimate reasons why this particular man, the writer, Lion F., became involved in that particular situation. The reader may call those reasons what he will—accident, fate, Divine Providence. I shall not importune him with any opinion of my own as to why I, at bottom a contemplative soul asking nothing better than to live in peace and to be able to read and to write, have been condemned to lead such a stormy existence so fraught with upheavals. I shall confine myself to describing just what I have been through, as sincerely as possible; in other words, as personally, as subjectively, as possible—I make no pretence of detachment.

It all began one evening toward the middle of May, just after sundown. Dusk was gathering in the little room on the ground floor of my house in Sanary where I kept my radio, but it was still not so dark that I had to turn on the light.

I was alone, listening to the news reports. Things did not look good, either in Belgium or in the Netherlands. Lying on the sofa, with my eyes closed, I was pondering the scanty items, lending half an ear to the public notices that succeeded the news proper. Suddenly the following came: "All German nationals residing in the precincts of Paris, men and women alike, and all persons between the ages of seventeen and fifty-five who were born in Germany but are without German citizenship, are to report for internment." Dates and names of places followed.

I did not stir. I simply lay there. To myself I said: "No panic, now! Let's think things over quietly. Very probably the regulation will apply only to Paris. It will certainly not be applied to the South of France. That part of the country is not threatened by the war." But an inner voice told me that these purely rational considerations were utter nonsense. From the first day of the war it was one's worst fears that had come true, not the good things one hoped for.

The radio went on to other matters. I lay there on the sofa, with my eyes still closed. Finally I got up and noticed, to my surprise, that night had fallen. All of a sudden a great fatigue came over me. I stepped out into the garden. I strolled about among our flower-beds, climbed our little terraces, came down again, my dazed thoughts drifting from one thing to another.

It was simply infamous. There I had been for three-quarters of a year caught in that mousetrap of a France, unable to get permission to leave the country. Now, for a second time, I was to taste the pleasures of an internment camp.

The landscape around my house was beautiful, filled with a deep peace. Mountains, sea, islands, a magnificent stretch of coast, olive-groves, fig-orchards, pines, a few scattered houses! A great silence reigned. A light breeze was blowing. One of our cats was capering playfully around me. She would run ahead, dash back to turn, and run ahead again, mewing insistently. I bent over and stroked her back. She purred. It was not a warm night, yet one could not call it cold. All the same I felt a sudden chill.

I hurried back indoors and looked for my wife. The large house was empty. But then, I reflected, the married couple that worked for us probably had the night off. I went on into the kitchen and there, in fact, my wife was preparing supper for the cats. She nodded without looking up.

"Something more to drink?" she asked. "There's grapefruit juice."

"Thanks," I answered. "Later on, perhaps."

She followed with some remark of no great moment, the fact that Léontine, our maid, was always putting too little rice and too little milk with the cat's meat, or something to that effect. I sat down on a kitchen chair, gazed at her as she moved about, and wondered: "Shall I tell her at once? People in the village will have heard too. If I don't, Léontine will. I had better tell her myself."

She poured the food into a large plate and set it down on the floor. The cats made for it and began eating greedily, pleased, purring. We watched them.

"So," I mused, "her great worry now is whether the cats should not be getting more rice and more milk. Well, I'll leave her with it for this one minute more...and then this one...and then this last."

I told her.

She looked at me, and I at her. Finally she said: "We must write to Paris at once, or better wire."

"Of course," I said, "the first thing in the morning. At least," I added, "the frosts are over."

French internment camps were not heated, and in winter it had happened on occasion that an internee would lose a finger or a toe from freezing.

We had had our supper, but I was suddenly conscious of a great hunger.

"Please," I begged, "something to eat."

I was eating when a knock came first at the one door, then at the other. Most unusual! At that hour we rarely had callers save by appointment.

"Who is there?" we called.

It proved to be neighbours of ours, a German artist and his wife. We had seldom seen each other, having had nothing particular in common. Now we found it quite natural that they should have come.

"Have you heard?" the artist asked.

We discussed the order from various angles. There could be no conceivable reason from the military point of view for interning those of us who lived there in the South. We had been investigated time and again. The government had made certain that we were enemies of the Nazi regime. But had even the Germans in Paris been interned because they were considered dangerous? More probably the government was proceeding against them simply to give the French public the impression that something was going on. If this were the reason, how could Germans in the South expect any different treatment? We could find but one point of comfort, and it was a small one indeed: given the slipshod methods of French officialdom, it would take a long time before the necessary papers reached the South.

How I spent the next few days I do not really know. I kept a diary during those weeks in France, but my notes are not at present with me, and I cannot say whether I shall ever recover them. Without them I am wholly dependent upon my memory—an advantage, perhaps.

Memory, of course, is a tricky thing. My mind, like the minds of most people, oftentimes refuses to retain things I should dearly like to remember, remembering of its own accord things to which I am altogether indifferent, thrusting important matters into the background and unimportant ones to the fore. My memory follows rules that my conscious being cannot explain, though they may have something to do with my subconscious being.

On the whole, I consider this wilfulness on the part of memory a benefit to a writer. It holds him to that uncompromising sincerity which is the prerequisite of all literary composition. It prompts him to keep to sensations which are really his own. In this particular case, the loss of my diary, the lack of factual notes, obliges me to stick to only those matters which touched me spiritually. As a result, from the strictly external point of view, many essentials may be lacking, but from the personal, the subjective viewpoint, my narrative will be sincere, artistically true, not cramped by documents, by the minutiae of reality. Whether I like it or not, the loss of my notes will oblige me to give a picture, not a bald photographic record.

Is it presumptuous of me to confess that I am glad of this? Is it presumptuous of me to believe, as a matter of principle, that a photographic, factual account of an experience contributes very little to an understanding of its essential character? It is nevertheless my considered opinion that an experience often changes in physiognomy according to the capacity a person has for experiencing. Yes, I am unalterably convinced that the translation of an experience into words depends more upon the temperament of the man who has lived through it than upon its actual content.

Fewer people are capable of experiencing things than is commonly supposed. The average person is too much under the influence of the evaluations that are commonly made by the people about him. He feels called upon to consider certain things significant or important, other things trifling or unimportant, because "competent judges" have applied those measures to similar cases. The emotions, quite as much as the conduct of the majority of people, are prescribed now by convention, now by fashion. The plain man can catalogue his experiences only with reference to a few familiar norms, norms that are hammered deeper and deeper into his brain by radio, film, and press, so that his own particular capacity for hearing, seeing, feeling, and evaluating becomes more and more restricted. The plain man's powers of experiencing are slight, the range of his sensations narrow. Occurrences in which he may be directly involved leave him untouched, make no impression upon him, fail to enrich him in any way. Whatever quantity of a liquid one may try to pour into a small pitcher, the pitcher can hold only so much.

A man of imagination has an advantage over other people, in that an actual experience is almost always less intense than his expectations of it. An actual misfortune is almost always less painful to him than his fear of it, just as, of course, his actual experience of joys is almost always less stirring than his hopes and anticipations of them.

How I spent the last days in my beautiful house in Sanary I cannot, as I have already said, describe in detail. But this I know: they were not pleasant days. Everything that I saw, heard, said, thought, or felt during those days was framed in uneasiness.

During the seven years of my stay on the shores of the French Mediterranean I drank in with all my senses the beauty of its landscape, the gaiety of its manner of living. Whenever I returned from Paris on a night train I would catch sight in the morning of the azure coast, the mountains, the sea, the pines, and the olive trees climbing the hillsides, and as I would sense again about me the expansive geniality of my Mediterranean neighbours, I would draw a deep breath and thank my stars that I had chosen that sky to live under. Then on the drive from the station, I would climb the little hill to my white, sunlit house, traverse my garden, which lay in its deep peace, enter my spacious, well-lighted study, look out through the windows at the sea, at the coast with its whimsical indentations, at the islands, at the endless distances beyond, and, with my beloved books about me, I would cry inwardly, with all the intensity of my being: "This is where I belong! This is my world!" Or again, after a good day's work I would relax in the evening quiet of my garden, a silence broken only by the wash of the sea or by the gentle call of some bird, and my soul would be filled with a deep sense of harmony, communion, happiness.

But the moment I was obliged to consider the possibility of being interned a second time, the landscape lost its colour for me, my whole life its relish. There was nothing definite, to be sure, but I knew in my heart that it was all settled, and the painful expectation of what was to come ruined my capacity for enjoying what was still to be enjoyed. I went on with my work, of course. Decades of arduous training had taught me how to concentrate on the work I had in hand whatever might be happening. When I am working on a book not only the hours at my desk but my whole life is engrossed by it. Everything I see, hear, read, or experience I automatically apply to it. Now, however, the moment I left my desk my book passed completely from my mind, to be replaced by anxiety as to what was in store.

I often used to watch my cats eat. They chewed and swallowed greedily, but they were always on the alert, never free of an inherited, an instinctive feeling that dangers lurked all about them. Deep down in all of us no doubt lies a similar sense of constant menace; only we humans have learned how to banish it from our minds, and so have grown unaccustomed to fear. During those days of waiting, I felt the way my cats felt. If a car drove up the little hill, if a caller knocked at the door, my thought would be: "Now they are coming! Now they are coming for me!"

My secretary could not help lamenting: "Oh, why didn't we go to America while there was still time!"

Ordinarily I detest such remarks, whimperings about what one should or should not have done. They lead to nothing. All the same, as I had to admit, in our particular situation outbursts of that sort had a certain justification.

Of course, it had not been in my power to leave the country after the outbreak of the war. The French government had not permitted me to do so. But far in advance I had seen the war coming. In February 1938, shortly after the annexation of Austria, I had thought seriously of emigrating to a country that offered greater security than France. My secretary was now quite right in bemoaning the fact that I had not carried out that intention.

But what, really, had kept me in France? Well, in the first place, this: back in 1933 I had publicly declared: "Hitler means war. Without war we shall never be rid of the Nazis." Now at last my war was in sight, and I had my share in it if anyone did. Could I then, with any decency, simply take to my heels, make for some safe spot? No, I had to stay. I thought seriously that I might help. After all, I had had a million readers in Germany. Many people there still listened to what I had to say; many, in spite of the danger, were still getting messages out of Germany to me and wanted advice. I thought that it was more especially in time of war that I could be of use to Hitler's enemies.

Then again I had been held by a writer's curiosity. All my life long I had made it a principle, not exactly to seek adventures, but at least not to avoid them. There had been still a third consideration: I was loath to interrupt work on my novel *Paris Gazette* by an inconvenient change of residence.

At the very beginning of the war, to be sure, I came to know what a grave mistake I had made. The French not only refused any co-operation from us German anti-Fascists, they locked us up. Protests in England got me out of the internment camp after a few days, with apologies from the French government, explaining that my detention had been due to a misapprehension among subordinates. All the same, the exit visa which I had asked for after that unfortunate experience was withheld from me.

At this point I must interpolate a confession or, rather, two confessions.

First confession: As I think back today to what kept me in France in the year 1938, I find that there were probably reasons different from those I have just given, reasons more personal, more deeply rooted in my character. What held me was the pervasive comfort of living in Sanary, the beauty of the place, my well-furnished house, my beloved library, the familiar frame of my work that suited me and my methods down to the last detail, the hundred little nothings of our life there that had become dear habits which would have been painful to give up. As, I believe, I have said already, I am always being torn against my will from environments which I have thoughtfully, lovingly moulded to my tastes and my needs. Again and again I have surrounded myself with things that I enjoyed owning; again and again I have set up a very ample writing table at a place from which I could look out over a beautiful landscape; again and again I have ranged a few thousand books about me; again and again I have reared a number of cats and each time thought they were devoted to me for my own sake; again and again I have bought a number of turtles and watched their slow, antediluvian movements; again and again I have put by a few bottles of choice wine in an air-conditioned room. And however often circumstances over which I had no control compelled me to forsake abodes that I had furnished with so much solicitude, I never learned my lesson. I would always begin building over again, then cling spiritually and literally to what I had built, confident that this time I must surely be able to keep it. Beyond any doubt it was also my love for my house in Sanary and for everything in and around it that kept me in France. In other words, without too many evasions, what held me was my fundamental laziness, my attachment to my comforts, my lack of imagination.

Second confession: I am very shy of public officials. The clerk in a public bureau is an agent of the State: he represents millions of people. How am I, a lone individual, to cope with him? This shyness of mine may be an inheritance from the days when my forefathers trembled before German officials in German ghettoes.

Reasons of this sort undoubtedly played their part in preventing me from securing a passport for immigration into the United States at the proper time. I rested content with a visitor's permit. The procuring of an immigrant's visa I pictured to myself as an exceedingly difficult matter. One day, in Paris, however, I plucked up courage and actually made a start. Finding myself in the neighbourhood of the American Embassy, I strode boldly in with the idea of getting information as to the required procedure for obtaining the visa in question. I had in my possession letters of introduction to the American consul, and on occasions I had also met the American ambassador socially. Nevertheless, a mixture of pride and shyness kept me from approaching either of those gentlemen directly. I turned in preference to a nameless table where I saw the sign "Information." An indifferent young woman, speaking in an indifferent tone of voice, gave me a few hasty instructions from which I gathered that if I applied for an immigrant's visa, my visitor's permit would automatically lapse. In truth, such information was the very thing I wanted. I felt myself excused from taking any further annoying steps. I accepted the words of that indifferent young woman as a sign from fate that I should be satisfied with a visit to America and not try to make my permanent home there.

So, after all, I am prone to call myself a believer in fate, but that, I fear, is merely a way of cloaking my love of ease becomingly.

No, my fatalism is yet not as primitive as that. It is rather the logical outcome of unfortunate experiences with the consistent application of intelligence. I have too often seen in myself and in others how the best-calculated devices not seldom have results directly opposite to those desired. My wife and my secretary, for instance, had insisted on our taking precautions in the matter of safeguarding our money. Through curious twists of chance the measures they proposed could not have proved more disastrous. I kept depositing money in countries that seemed safest from war—Sweden, Holland, Canada. Those were the very countries where my funds were either confiscated or frozen. My friend Brecht chose Sweden as a safe place to live. At the outbreak of the war, events seemed to indicate that he had made a very shrewd guess. But as things turned out the "safe Sweden" proved to be a trap for him. My German-born secretary seemed lucky in obtaining her Swiss citizenship. The only result was that the French continued to regard her as a German and shut her up in an internment camp, while the Americans considered her safety sufficiently assured by her Swiss passport to refuse her an emergency visa.

In view of such experiences I can hardly blame myself for letting my bark drift once in a while without trying very hard to steer it. I am not very much impressed when people say to me: "You see, I always told you you should do this or that. Why didn't you do it?" I know that in times like the present there are exactly as many reasons for doing a thing as there are for not doing it, and "all omitting and committing" has become a mere game of chance. So I only shrugged my shoulders when my secretary wailed: "Oh, why didn't we go to America while there was still time!" I had no regrets. Nor did I have any when at last it became certain that I had to return to the internment camp.

The person to bring me the confirmation was our maid Léontine. She entered the room, excited, important. The notice, she said, was now posted at the town hall. More than that, I was to appear at the camp at Les Milles again. The notice, she went on, specified all persons of German birth but without German citizenship who had not reached the age of fifty-six on the first of January.

I have been called upon to listen to a good many pieces of bad news in recent years and have developed a certain technique on such occasions, a way of switching off my emotional engine, so to say, and thinking coldly and calmly. The news was no great shock to me. I had been expecting it. I began wondering whether, as I was going to be fifty-six in a short time, there might not be a way of escaping the order. I am quite certain that, even as Léontine talked, I was counting up the days still lacking until I should be fifty-six. It must then have been the eighteenth or nineteenth of May. I would be fifty-six on July 7. I am quite certain also that I took mental note of the mixed emotions that were apparent in Léontine's manner, in her facial expression, in her choice of words, in the tone of her voice, in the movements of her body. Léontine was a plumpish, pretty girl approaching her thirties. Like her husband, she had worked for us for six years. I am certain they were both devoted to us and probably still are. Léontine's face expressed honest regret, but at the same time a certain delight at being the one to bring us the news, then curiosity as to how I would receive it, anxiety as to what might become of her if my wife and I were sent to camp, and, finally, in spite of all her loyalty, just a suggestion of malicious satisfaction that now I too, her employer, her "master," would be getting my taste of the war's bitterness—and even a worse one than she.

I had forty-eight hours left for my preparations. One could take sixty pounds of luggage. Judging by the experience of my first internment, I knew that the first essential was that my things be easy to carry—one had to look forward to carrying them oneself and sometimes over long distances, marching in line. That is what had happened to me the first time. Lively debates began as to what I had best take with me. The most important item was blankets for nighttime, and hardly less important was a little folding-chair, for the camp provided no seating conveniences. As to suits and underclothing it was best to take the toughest and roughest one possessed, for clothing went to pieces in no time. Books? Size and weight were more important than subject matter. Handy, thin-paper pocket editions were the most practical. I decided on a thin-paper Balzac that contained six novels in smallest compass.

The next day I was ordered by telephone to report at the town hall where a pass for my trip to the camp would be issued. We non-Frenchmen were forbidden to stir from our places of residence without special permits, and such papers were required even for the trip to the internment camp.

The clerk at the town hall was a man with whom I had had frequent dealings during my years at Sanary. He was obliging, not to say solicitous. At the same time, like most of the natives, he showed a certain embarrassment, a mixture of curiosity, genuine pity, and wariness about getting too deeply involved with people whom his government was putting under lock and key and who, thus, must be dubious characters. He applied himself industriously to drawing up the papers. Ordinarily two weeks were required to obtain a permit to go to the town eight miles away, say to see a dentist. This time the sergeant at the nearest police station reported promptly by telephone that he was ready to come over at once and take charge of the necessary scrivening.

Three other Germans from Sanary had also been ordered to appear. We waited in a room on the ground floor of the town hall, which commonly served as a temporary detention place for criminals until the police came to take them away. The veterinarian also used the room when he made his weekly call to treat the town's sick cats and dogs and other small fry. Now it was our turn to wait there—four of us who would start off on the morrow for Les Milles: my neighbour, the artist R.; his son, who had just turned seventeen and so also had to pay the penalty; myself, and finally the writer K., who had fought in Spain on the side of the Republic.

We stood about and waited. We had all thought things would be quite different when we first came to France. The words *Liberté, Egalité, Fraternité,* were painted in giant letters over the door of the building we were in. We had been celebrated on our arrival some years before. The newspapers had published editorials of cordial and appreciative welcome. Government officials had explained that it was an honour for France to receive us as her guests. The President of the Republic had given me an audience. Now they were locking us up! We accepted our fate with a sort of bitter indifference. The years that had passed had displayed vividly before our eyes the fickleness of human attitudes. We indulged in no complaining, but kept to essentials—the best way to reach Les Milles, how much money we should take with us, and the like.

At long last the police sergeant appeared. He had picked up a vagrant on the way. The vagrant was drunk. The sergeant himself was drunk. He had been promoted during just those days, an event which he simply had to celebrate, he said. The vagrant and the sergeant slapped each other on the back. The sergeant slapped us on the back. He had nothing whatever against us, he gave his word. The room reeked of hard liquor.

The blank forms were detailed and complicated, as are all official papers in France. The French apparently could not let us pass unless they knew the full names of our fathers and mothers. The drunken sergeant found the maze of questions quite beyond him. He had managed to understand from our certificates that two of us were father and son. But he wanted me, a man of fifty-six, to be the son of the artist R., a man of forty-eight. He could make neither head nor tail of our relationships. He could make neither head nor tail of anything. He was at his wit's end. Finally we called the Mayor's secretary to the rescue.

The next day we drove to the camp in a taxicab.

I have an exact remembrance of my unsentimental leave-taking from my wife. At the moment we were as busy as could be stowing the luggage in the old, ramshackle vehicle. My wife said she had to get more paper to make a better wrapper for something and ran into the house. Things of that sort took up our last moments.

We were halted by police at one point along our way and had to show our papers. In answer to the question as to the "purpose of the journey" the secretary and the drunken sergeant had written: "Government business." The police looked at us, looked at each other, divined what sort of government business it was, and exclaimed sorrowfully: "Aha!" Then they saluted with embarrassed sympathy and wished us good luck.

We reached Aix. We reached Les Milles. We drove straight through the village and then along the low walls of the brickyard that was to swallow us up, and finally stopped on the dusty country road in front of the high gate. Just inside the grating was a small guardhouse, with soldiers in uniform standing or lolling about. I paid the chauffeur and gave him an affectionate message for my wife.

The clock on the main building of the brickyard pointed to one minute past five. I noted the fact mentally. So, the first minute past five on May 21, 1940, was my last minute of freedom in France!

I picked up my luggage and started to carry it across the yard to the receiving office. I am not very apt at such things: I simply could not see how I was to carry the big valise, the little valise, the blankets, and the folding-chair, a distance of seventy-five to a hundred yards. I tucked the folding-chair under my left arm, the blankets under my right arm.

Then I reached down for the big valise with my left hand and for the little valise with my right hand. The blankets slipped. I set everything down and got the blankets in place again. Just when everything was in order, down came the folding-chair. Grave, dull, unmoved, the soldiers looked on.

"Let's get going," said the sergeant. "Allez hop!"

That was at two minutes past five, and I was desperately unhappy.

At three minutes past five I was very happy instead.

Coming toward me across the yard I saw two young men whose names I could not remember, but whose faces seemed familiar. They had been there at Les Milles with me the first time I was interned.

"Get back there!" the sentry shouted. "Get back there!" They were not intimidated, nor did the sentry seem to take the matter seriously.

"Hello. You really here again?" one of the boys said. "We would never have dreamt of such a thing!"

They fell upon my luggage and carried it to the receiving office.

There came another round of papers, whereupon our luggage was searched—with no pretence at thoroughness. The lieutenant in charge of the office was a manufacturer from Lyon, a well-groomed man with greying hair, habitually wearing a somewhat tired expression on his face. He greeted me courteously, invited me into his office, asked me what I thought of the political and military situations. He expressed regret that circumstances had forced the government to intern us again, and hoped that this time our detention would not be of long duration.

Returning to the receiving desk, I was asked how much money I had with me. I hesitated a second.

"Don't be afraid," said the sergeant. "Tell us the exact amount. We are a sort of bank here. We will give you back whatever you want at any time. In a camp like this there's always a good deal of stealing. Your money is safer with us than it would be on your person."

I did as he suggested—a mistake, as the event proved. Small sums were paid out to us on occasion, but only at long intervals, and after no end of petitioning and manoeuvring of all sorts.

With all that out of the way I was given a number, Number 187; and Number 187 I was to remain from then on.

Les Milles is an ugly little village, though the surrounding country has its quiet charm: hilly fields with blues and greens, placid little streams, old farmhouses, olive-groves, vineyards, some green grass (a thing rare in that region), and, visible in the distance, an aqueduct, lofty, bold. In the midst of that lovely country our brickyard lay, indescribably ugly.

The main building, wide, low-studded, was surrounded by bare white yards. A smaller building to one side served as office, guardroom, infirmary, kitchen, wagon-shed. The whole area was enclosed on two of its sides by a brick wall, on the other two, by an earthwork or terrace, all thoroughly fenced in with barbed wire and guarded by sentries. The internees were in the habit of hanging their wash on the barbed wire in the back yard. There it fluttered gaily in the wind while on the other side the guards idled up and down, bored. It was a strange sensation to gaze out from there upon the lovely, rolling, soft green fields, so near yet so far beyond our reach.

Looking into the main building from the yard through one of the great doors, one saw nothing but a huge black hole. Every time one entered one had to accustom one's eyes to the dark. Especially on the ground floor one was always stumbling over something. Dusky runways that led past the openings intended for the brick kilns made the approach to the straw piles on this floor particularly narrow. The whole place reminded one of a catacomb.

A crude flight of wooden steps, narrow, shaky, covered with dirt, led up to a second floor. There the room was more spacious, but because of the danger from air raids the windows were partly boarded up and the few panes left uncovered were painted a dark blue so that no ray of light might make its way to the outside. As a result this second floor was always in a semi-twilight, and such a thing as reading was out of the question. At night there were a few very feeble electric bulbs that served rather to emphasize the darkness than to relieve it.

The inside of the building seemed twice as dark as it actually was because the yards outside lay, for most of the day, under a dazzling sunlight. Brick dust was everywhere about the building. Thick layers trodden hard underfoot made the floor uneven to walk on; bricks that seemed to be crumbling to dust lay about in piles. Dust, dust everywhere!

We were obliged to spend a large part of our time on the inside of this building. There we slept, there we had our meals. We depended on those rooms whenever it rained or whenever, as happened frequently in that part of France, the wind was strong and turned the yards into one great dust cloud. Many of us would take refuge inside the building even on calm, bright days, for the yards lay under a glaring sun without a trace of shade, and the sun of Provence is unbearable for any length of time in summer. We therefore spent a great deal of our time in dust and darkness.

Space on the second floor was considerably reduced by racks made of laths that lined the walls and jutted out into the room. The racks themselves were too narrow to sleep in. We used them as places for storing our belongings, but always with the greatest prudence, for smaller objects fell between the laths and the compartments were too low to accommodate anything sizable.

Aside from these racks the room was completely bare. We were given a little straw for our bedding, and the rest was left to us. There were no chairs, no benches, no tables, nothing but piles of defective bricks. Out of these we tried to build seats and tables, but they would always fall apart.

This second floor was only a great yawning, empty hole, but I was pleased rather than not to be lodged there again; for that had been my "residence" during my first internment. I knew every board across the windows, every lath, every brick. Strange how soon a human being becomes attached to his surroundings. He seems to share something of himself with the inanimate objects about him so that they belong to him ever after and become, so to say, a part of his being. The dark, low-ceilinged room with its dust, its dirt, its straw, had no terrors for me. From my once having lived in it, I had formed ties with the things about me: this post that I kept knocking against was an enemy; that wide, bulging corner had become almost a friend. The young men who had come to my rescue at the gate helped me whenever they could. They hunted out the lightest spot in the room, the one best protected from draughts—a spot near the racks. There they made a straw bed and spread my blanket over it. They unpacked my bags and stored in one of the racks whatever they could cram into them. They gave me something to eat and I shared with them what I had brought in the way of food. True, we had nothing to drink. Water was scarce, and even the camp authorities considered the water of only one faucet drinkable, and that too was suspect.

One of the young men who had helped me, an Austrian, Karl N., appointed himself my valet. A slow-moving, sleepy sort of fellow, he was at the same time efficient, good-natured, helpful, and extraordinarily devoted to me. His one interest in life was sport. Big, lumbering, lethargic as he was, he fairly came to life when the talk turned on boxing, and more so on swimming. He was an excellent swimmer himself. He had

40

once received a serious injury in a boxing match and it seems that that must have altered his mental and temperamental processes. He expected me to pay him, of course, but money considerations alone could surely not account for his devotion and for the solicitous care he took of me.

By evening on that first day I was very tired and looked forward to stretching out on my straw and blanket. But the little difficulties that were to make up my life for the following months began just there. It is not altogether an easy matter to undress and get ready for the night when you have no chair, no bed, no table, no water, only a little straw, and are thrown in with numbers of other people in a dark room. You don't know where to put your things; the floor all around is horribly dirty and anything that touches it is at once soiled. What is one to do with one's watch, with one's eye-glasses? The best place obviously is in your shoes. But then where are you going to put your shoes? Karl did his best to help me, but I could hardly have called it comfortable. A man of fifty-six, who has been all his life accustomed to his own room and a clean bed, does not find it very easy to sleep on the floor on a pile of dirty straw. He simply cannot master the technique of the thing.

In the end the fatigue of the busy day won out over the little vexations, and when the rising signal sounded at half-past five in the morning, it woke me out of a deep sleep.

The next day a sort of roll-call was held for the first time, and we were divided into groups. There must have been about seven hundred of us in all.

The man in charge of the grouping was a sergeant, or perhaps even of higher rank—I can never tell the differences of military rank. Our guards wore red fezzes, but they were not Arabs. As they stood on the rampart-like terrace, in their colourful headgear, with their gleaming bayonets, before them the glaring white yard and behind the soft green of the Provençal countryside, they made a picturesque but hardly a soldierly appearance. They were not soldiers, in fact. They were peasants or else small rural artisans who had been thrust into uniforms. The sergeant who called the roll was a stately individual with a bushy moustache, a puffy face, and a powerful voice. But even he, for all his military trappings, was merely a good-natured citizen, not the least bellicose.

As a first step he divided us into three groups: Germans, Austrians, and ex-Foreign Legionnaires.

Absurdly enough, not even Central Europeans who had served in the Foreign Legion had been exempted from internment. Some of them had served France in arms for as long as twenty or thirty years. Many of them had been under fire for France, and several had lost arms or legs battling for French interests. Almost all had military decorations. There they were tramping grimly about, chests aglitter with ribbons and medals, empty sleeves flapping limply around stumps of arms, wooden legs clattering over the dirty floors of the main building and the ground of the courts outside. Tough customers, not a few of them—not the sort one would care to meet alone at night. Many had forgotten their German altogether and spoke nothing but French. Even the guards expressed their anger that France should be repaying such men for their services in such a way.

So there we were divided into Germans, Austrians, and Legionnaires. That meant that I had to be parted from my Karl and the other helpful Austrian. We were then directed to line up in squads of twenty men each. And this haphazard arrangement was to be decisive for the next weeks, indeed even for the next months. Thenceforward the individual's lot was to be the lot of his squad as regarded lodging, distribution of food, labour; in other words, as regarded his whole life by day and by night. The members of his squad were his bedfellows, his messmates. They were to witness all his bodily operations. He was dependent upon them in a hundred little matters of daily routine. Yes, we were to be permanently dependent upon one another, upon our neighbours, upon the members of our squad, and the chance of that first arrangement sowed the seeds of friendship and enmity for a long time to come.

The separation into squads finished, we were led back to the second floor. On our first day we had been able to choose where we would spread our straw; now each squad was assigned its own particular area. My squad did not get a very pleasant location. We drew the middle of the room, where there was least light and where we were farthest from the windows and the racks. Not only that, standing or lying down we were in everybody's way, and they all trampled on our straw bedding whether they intended to or not. Worse yet, the space allotted to us was exceedingly cramped: measuring it off, we found that each of us had a breadth of some thirty inches at his disposal. There was no passageway between our straw piles, so that we lay not only side by side, but head to head.

The men spread out their straw. My Karl was not in sight. He could not leave his Austrians and they had been assigned to another room. There was no more straw left for me. There I stood, quite helpless.

"Come here," said one of the men finally. "Come over by me!"

That man was thenceforth my neighbour. He was a workingman, a mechanic, a quick-tempered but good-natured little fellow in his middle forties. He spoke with such a heavy Saarish accent that I had difficulty at times in understanding him. He made a very pleasant neighbour, resourceful, adaptable. At the very outset he helped me by an advantageous use of my valise to erect a sheltering partition between me and the man at my head in such a way that we would not bump our heads together. The valise meanwhile provided a place for my shoes, and in them I could keep my watch and my glasses at night so that they would not get lost in the straw and broken. As time went on, my friend from the Saar did me many another good turn. He was assigned to work in the "workshop," where the personnel was French. He got better food than we did and would always turn up in the evening with some titbit or other, not seldom wine, and also with news that he had gathered from his French comrades. I could hardly have found a better neighbour. He had only one unpleasant trait, and it was certainly not his fault: at night, after his day's work, he had a very bad smell.

Yesterday the rack where I kept my things stood me in good stead. I had now been ousted from that particular spot and, according to our unwritten law, had lost my right to use those shelves. However, the new occupants of my former space allowed me out of hand to keep the part of the rack that I needed. These men, like the majority of my squad comrades, were men of the working classes. They treated me with kindness and respect. They ripped a number of laths from one of the racks—though that was quite against the rules—and from them devised a sort of bench and table for me near the gable window. That gave me a chance to sit down at a point directly in line with my sleeping place, and, sitting down, to eat, to read, and to write. Before long my straw bed and the niche opposite with my lath table and chair I came to think of as "home," my natural frame, something saturated with my being.

Among the workingmen in my squad and the squad adjoining were four, Saarlanders all, with whom I particularly enjoyed talking. Many among our number came from the Saar, for that matter—men who had got into trouble by conspicuously siding with France in the days of the plebiscite and then could do nothing but flee to France. France had promised them special protection. She was now protecting them—in an internment camp!

One of these four friends from the proletariat was a factory stoker, another a furniture maker, then came my "straw-fellow," a mechanic, and finally another mechanic who had the place directly at my feet. All four spoke French as their mother tongue; three of them had married Frenchwomen. They were delighted to help me and did so with great success, and they were always ready for a good chat. From them I learned much about the lives of the working people in the Saar and in the South of France.

Not far from me there was a jolly Saxon tailor. He was a great eater and regularly reported for kitchen duty because in that way he could get a bit extra to eat. Then came a hairdresser, as tiny as a dwarf, not a little selfish and always on the look-out for an advantage. Finally I remember a jovial, worldly-wise fellow who had kept a tavern in Toulon. Those three made good company too, but unlike my Saarlanders they never ventured a political opinion. They were concerned to appear more as Germans living abroad than as refugees—Germans, to be sure, who were not in favour of the Nazis, but who had left the Reich with their papers in order and with the full consent of the government.

The tavern-keeper from Toulon was our squad leader. That post carried no privileges with it; rather it involved much work. All the same, there were several men in each squad who wanted to be leader. Some of them proved flat failures and had to be discharged, whereat their feelings were hurt. It was truly extraordinary how many men there were who felt the need of organizing something, of being important.

Paris had by now extended its internment decree to include Austrian and Czechoslovakian refugees, so in the days that followed hundreds of new arrivals appeared in our camp. Many were delivered in police wagons, usually two by two and handcuffed to each other. Strictly speaking, only persons under fifty-six were to be interned, but the authorities were not very particular on that point. A very reputable gentleman from Marseille, for instance, born in the year 1882, was brought in in handcuffs. He had shown the police his passport in proof that he had passed the age limit for internment. The officer in question replied that his job was not to do sums in arithmetic, but to make arrests.

The brickyard now became crowded; every inch of space in our room on the second floor was occupied. There were men of every age and every sort among us. Most of their names I have forgotten, but many faces and individualities stick in my memory.

I am thinking among others of a manufacturer, also from the Saar, a quiet, altogether decent person. He would sit most of the time with a little typewriter on his knees, writing letters and compiling market statistics. He managed to create an atmosphere of comfort about him. In a thousand different ways he would get news reports, newspapers, and extra food smuggled in to him, sharing everything generously with others.

Then there was a man of very positive personality who always had a little group about him listening to what he had to say. He was a dentist from Monte Carlo, and, as it later proved, a Nazi. From the first he struck me as very much the dictator, though I may have perceived the authoritarian trait in him largely because, as it chanced, he was the only person to have sleeping space apart from the others. His was situated between two approaches to the racks. The man was neat to the point of excess. He built a little wall of bricks around his bed. There, mornings and evenings, he could be seen lying outstretched in his brick frame as on a catafalque. It was most impressive.

Some twenty straw piles from mine slept the writer Walter Hasenclever, one of the founders of German expressionism.

Also among us was a quiet patient fellow, a born philosopher. He had been caught in India in the First World War and interned there for the duration. He had brought a little folding-chair and was quite resigned to sitting out this war too in an internment camp perched on his little chair.

A short, stocky man, middle-aged, merry, crafty, accommodating, proved to have been for many years the proprietor of a cinema theatre in Marseille. He was always lounging about in a pair of unspeakably dirty pajamas that had once been white, wearing a tasselled cap on his roundish head and, in open defiance of camp rules, leading a little dog on a leash. The guards and the sergeants all liked this jolly little fellow, and he oiled their palms so bountifully that they put up with his dog. The dog slept next to him in the straw. Once in a while he would bark, and everyone would do his best to induce him "for God's sake to keep quiet." Let an officer draw near and twenty voices of guards and internees alike would rise: "Weinberg, your dog! Get your dog out of sight!" The dog would vanish as if by magic under Weinberg's blanket, and the officers always tried to look the other way.

In other circumstances I should never have come to know most of the men who were in camp with me. If I had encountered them I would either not have noticed them or have forgotten them immediately. Now the character of our prison and the fellowship of our common plight forced me to draw close to them. Each of them felt a need of expressing himself, of telling his life story, of unburdening himself of his hopes and fears, of receiving friendly advice. In the course of my fifty-six years I have had dealings with thousands of men of all sorts and conditions. I no longer have any curiosity about people. What I found most difficult about the camp was the fact that one could never be alone, that constantly, day and night, every act, every physical function, eating, sleeping, voiding, was performed in the presence of hundreds of men, men who were talking, shouting, moaning, weeping, laughing, feeding, smacking their lips, wiping their mouths, sweating, smelling, snoring. Yes, we did everything in the most public view, and no one seemed to feel the slightest embarrassment.

But much as I sometimes wished to be rid of all that throng, I am not sorry now that this exuberant "fullness of new faces," to adopt Goethe's phrase, pressed about me. It enabled me to feel again and very deeply how uniquely individual is every human face, even the plainest, how uniquely individual each human being's way of doing things.

Among my more or less close neighbours I must mention another, an orthodox rabbi, slight of stature, bearded. He was always saying prayers, and in orthodox regalia—phylactery and prayer shawl— secluding himself as best he could from the public gaze by withdrawing between the racks.

There were orthodox Jews in goodly number at Les Milles. They adhered strictly to their observances, deporting themselves meanwhile in a modest, inconspicuous manner. They had the camp authorities assign places for their worship where they would cause no disturbance to others. For that matter the French were very co-operative on this point. During my first detention I had spent the most solemn of Jewish festivals in camp, Yom Kippur, the Day of Atonement. With permission of the camp authorities the orthodox Jews had built out of waste bricks a sort of synagogue, an altar, the *almenar*, a shrine for the Torah scrolls, and a sort of lectern for the cantor. As the long day drew to an end and the bricks had to be taken down again, a number of internees insisted on having their fun. They went up to a group of men who were suspected of being

Nazis and shouted: "Jew-baiters wanted, to destroy the temple!"

The frail rabbi to whom I have referred, a quiet, unobtrusive man, had the bad luck to have a most unpleasant straw-fellow, an elderly man with an actor's face, who had a fancy for imitating the calls of animals. The moment reveille sounded at five-thirty in the morning, one would be sure to hear his lusty cock-a-doodle-do. One would be standing, lying, or squatting somewhere and suddenly one would hear the mooing of a cow, the barking of a dog, the whinnying of a horse, the trill of a nightingale, and then the man with the actor's face would come walking by unconcerned but inwardly chuckling at his good fun. For some reason he bore a special grudge against his neighbour, the rabbi. He tormented the poor fellow cruelly, not only mooing and whinnying in his ear, but even cuffing and pommelling him, so that oftentimes bystanders felt obliged to interfere.

Was the animal-imitator altogether in his right mind? One could not say. Many of the internees had acquired a mental twist during their bitter years of exile, and particularly during this first year of the war.

In the infirmary was a well-bred gentleman of charming manner who exercised in the yard during the hours when the slightly ill were allowed that privilege. He came up and spoke to me and told me his story. He had been a sports instructor at one of the health resorts on the Riviera for many years. He thought of himself as a Frenchman, but had neglected to take out naturalization papers. During a first internment, he told me, he had suffered a nervous breakdown and had been sent to one of the army's insane asylums at Marseille. He was finally discharged from there and sent to the infirmary at Les Milles. The trouble was that he happened to possess a very special faculty—a faculty for telling a person's character simply by smelling him. He could smell out the innermost souls of people. During his first stay in the infirmary he had immediately smelled out the fact that not less than eight of the thirty inmates were Nazis. He asked to see the commandant at once and said: "There are eight Nazis in this infirmary, sir."

To which the captain replied: "Clear out! Back to the asylum for you."

This time, on his second internment, the doctors had clapped him into the infirmary immediately on his arrival. And this time too he had smelled out Nazis, four of them in fact. Now if he were to tell the captain, the latter would send him straight back to the asylum in Marseille.

"How would it be if you were to go to the captain," he asked me, "and tell him about the four Nazis?"

An elderly Austrian among the internees, a scholar, formerly a teacher in the *Volkshochschule* at Vienna, was a remarkably ugly man, perhaps the ugliest I have ever encountered. A face with over-prominent bones, a bushy beard always unkempt, glasses. Woebegone, bedraggled, dirty beyond words, he was always chewing on something, smacking his lips audibly, and when he was not munching, his lower jaw sagged, leaving his mouth wide open. He walked with a stoop, a pair of inordinately long arms dangling in front of him, and so far he reminded one of an ape. But he hopped around with a nervous, unsteady gait, and that suggested rather some aged, mangy bird. He was by no means a fool, and not seldom came out with surprisingly shrewd remarks, but he had lost all perception of bounds and limits, all sense of realities. Doubtless the tortures to which he had been subjected in the Nazi concentration camps had unbalanced him. He was learned to a degree and had exact information on all conceivable subjects—in short, a walking encyclopaedia. His head was crammed with details from my books, for instance, things I myself had long since forgotten. He had a beautiful voice—perhaps a trifle unctuous, for in the end it got on one's nerves. His habit was to discourse at length in long, rounded sentences, taking part in every discussion, often importunately. On such occasions he had a way of poking one of his huge ears forward as though listening, and then coming out with something scholarly, polished, ready for print, but not pertinent to the subject. He evidently thought of himself as something of a Socrates, going about among the throngs, questioning everybody, teaching others and himself. His discourses were to him the centre of all things. He would point to some spot or other near the latrines. "There," he would say, pushing a bit of bread about inside his mouth, "on the sixth of February at five o'clock in the afternoon I began my memorable discussion with Professor K. on the ramifications of Leibniz's doctrine of monads in the thought of our day." Among all the denizens of the brickyard at Les Milles he was probably the happiest. Inside that enclosure he could be certain of an audience. Many people liked to listen to him, and a circle could often be seen gathered about him. That they took him as a sort of clown did not in the least disturb him—he even liked it. Just as long as someone was listening, so long as they paid attention to him. His worst fear was that these happy days at the camp might come to an end. On his release from his first internment at the beginning of the present war he had flatly refused to leave the camp. The soldiers had been obliged to set him on the road forcibly, after which they passed his bundles out to him on their bayonets over the brick wall amid jesting and laughter.

About this time I had a somewhat lengthy conversation with Captain G., commandant at the camp, and asked him what my chances of an early release were. The captain was a hat manufacturer from Paris, stout, with a puffy, over-ruddy face that struck me as sly, secretive, stubborn. I had found him invariably correct and courteous during my first stay at the camp, and so he was this time. He explained that he, as well as his superiors, knew quite well who I was. I would certainly be set at liberty soon, but the weeding-out process, the real purpose of our internment, could not begin until all of us, absolutely all, had been brought into camp. Would we have much longer to wait for that? I asked. He could not give me a definite answer, he said, but personally he was assuming that the time limit would expire within a few days.

"Within a few days." That is what the officers kept assuring us. No one really thought so, but we all clung to the hope. During those first two weeks of our detention the main subject of conversation was: When will "le triage" begin, that sifting, that weeding-out, of which we had heard so many tales? And on what basis would the sorting be done? How would the commission be made up? Where would it sit, at the camp or elsewhere? These, and others of the same sort, were the questions that exercised us.

The commission never arrived. The sifting process never began, and even had events not come rushing in a deluge and rendered it impossible, one may wonder whether it would ever have been undertaken.

The official version was that we had been interned for military reasons, that a suspicion prevailed that Nazi sympathizers, members of the Fifth Column, lurked among us Central Europeans, that it had again been deemed desirable to have a sifting and a very thorough one. Few among us believed that this was the real reason. We refugees from Germany had been sifted ten times. From the first days of the war we had been under strict and constant surveillance by the police. We had not been allowed to leave the towns where we lived. No, the responsible authorities knew perfectly well that the spies, the saboteurs, the Nazi sympathizers, the leaders of the Fifth Column, were to be sought quite elsewhere than among us, that they were sitting in very high places, powerful, influential. We had been interned simply to put on a show for the French people, to divert public attention from the men who were really to blame for the French defeats and who could not be reached.

There was, I believe, no particular cruelty in the measure. Our internment may have wrecked the happiness of many of us, it may have cost the lives of many of us and broken all of us in spirit and in body, but those consequences followed not from malicious intent but from pure inconsiderateness. Of a man who was living well we Continentals used to say that he lived "like God in France." The expression conveyed a feeling that God found life pleasant in France, that there people lived and let live, that there life flowed along smoothly and comfortably. But if God had a good time in France, in view of the slatternly conception of life that prevailed there the Devil did not have a bad time either. The French have coined a phrase for their slipshod indifference, their way of letting things take care of themselves. They call it "je-m'en-foutisme," an attitude toward life that may be somewhat inadequately translated as "I-don't-give-a-damnism." That is why I do not attribute our misfortune to any deliberate intent. I do not think that the Devil with whom we had to deal in the France of 1940 was a particularly truculent devil who enjoyed practical jokes of a sadistic nature. I am inclined to think that he was the Devil of Untidiness, of Unthoughtfulness, of Sloth-in-Good-Will, of Convention, of Routine, the very Devil to whom the French have given the motto, "je m'en fous"—"I don't give a damn."

Of course the manner in which our internment was carried out is hard to understand if one assumes that government officials consider the consequences of their measures before they order them. The French authorities simply did not think ahead. We asked ourselves, if there was no intent to harm us physically, why did they hunt up for our accommodation a dark and dust-choked brickyard where there was not enough water for washing and none at all fit to drink? To such questions our French officers would reply: "Our soldiers at the front are no better off." They probably had no intention of treating us badly, of treating us as enemies. They knew very well that ninety-nine out of every hundred of us were definitely innocent, that we were friends of France who had come to France with full trust in French hospitality, warmly welcomed by the French people and their government, natural allies in the war on Hitler. If, in spite of all that, we were given such wretched quarters and our health was ruined through neglect of the most elementary rules of hygiene, it was due to pure thoughtlessness, a lack of talent for organization.

Execution of the internment order was being rigorously pressed: subordinate officials had evidently been instructed to lock up too many people rather than too few. Not only were Germans, Austrians, and Czechs being detained as the decree specified; we were getting people from Luxembourg, Holland, Belgium, and Scandinavia. There was no appeal. Once a man had landed in a camp—it made no difference whether by an evident mistake on the part of the police or by an equally evident abuse of their authority—he never got out again.

It was ridiculous to see the sort of people that were herded together there on the pretext of their having possible connexions with the Fifth Column. Among others was a man whose four sons were serving in the French army. Another had a brother who was an officer on the French General Staff. More than a dozen of us internees possessed French decorations. Several were knights of the Legion of Honour. I myself had been received by the President of the Republic. Leaflets dropped by English flyers over Germany had quoted sentences of mine. I had written books whose background portrayed the barbaric ways of the Nazis, and they had been read by millions. The Nazis had denounced me as Enemy Number One in not a few of their manifestos. To intern so many people who had beyond any doubt proved themselves bitter enemies of the Nazis was a stupid, revolting farce.

Meanwhile, instead of mitigating the severity of the internment specifications, Paris stiffened them. The age limit was raised from fifty-six to sixty-five—a mere transposition of figures, we jested bitterly, a mistake of some clerk that had been ratified by the "higher-ups" in a spirit of malicious "I-don't-give-a-damnism."

New internees poured into our camp. Ground floor and second floor were now packed to the last dark corner. One's every step tripped over bricks, straw piles, men. We lay on top of one another, we squatted on top of one another. Crumbling bricks came to be much in demand and one was put to it to scrape together the four or five bricks required for making something that would serve as a seat.

Among the older men who were now being brought in one noted cultivated gentlemen of astounding knowledge. I remember one or two in particular. They were Viennese and took things philosophically. They had had the bad luck to get caught in the meshes of the French military bureaucracy. To approach that machine with considerations of common sense or humaneness was sheer folly. When one happens to be caught in an earthquake does one try to reason with the falling walls? These gentlemen preferred to sit on their little folding-chairs or their little piles of crumbling bricks and chat intelligently of books, of music, of the beautiful women of a day gone by, of the charms of an era that was no more. In their discriminating discussion of Mahler, Schnitzler, Gerhart Hauptmann, of the merits of this or that feminine beauty, or of this or that restaurant, one perceived a soft, reflected glow of the old days in Vienna, in Paris, in Cannes. Gentlemen in tattered suits that were soiled with brick dust. But one walked with them in a dusty yard glaring

white in the sun, elbowing one's way through a milling crowd, jostled
and shoved about at every step; one sat opposite them on a little pile of
bricks—careful meanwhile that the barbs on the wire at one's back did
not cut one's skin—exchanging recollections of those lovely things that
had vanished from our lives, or debating as to whether James Joyce had
really introduced a new element into literature or whether the alleged
novelty had not been there before, as, for instance, in this or that story
of Schnitzler.

They were Austrians, as I have said. The distinguishing trait of the
Austrian temperament is, to my mind, a certain indolence, a certain
resignation that you might call wisdom or sereneness, or, if you will,
inertness, lethargy, shiftlessness. In that camp one could observe the
trait in most of the Austrians, in Jew and in Christian, in bank president,
manufacturer, and plain workingman, in Communist and Legitimist.
The Austrians were in general more sociable than the Germans, less
reserved, less formal, more adaptable, more talkative. At the same time
they were noisier and more irascible. There we were all stewing in
the same broth, but, foolish as it was, a silly national hatred between
Germans and Austrians often manifested itself. The Austrians made
fun of the discipline that the German room-chiefs and squad leaders
tried to maintain. The Germans were proud that the French sergeants
who made inspections found their quarters more orderly than those of
the Austrians.

The change in the age limit brought the last two Germans in Sanary
to camp, one of them a man of sixty-one, the other of fifty-six.

The latter, like myself, was a writer. He had just passed the age limit
at the time of the first internment order, while I came a few weeks within
it. He had felt a sincere regret that I had fallen victim to the decree.

But he cherished a profound belief in himself and was positive that his having passed the age limit, as it were by a hair, was a personal merit.

How normal it is for people, whether they admit it or not, to regard good luck, when they have it, as a quality of character, though they of course refuse to think of bad luck in anything like the same way. Misfortunes they ascribe to the injustice of Fate or of God, and think they are to be pitied because of them; if a stroke of luck comes, it is an achievement of their own. The man who is lucky at cards likes to put on airs and see in it a confirmation by Fate of his personal superiority.

Be that as it may, my poor neighbour, who had been on the top of the wave ten days before, now walked around in the camp in a rage. Even more furious was my other acquaintance from Sanary, the man of sixty-one, an opera-singer still rather imposing to look at.

His luck had been particularly bad. He had been locked up like the rest of us at the beginning of the war. But elderly people against whom there were no specific complaints had, in general, been freed after a few weeks. He had been detained. As later came out, there was something special against him: he had very unfavourable papers in the police files. He had been reported a number of times. The good people of Sanary suspected that he was a German officer and had been sent to France by the German Secret Service for shady purposes.

By that time the man had been living for years in France. He owned a pretty house in Sanary, looked every inch the German, spoke French wretchedly, and no normal mind could see exactly why the Nazis should have chosen such an unsuitable person for their dark designs. On the other side of his balance-sheet was the fact that witnesses from the native population—French housemaids, gardeners, and the like—averred positively that they had seen a photograph in his house which showed him as a German army officer. He, the singer, averred just as positively that he had not served in the army in any capacity during the First World War, and that he had been a soldier only in his early youth and for a very short time. The fact that he thus disavowed his status as an officer during the World War was in itself suspicious, and his record looked bad.

Closer investigation had shown that the photograph under suspicion pictured the singer in the role of Don José in *Carmen*. But the suspicion had now become documental, and the Devil in his French edition as Shiftlessness and Bureaucracy held the man fast in an internment camp, and he was not going to get out again.

Heretofore he had always felt young. Now rage and a progressive desperation were eating him up. His hair turned white in three weeks' time. He became an old man. One of his sons, a boy of about twenty, had also been interned. He saw how the confinement was wearing his father down and was eager to help him.

There was a way of doing it. The French officers hinted in unmistakable terms that they would set the father free if, and only if, the son joined the Foreign Legion. Now, service in the Foreign Legion was considered especially severe. The corps had had exceptionally high losses in the World War. Not only that, anyone who enlisted in the Foreign Legion had to enlist for a term of years (this regulation was later suspended). The boy found it difficult to make up his mind. Should he, the youth, wreck his life for the sake of the few years his father still had to live? The father for his part did not exactly demand the sacrifice. He merely walked about the camp, silent, embittered, ageing visibly from day to day. The sacrifice was demanded by the stepmother, a woman of wealth on whom father and son were alike dependent. After much arguing one way and another the boy finally gave in and enlisted in the Legion.

He got a few days' furlough before being shipped to Africa. Father and son took a walk one day along the streets of Sanary, the once portly father now a mere shadow of himself. The good townspeople were in tears for a whole week over the nobility of the son's self-sacrifice and his love for beautiful, big-hearted France.

Unluckily the son's self-sacrifice proved to be in vain. The father was now under lock and key for a second time.

As for the photograph that showed the singer in the role of Don José and that played such an important part in his own and his son's destiny, the harm it did was bound up with the brainless routine of the whole French Secret Service. The way the counter-espionage functioned in the South of France was a sorry farce.

I may be allowed to relate my own experience with the French military police. Colonial troops had been stationed in Sanary since the outbreak of the war. They were not always the same troops; the regiments frequently changed. Each detachment, however, brought its own police with it, and each time the handful of foreigners in the place were asked the same stupid questions over again: when and where their fathers and mothers were born, when and where they were married. Such data had been taken and written down any number of times. They could have been found in a hundred different registers. Not only that, a special agent had been detailed to Sanary to keep an eye on us foreigners. (Sanary is a village of about four thousand inhabitants. At the outbreak of the war about two dozen Germans, Austrians, and Czechs were living there, along with many other foreigners.) The man whom the authorities had entrusted with our surveillance had once been a clerk in the little branch bank we had at Sanary. He knew us all and rather liked us, but he felt that he had grown in importance now that the foreigners in the little town were to some extent in his hands and he could give them—

especially the women—quite a fright by appearing on the scene. He was himself ashamed of the idiotic questions he was now and then obliged to ask. However, his superiors insisted upon having his report on them, he declared.

Why did my secretary type at night? The townspeople suspected it might have something to do with secret information to the Nazis. When my wife drove down to the village she was almost always obliged to pick up soldiers who asked her for a lift. The police wanted to know why she did that. People in town said she might be spying on the soldiers. After that she refused to pick them up. Then the police wanted to know why she did that—a manifestation of unfriendliness toward the French army? The townspeople found it provocative. I was asked what proof I had that I was a writer. I showed them French editions of my books. That was not enough. I showed them articles about myself and my work in the leading French newspapers. That was not enough. I received a money order from my American publisher. The police made a long investigation of the matter: where did the money come from, why was I getting it, and what had I done to earn it? The townspeople suspected it came from Hitler or from Stalin.

If one wanted to go to Toulon to do some shopping (Toulon was eight miles away), one had to fill in any number of forms, supply photographs, furnish data about one's parents and the like. Then if one had good luck, one got the permit in about ten days. The reasons for the trip and its purposes were never seriously investigated. The requisites were merely written or, even better, stamped papers of some sort. It was a case of papers for papers' sake. The official wanted to be protected by a rampart of papers with writing on them.

I was called upon to suffer more than most people from the devious ways of bureaucracy, and I am probably more sensitive to such things than most people. My common sense is always rebelling at the stupid formalism with which the world is run. Oh, those everlasting regulations! Oh, those "mesures générales!" In the vast majority of cases they leave untouched the persons they are intended for and fall full weight upon the innocent. How many of the things that official regulations compel one to do are without the slightest rhyme or reason! What a part of my life I have spent standing around in public offices, asking for something, waiting for it, using a thousand devices merely to have it confirmed in the end that I was born, and, to wit, in Munich, and in the year 1884. Only in rare instances have investigations been made in earnest. Most often it has been a question of exchanging one set of papers written out and stamped for another set of papers written out and stamped—and of paying money for it. I am a slow worker, but I could have written at least two books more in the time that I have been obliged to spend waiting around public offices and in the back yards of recruiting stations—waiting unnecessarily for unnecessary things.

While I lived in Germany I was inclined to think that bureaucracy was a typically German vice born of an excess of the German's impulse to have orderliness and sound organization. When I went to Soviet Russia I saw that the situation was still worse there. But I had to go to a free and liberal France to experience bureaucracy in a still more intensified form, mitigated only by the inefficiency and shiftlessness of those who administer it. Even in America I saw myself ensnared in a tangle of endless red tape.

The fact probably is that the progressive mechanization and rationalization of economic life has come to require a gigantic apparatus of documentation. And the more firmly the principles of a planned economy gain hold, the greater the danger that the life of the individual will be smothered under bureaucratic complications. There will be the further danger that schematic regulations, well enough devised in themselves, will work out in practice as a meaningless hindrance to the individual, that common sense will evolve into nonsense and benefit into sheer nuisance.

There is a remedy for this, it seems to me. The text of laws, of regulations, should be required to have attached to them a statement of the reasons for their existence and of the purposes they are intended to achieve. Then the deciding judge, the official who administers them, should have discretionary powers to enforce regulations prescribed by the law only when they achieve their purposes and to waive them when their application would obviously run counter to their stated aims. The principle of relativity should be applied with due discretion in the field of jurisprudence and governmental administration.

Prerequisite to this would be a careful selection and training of officials. The French officials, for instance, were wretchedly paid and anything but carefully selected. They could be bought and they failed to deliver. Their indolence, their corruption, their empty routine were among the forces that led to the downfall of France.

Our day at Les Milles was as follows:

In the morning at half-past five the rising signal—a pretty tune. The trumpeter did not always get it right, but we knew it and straightway many of us would take it up, whistling, bawling. Every morning, too, at the same time came the inevitable and mighty cock-a-doodle-do of the animal-imitator. Other regular features were a quarrel as to which window should be opened, then from all sides a general chorus of almost deafening grunts, groans, yawns, belches—all the possible sounds of men who were stretching their limbs, stiff from sleep, unwilling to begin their joyless day. One always heard the same expressions—smutty jests, gross obscenities. It was always the same boorishness.

So much for the second floor. As for the ground floor, meanwhile, that dark, catacomb-like room was crowded with some hundreds of men, most of them with some receptacle or other in their hands, waiting for the doors to open. The moment the great wings were pushed apart, there was a general rush out of the building, followed by a mad race across the yards toward the washroom, the water-trough, the latrines. Everybody ran, not a few quite awkwardly, for among our number there were many older men who had had little physical training and made haste comically. They came to a halt in lines in front of the toilets and the washing-places.

The standing line was one of the characteristic traits of the camp. We stood in line in front of the office when we wanted to make an application or an inquiry. We stood in line once every two weeks to obtain a small part of the money that had been taken from us on our entrance. We stood in line in front of the counter of the canteen. We stood in line when we were ill and ordered to report to the doctor. We stood in line to get the food that was provided by the camp authorities.

Lines stood in front of the latrines all day long. There were four closets built of wood at one end of the enclosure, three at the other end. At times up to a hundred men could be seen waiting in front of each of these conveniences. There was no flushing. There was no avoiding the excrement, no escape from the thick swarms of flies. One waited for one's turn, raging, jesting. Many men were ill; all became so. If one failed to succumb to the food, infection from the toilets was inevitable.

That so many of us survived the internment camp at Les Milles is a devastating refutation of current notions as to the necessity of proper hygiene. "In fæcibus nascimur, in fæcibus morimur," said St. Augustine. Some melancholy wag had written the quotation out on one of the toilets, but completing it this way: "In fæcibus vivimus." (In muck we are born, in muck we die, in muck we live.)

Even today as I think back to my long waiting in those lines, a feeling of depression, utter degradation, and indignation takes possession of me. Certain details I must spare the reader, for the mere thought of them turns my stomach.

Soldiers had priority over us as regards the toilets. If a soldier came up, no matter how long the line was, it was his privilege to go to the head of it. Once, when I was seventh or eighth in line, a man came and placed himself at the head of the line. Another shipment of internees had just been delivered. I thought the intruder might be one of the new arrivals and did not know the rules. I suggested politely that he go to the end of the line. At that he turned on me, red in the face and with fists clenched, assailing me with lewd words of menace. It turned out that he was a soldier. He had taken off the regulation tunic so that there was no way of distinguishing him from the prisoners. I was in great distress at the moment. The ridiculous misadventure depressed me greatly and enduringly.

For that matter there could be consolations even in that repulsive environment. One day, I remember, I was something like twentieth in the line but those ahead of me all insisted that I should go in first. I have had many honours conferred upon me in my time. This was the highest.

Courtesy was so much a matter of second nature with some of our number that they did not forget the outward forms of politeness even under those revolting circumstances. As they squatted there, grunting, panting, one would inquire of the other, with all the German's meticulous attention to rankings and titles: "How are you today, Herr Professor?" "How is your health this morning, Herr Geheimrat?" "Did you sleep well last night, Herr Ministerialdirektor?"

Near one of the toilet cabins was what might be called the urinal. But there no lines formed. The men relieved themselves almost anywhere in the neighbourhood, and this whole section of the yard was a most forbidding quagmire. At just this point the yard was bounded on the one side by an escarpment guarded by a patrol, on the other by a high iron fence, with a second fence of barbed wire just beyond. A very pretty park began just beyond the fence and one looked out across it upon a lovely landscape. That was where we urinated.

We soon lost all sense of privacy in the camp. There was no effort to conceal ugliness and deformity, whether of body or of soul. One saw much that was ugly beyond words.

Some twenty minutes after the rising signal two men from each group brought their comrades a bucket of coffee and the bread ration for the day. Each man went and got his share of coffee in a tin cup, dipping his bread in it. There was much complaining over the quality of the bread. Doctors among our number declared it was the main cause of the illnesses that afflicted us all.

At half-past seven roll-call was sounded. This ceremony took place in a veritable hullabaloo, though good-humouredly as a rule and not at all in a military atmosphere. A strong guard of soldiers would first march out, some twenty middle-aged farmers and artisans in uniform. They stood about yawning and terribly bored. Then two or three sergeants would appear in their red fezzes. A lusty voice would roar: "Attention!" But no one came to attention. The older men among us did not know how it was done, and they probably considered the whole thing nonsense anyway. The same command would be repeated three or four times: "Attention!" The squad leaders would be reprimanded, but the thing just would not work. A contributing factor in the trouble was that we had among us about a dozen men who were slightly insane. Our Austrian polyhistor, for instance, was to be seen wandering about between the ranks at every third roll-call after the command to come to attention had been given. Voices would call out to him: "This way! This way!" but he could not or would not understand. Finally he would turn to one of the French officers and explain: "I am Professor P., Squad X. Where shall I stand?"

Other old men would be wandering around during the whole calling of the roll. Half blind and half deaf, they could not adjust themselves. Meanwhile behind the ranks of internees, or indeed between them, Foreign Legionnaires would be going to and fro, carrying large barrels of refuse from the latrines out in front of the camp, and they would never fail to call: "Ice-cream! Get your ice-cream, please! Chocolate! Vanilla!"

Notices would then be read out and the day's work distributed. The first call would be for a certain number of specialists—electricians, mechanics, tailors, shoemakers, cooks. There would be many applicants to respond to each call—the day was long and lack of occupation depressing. Whatever was asked for—a shoemaker, a tailor, anything—the Austrian scholar would always volunteer. He had studied the manuals of all the trades, he said. Some of the other eccentrics were equally faithful in offering their services.

Next came the distribution of general tasks. These were done by squads. Squad A, for instance, would be ordered to clean the yards, Squad B the inside of the building, Squad C would have kitchen duty, other squads bricklaying or trench-digging.

The cleaning of the rooms, like the cleaning of the yard, was a matter of stirring up the dust. Two or three men would have been sufficient for such room service as we had, but twenty or thirty were detailed to it. Only those assigned to such duty were allowed inside the building while the work was in progress. When intruders were caught there it was their practice to say that they were doing guard duty, making sure that nothing was stolen. On one occasion I was found in the building during the forbidden hour. When I explained that I was a guard, the commanding sergeant observed: "There are four guards here already."

"I am keeping an eye on the guards," I replied saucily, with a presence of mind unusual to me.

Kitchen duty came down to cleaning carrots, peeling potatoes, and the like. So many men were assigned to this work that, putting it high, one never had more than twenty potatoes or ten carrots to prepare. We spent the time chatting.

Those who had not received any work, lay, squatted, or strolled around the dusty yards when they were not standing in line somewhere or waiting for something. Many tried to read, to learn new languages, and so on. In fact, one could always see people walking about the yards mumbling to themselves, with their fingers stuffed into their ears. They were memorizing vocabularies or rules of grammar. Others would be sitting about on piles of broken bricks, giving and receiving language lessons. There was little profit in all such things, however, and most of us soon gave them up. You simply could not get your mind to work in all that sunlight, dust, and noise. Merely to sit by yourself and doze was equally impossible. You were always disturbed; someone always had something important to tell you or else felt an urgent need of advice. If you got rid of one, another was sure to turn up. Even if you were not molested for a moment or so, any concentration was out of the question with the everlasting comings and goings all around you.

So there was nothing left but to talk the whole livelong day, and of the same things always, the same little hopes and the same big worries. Optimists were optimistic, pessimists pessimistic, and the in-betweens listened to the optimists one day and to the pessimists the next. Always there were the same complaints at the senselessness of the whole thing, the same execration of French inefficiency, the same boiling resentment against a France that we had all loved so warmly at the beginning. There were those, of course, who made an effort even in that situation to understand and forgive the internment policy of the French, but there were evident traces of strain.

Newspapers were barred; letters came at rare intervals and during the first four weeks not at all—we were cut off from the outside world. The result was an unending series of rumours both as to our own situation and as to the political and military situation in general. They sprouted in the early morning as we assembled in lines in front of the latrines. They gained in strength and in substance as the sun rose higher. By three in the afternoon they had blossomed out into facts. Around four they began to fade. At six they were dead. At half-past six one man would be denouncing another for having believed the rumour and passed it on. Then the next day the same thing over again.

The man who caught a rumour fairly early before the others got hold of it thought himself very important. That was probably why our two interpreters enjoyed such great prestige. They had been chosen from our midst—they were internees like ourselves. They had a hard job. They acted as intermediaries between ourselves and the camp authorities. They were the ones to make the commandant's orders known. We had to use their services when we wanted to see the commandant. The squad leaders got our mail through them, and when anything went wrong they were reproved by the officers and abused by us internees. On the other hand—and this was probably their great compensation—they were constantly being questioned by everybody as to the ever-shifting prospects of the group as a whole and of the individuals in it. It was taken for granted that they were always in close touch with the camp commandant and therefore learned about everything of interest at the source. They were told nothing at all, of course. People would sometimes tell me importantly that they had heard this or that from the interpreter, who had it straight from the commandant, and I was always reminded of an amusing story from the First World War, the story of Pierre, Marshal Foch's chauffeur. Pierre was always besieged by his comrades with: "Pierre, when is the war going to end? You ought to know!"

Pierre tried to satisfy them. "The moment I hear anything from the Marshal, I will tell you."

One day he came.

"The Marshal spoke today."

"He did? Well, what did he say?"

"He said: 'Pierre, what do you think? When is this war going to end?'"

The interpreters at any rate felt very important in their role as Pierres. Indeed, the man who had just heard something from the interpreter thought of himself as a sort of little Pierre and correspondingly important. Many thought they would be losing prestige if they were not the first to know everything. When they heard a new rumour, they would declare, quite untruthfully, that they had known it all along.

So we stood around and talked the livelong day. Within a week's time everybody had told everybody else everything he had to say. Nevertheless, there they were any number of them who scurried busily around, earnestly inquiring whether somebody had seen somebody else, for they had something of great importance to communicate to him.

Of course it could not be said that all the talk was equally empty. I have previously alluded to my conversations with those very cultivated gentlemen from Vienna on the subjects of painting, poetry, and music.

But there were people from all walks of life with whom profitable intercourse was possible.

I recall in particular Herr H. and his son. Herr H., a small man, gentle, approachable, had been a reader in a Berlin publishing house. Neither the First World War nor Hitler had operated to alter his temperament. He had married a Frenchwoman. The eldest of his sons was an officer attached to the French General Staff. Herr H. lived in the camp as though it were the cosmopolitan Berlin of the year 1913. One could never decide whether his smiling, head-bobbing sereneness indicated profound philosophy or mere lack of comprehension. His younger son had limped from childhood. He had been subjected to most trying experiences at the beginning of the present war in a Paris internment camp. In spite of his youth he was just as even-tempered as his father. Both were agreeable souls, both thankfully enjoyed the thousand little pleasures that brighten even the gloomiest existence—the fact, for instance, that the bread seemed a little better today than yesterday, that the water-ration was a little larger, that one could now buy cigarettes at the canteen. It often struck me that father and son were trying to hide their worries and anxieties behind the brisk, appreciative interest they took in little things of that sort. The sufferings and humiliations of life in the internment camp certainly took their toll on the father: he survived only a few weeks after his release.

A man I especially enjoyed talking with was the writer R., who had been born in Dalmatia. A tall, fine-looking man, he had always been a great favourite with the women. Now in his fifty-second or fifty-third year he was putting on weight and showing the effects of hard drinking. He was a man of the world, spoke German, French, and English perfectly, was at home in an incredible number of arts and sciences and passionately, judiciously had read, mastered, and enjoyed all the great books of world literature. He was probably not a writer of any great importance. He was a connoisseur with whom it was well worthwhile to talk. He drank heavily, even in the camp. Heaven knows where he found the money or the guile required for keeping so constant a supply of liquor. He was not a strong man in any sense of the word. Tall and stately as he looked he was inclined to avoid the final push, the courageous decision. One flash of resolve and he could have escaped with us later on, but he lacked the toughness and the decisiveness for such an adventure. He frittered his intensity away in a sort of petty bustling that was applied to procuring little comforts. He was, however, a man of knowledge, of taste and charming manners. To chat with him was a solace and a pleasure.

For that matter I was almost always the gainer in conversations if I could induce the person I was talking with to tell me something about the work he had previously been doing for a living: a lawyer about his cases, a physician about medical science and his practice, a real estate dealer about land values. For a large part of what I know about people and things I have to thank an art of listening which wise teachers taught me early. Applying that skill in the camp, I learned all sorts of things—I learned about the lumber business in France, about a certain brand of fish food, of which one of my fellow-internees had a monopoly, about sponge-fishing in Greece, about the effects conveyor-belt work has on the workman, about the fireman's technique of stoking in a large factory boiler-room, about the human soul.

There were many painters there, painters of every sort and of every degree of eminence—Max Ernst, for instance, one of the founders of surrealism. There was also a portraitist of great reputation whose dramatic style did not suit my taste. There were many doctors of any and every school of medical thought. There were Catholic priests. Dressed in their cassocks, with their round, fat Bavarian or Austrian faces, they looked like men in disguise. There were people who had had dreadful experiences in the vast prison camp that the Nazis have made of Germany and especially in the Nazi concentration camps. I listened to them all with sympathy and with profit besides.

I am ever being tempted to write about the numberless different faces and characters that one encountered in the camp. We were all living under the same conditions and more and more as time went on we all looked alike, thanks to the dust and the dirt, but each man's personality was visibly stamped upon him. We squatted side by side in a close pack. We saw each other in every possible circumstance. Whether we liked it or not we were involuntary witnesses to every man's behaviour, to the way he walked, the way he ate, the way he slept, the way he washed, the way he put on his clothes. No one could hide anything from anybody. We knew out of hand just what sort of fellow each person was—and without asking him for his opinions. Everybody every day had to put up with all kinds of little annoyances. The balanced man took them in his stride, the irascible individual smashed his bricks, the quarrelsome and dogmatic fellow insulted his neighbour, the good-natured soul tried to help, the grab-all went on grabbing.

I remember an Austrian physician, a well-educated man who hid his troubles behind a somewhat strained joviality. I remember another Austrian, also a physician, very young, Dr. L., an especially agreeable person, ever ready to help others, ever urging calm upon the impatient. But on closer observation one recognized how nervously consumed he himself was. Among the many writers was one who had proved himself a good fighter in Spain and a good Marxist. He was constantly preaching that the things that were happening, even the things that were happening to us, were necessary and all contributed, in roundabout ways perhaps, to progress. In spite of this conviction he was always having outbursts of black despair, devastating attacks of what the French call *le cafard* and what Americans call "the blues." I remember a young painter, sophisticated, something of a spoiled child, but full of the joy of living, who clung to every hope and every rumour even when everybody else had abandoned them. I remember an architect in his late middle age, obdurate, cantankerous, a congenital nihilist, a pessimist to the bitter end about everything touching our own situation. He did his level best to demolish every argument that a hopeful soul among us would put forward; but let there be the slightest chance to do anything at all to better our situation and he would be right on hand.

Such was our company by day and by night, and by day and by night we talked and talked.

There was of course a good deal of political discussion. Workingmen and peasants not seldom manifested considerable understanding in this field, viewing things in a certain perspective. But I was being continually astounded at the paltry, over-simplified motives to which most of the other inmates of the camp attributed historic events, at the extent to which their view of the whole was obstructed by their narrowly personal interests, at their utter unwillingness to face the unpleasantness involved in looking at larger causations even from a distance, let alone from near at hand. "An experience opens many windows," an Anglo-Saxon writer once said. That seems to me only partly true. For my comrades in the camp who came from the middle classes most windows remained closed in spite of their experiences—those windows at least that afforded a long view of the events of our time.

The midday meal came very early, about eleven o'clock. It was usually a lentil or bean soup with some meat in it.

The food could not be called poor exactly. It suffered somewhat in flavour from the bromides that were added to it to lessen sexual appetites.

What annoyed me more particularly was the general hurly-burly of the meals. We could not afford many eating utensils—there was no place to keep them and no water to wash them. We had to use the same receptacle for all the food we received, an aluminum cup that one could never get entirely clean. The morning coffee tasted of the fat in the evening soup, the evening soup of the morning coffee. Soup and coffee were both ladled out of the pot that each squad had in common. They were hot when we got them. The aluminum cup heated through instantly and it was especially hard for my clumsy self to carry the hot cup safely to my place. Most of the men sat on their straw piles on the floor. The dust got into everything. A thin layer of it always floated over the soup. "Dust shalt thou eat—and like it," was an often heard quotation. There was a quarrel somewhere in the room at every meal, someone contending that he had not received his due share. It was all very unpleasant.

We had been promised a canteen from the very first, and in about ten days it was really opened. It was poorly stocked and one could procure things there only with difficulty. It was strictly reserved for members of the Foreign Legion during the forenoon; we others could not apply until twelve o'clock, and by that time as a rule nothing was left. The Legionnaires had bought the place out with the idea of reselling at a profit. If you had money, not only were you able to eke out the regulation meals with food purchased directly or indirectly at the canteen, but soon all sorts of food and drink were being smuggled into camp, especially by the guards. The little village of Les Milles had a sudden and very considerable spurt in business. But not only Les Milles. For the whole region including Aix, our camp, which had now grown to two thousand men, was a windfall. Underground trading grew steadily in volume.

Twice a week a farmer drove to camp to collect our garbage for his pigs—potato peelings and the like. The man brought pork with him, cooked, sliced, and carefully weighed out into packages that were wrapped in newspapers. We had to make our purchases furtively when the guard had turned his back. There was thus no time for examining the goods—we had to take everything on faith. The prices were high, but the farmer was an honest man and what one found inside the newspaper wrappings, though blindly bought, always corresponded in quantity and quality to the price asked.

What I missed especially was vegetables. There were scarcely any of any sort. Fruits, greens, lettuce were sadly wanting. Two dried figs (or else plums) and two small leaves of lettuce once a week—otherwise nothing but dried peas, beans, and lentils. Such a diet was not calculated to improve one's health. I suffered severely under it. On one occasion my hankering for fresh vegetables drove me to a business transaction that may seem surprising. One of the inmates had managed to procure some tomatoes. I traded a can of lobster for one of them and we both were content with the bargain.

As a rule my two "valets" kept me lavishly supplied with food. I say "two," for I had acquired a second servant meanwhile. He, like Karl, was an Austrian. He had been a restaurant-keeper. Of his experiences in the concentration camps of Buchenwald and Dachau he told ghastly stories and exhibited scars from the maltreatment he had undergone. He had occasional fainting spells and attacks of dizziness which could be attributed to the hardships he had been subjected to. On account of them he had come to expect a good deal of consideration; far too much, many people thought. He was always talking of what he had gone through, and before long when he would come and tell us that he had fainted for the second time on a given day no one manifested any sympathy. He deserved sympathy nevertheless, and when he begged me to take him on as a servant, I could not refuse. On the other hand, I did not want to give up my Karl, so I invented ways to keep them both busy. They divided the little chores of my daily living between them.

They could not endure each other. The restaurateur was always expressing amazement at Karl's inefficiency. How was it he found so little food for me? Karl on his side would explain at length how thoroughly the other man was trimming me by over-charging on the sugar, mineral water, and other things that he was having smuggled in. Karl could not understand why I did not put a stop to it, and he would make frequent point of delivering to me in the other man's presence something or other that the latter had previously been buying, mentioning two or three times, loudly, the much lower price that he had paid.

Between the two of them at any rate I had plenty to eat, with the exception of fruit, lettuce, and other green vegetables. The food we smuggled into camp had to be quickly consumed on account of the inspections and on account of the rats.

I may already have said that there were six or eight café owners among the internees and they were still doing business at, so to say, their old stands. They had managed to procure—heaven knows from where—supplies of tea and coffee, and they offered these beverages for sale after the midday meal at various points about the camp. Salesmen of theirs would circulate among us: "Coffee [or at other times tea] now being served. Room Two [or Room Three] in the rack on the south side. Get your cup right away. Inspection due at any moment."

There would be watchers aplenty to warn of a guard's approach. The various café men carried on a sharp competition with one another and spoke disparagingly of one another's drinks. As in the establishments they had formerly managed, they went about among their customers welcoming with deep bows those who had honoured them with their patronage. "Good day, Herr Professor, everything satisfactory?" One of them even received a smuggled newspaper which we were allowed to peruse for a moment if we bought our coffee from him.

A cup of coffee was cheap, about two cents. Many people could not afford coffee even at that price and went without unless invited by others. Though we were all living under the same conditions, differences between poor and rich soon became evident. The man who had money to spend could procure no end of comforts that the poor man had to forgo.

Noontime brought dreary hours. With our meal fixed at eleven, we were left with three empty hours ahead before roll-call sounded again.

Most of the men tried to take a midday siesta. That was not my practice; I was anxious to save all my sleepiness for the night. Even had I wanted to sleep, I could not have done so. Our semi-dark room was always in a hubbub, with people stumbling over one, with bricks falling and breaking. Yet there were always those who did not allow the discomforts of the room to keep them from playing cards. They would sit on their little piles of bricks, slam the cards down on other piles of bricks or on an unsteady board, shouting, wrangling. Cards were virtually illegible from the dirt. Winnings and losses were settled with promissory notes drawn against such times as the camp authorities should make the small repayments from deposits. In one of the alcoves between the racks a number of orthodox Jews squatted or stood, praying or "learning," their heads bent low over the Scriptures or the Talmud. And in all that uproar men who were sick would lie on their straw piles and groan, and men who were well would lie on their straw piles and snore.

Sometimes I tried to read, but that would not work. It was all too noisy, too hot, too dusty. So I would spend the time wandering about the yard or else sitting on my bench in a half-doze, or I would squat with bent back on a brick pile in front of the barbed wire in the vibrant sunlight.

Procedure at the two o'clock roll-call was the same as at the first. It was if anything harder to keep us occupied during the afternoon than it was in the forenoon. They had us move bricks around to no purpose whatever, or else dig in the ground. But even at that only a few of us could be provided for. The rest—and they were the great majority— walked round and round the yard in a more and more industrious tedium.

There were four barbers among us, all told, some one of them could be seen doing business almost anywhere. They were necessarily not very clean—they had little soap and little water—but at any rate it was a change to get shaved. Many men went to the barber's daily, some twice a day. You sat on a pile of crumbling bricks, with a crowd of men standing around in a circle talking. With us as in all places at all times, the "barber-shop" became the centre of gossip and rumour. Sometimes as you squatted there the pile of bricks would give way under you, but no one laughed at that by now; it was an old story. One merely stood around talking, arguing, stimulated, earnest, but at the same time bored.

The call to supper sounded at five o'clock. The fare was scantier than at eleven. Sometimes there was just a bit of dubious sausage, a bit of cheese, and a sardine.

But the hour following was a rather pleasant time. It began to grow cooler around six o'clock. The wind fell and it became possible to stay out in the yards. The atmosphere improved. One felt more confident, more hopeful. There was less anger in the air.

There chanced to be a good number of trained football players among us and they would get up a game—as much of a game as the grounds allowed. On one occasion the ball went over the wall. A soldier was standing on guard with his bayonet fixed, watching the game. The players asked him for permission to go out and throw back the ball. The soldier said that it was strictly forbidden, that he could not allow it, but that if someone would hold his gun for him, he would climb over the wall and bring the ball back. And so he did.

THE FIRST NIGHT

A painful moment came when the bugle sounded: "All indoors!"

Black through the wide doors the interior of the building yawned. Unjoyously the prisoners crowded in, urged on by the keepers, good-natured fellows who, on this occasion, could become very gruff. Inside the building one pushed and shoved first through the corridor of catacombs on the ground floor, then up the narrow wooden steps to the floor above. Here and there a weak electric light shone faintly, making us only more conscious of the dark.

Preparing for the night was not a pleasant task. Karl was there to help me. My valise, as I have explained, separated me from the straw pile of the man at my head. On it I set my shoes, placing my watch and eye-glasses inside of them (without glasses I am helpless).

Half an hour after the "All indoors!" signal, the bugler sounded a second command: "Lights out!" In the interim we talked. My neighbour on the right, the mechanic from the Saar, felt constrained evening after evening to open his heart to me. He suffered from the confinement, longed for his French wife, longed for his work. The firm that employed him was making every effort to have him released, but it was getting nowhere with the military authorities. The thought that he had to sit there to no purpose whatever would not let him sleep.

My neighbour on the left also grew very eloquent in the evening. He was a biologist. Slight of frame, of delicate health, he bravely made the best of a serious case of asthma using a bitter, ironical humour. He talked politics objectively, dispassionately, and I have to thank him for much new and interesting information in his special field, the theory of heredity.

So then: "Lights out!" We had to turn them off ourselves, and we were in no great hurry. Eventually one of the three anaemic lights in the great room would go out, then a second. The last would go on glowing until impatient voices finally demanded that it be extinguished. If the delay were too long a harsh warning would come from the French guards in the yard.

The darkness we dreaded would straightway be filled with quarrels and bickerings as to whether the unbarred portion of a given window should be closed or left open. Some would declare that they could not stand the stench if the window were closed; for others it would get too cold and too draughty if the window were open. "Window open!" "Window closed!" It lasted a good quarter of an hour every night, and the disputing grew increasingly vehement.

The window problem settled, there would always be a few dozen people who would keep on talking in the dark. They would laugh, talk business, exchange obscene jests. They had done nothing but talk all day long; now they needed the night for more talk. A chorus of voices would shout, implore, threaten: "Quiet! We want to sleep."

But there was to be no quiet. Tempers were overstrained, people were quarrelsome. Some kind of dispute was always going on. Someone had jostled someone, somebody had stepped on somebody, somebody was taking up too much room. Not seldom the wrangling would go too far. Then from an entirely different quarter in the dark a brutal voice would suddenly rise: "I'll put an end to that now!" and one would hear someone charging the whole length of the room over protesting sufferers toward the wranglers.

There was no period during the whole night that could be described as quiet. It was one round of complaints, oaths, insults from the trodden as no end of treaders went stumbling through in the dark to or from the toilets.

It was indeed an adventure to get to the toilets in the dark. As I have said, there was no light at all, on the whole second floor. One had to pick one's way through a narrow lane between the sleepers, then at the proper point try to find a broader but very irregular lane that led to the right between more sleepers to the wooden stairs up which a faint glimmer of light forced a passage from the floor below. Going down the stairs one made a left turn and on the ground floor followed a ray of light till one finally came to the four indoor latrines.

These four latrines were kept strictly closed during the day. At night they were icy cold. All night long men stood waiting in line before them. We waded ankle-deep in excrement. The return trip was, if anything, more perilous still. It required time, exertion, and nerve to grope one's way up the stairs in the dark to one's own straw pile. I never could make it at one try myself. I would inevitably land on the wrong straw pile, to be thrust off by its startled and angry occupant. My neighbour on the left tried to help me by holding out his raincoat as a sort of sign-post, but I could never get my fingers on the thing. My neighbour on the right was seldom asleep. Hearing me stumbling or creeping about, he would call to me in a muffled voice: "This way, this way."

During an attack of dysentery I had to make that trip several times every night for a whole week.

Quite aside from this dreadful journey our nights were hideous and even the hardiest among us were unable to get sound sleep. One had a downright feeling that the room was peopled with tormenting apparitions. Fears that one had managed to dispel during the daytime, by use of common sense and will-power, towered before one again vapoury, gigantic in the grunting, malodorous night. That was the experience of the majority. If I whispered: "Are you asleep?" my neighbour on the right and my neighbour on the left would whisper back: "No." When, with the early dawn, the first rays broke through the cracks in the wooden shutters, I saw the outline of my little proletarian side-partner crouching wretched among his worries on his straw pile, while to my left the biologist would be lying flat with wide-open eyes.

All night long the cold dark room was filled with noises of the snorers, the flatulent. Here a cough that was more like a bark, there a gasp as someone struggled for breath, there a groan, there someone cried out in his sleep. Here a man groped toward another to console him, there a low voice would be heard calling for one of the many physicians among us.

Many who could not sleep at all groped their way down into the catacombs to stand around in the full light near the latrines. As many as two hundred men would sometimes assemble there, and in case of an inspection one could always say one was going to the toilet. There was something weird, pitiful, ludicrous about those nightly gatherings of men of all sorts in their tattered nightclothes, many of the older men with funny nightcaps on their heads. Excitedly, but in whispers, they debated questions that had already been discussed all day long. If voices grew too loud, curses and threats would be sure to come out of the adjoining corridor, where the Legionnaires were quartered.

My neighbour on the right, the biologist with asthma, groped his way down to that company every night. The Dalmatian writer R. was also usually to be found in the catacombs in the early hours of the night, clutching a bottle of wine under his arm and inviting all his acquaintances to have a drink. Not a little business was transacted down there. While their comrades nearby lay cursing at our noise, Foreign Legionnaires tried to dispose of the commodities they had snapped up in the canteen in the forenoon. On the floor of that Bourse also the café men negotiated with the kitchen workers to make sure of their supply of hot water for the next day. Business was in the air everywhere in the catacombs.

The real centre of the trading was an Austrian of some years. He had been a barber and a barber of fame and repute. He had scraped the chins of several archdukes and, I believe, of one emperor. He averred—and seemingly on good grounds—that nothing human was alien to him and that he knew all the ropes. In any event, he was able to supply a most varied assortment of articles to anyone who could pay for them: small folding-chairs, blankets, wine. He was boasting one night that he could smuggle everything and anything into camp.

"Well, then," asked the Dalmatian writer, "can you get a riding-horse for me?"

"Of course," said the barber, "but, you understand, a pound at a time."

I did everything I could to make sure of a good sleep at night. I exercised all day long and sat down as seldom as possible. In spite of that I often had to be satisfied with three or four hours' sleep, and I could get no more than five or six on my best nights. The rest of the time I lay awake in the midst of all the snoring and grunting, within me an impotent exasperation at the wretchedness and indignity of my situation. Reason was of no avail. I could say to myself: "At this very moment, now, people in every country in the world sit reading my books about the barbarism of the Nazis, filling their hearts with wrath at those barbarians; but here am I lying in wretched confinement, beyond the human pale, suspected of being a confederate of those barbarians!" Anger at the senselessness of my situation, at the stupidity of French bureaucracy, filled me to the very pores. My intelligence failed to offer the argument that I was dealing not with individual men but with a system.

I would try to invent distractions, strive to recast Latin, Greek, or Hebrew verses in German, playing all those mental games that an older generation used to call "exercises of the wit and intelligence." I would try to figure out just when I had done certain things for the last time. I am fifty-six years old and even before my internment I would sometimes ask myself: "Is this the last time I shall do this?" In reading a book that I liked, I would ask: "Is this the last time I shall read this book?" And I would have the same habit with pictures that I saw, with clothes I was taking out again to put on, with music that I heard, with people I met. After all, unwittingly, unforeseen, we take leave of something every day of our lives.

So now during my sleepless nights in the straw and the dirt of Les Milles, I would ask myself: "When did I go bathing in the sea for the last time? This woman, that woman, when was I with her for the last time? When did I read Shakespeare for the last time?"

A camp comrade had told me that he had once seen a performance of one of my plays. Though it had been long ago he still remembered every detail of the plot and questioned me eagerly about certain incidents. I could give him no information. I knew much less about the play than he did. I had wholly forgotten even the plot sequence. The thing preoccupied me and during those sleepless nights I made many tests to see how far my memory could still be trusted.

In my younger days I had been made to memorize a great deal, some of it useful, much of it useless. My memory was trained in every way. Testing it now I came to see more clearly than ever before to what an enormous extent it functioned arbitrarily, as by a will of its own. With an alarming obstinacy it would refuse to share with me important things which I knew perfectly well, while, spontaneously, importunately, it would prattle to me about things that I did not care to remember at all.

A lifetime's experience has failed to lessen my wonder at the wonders of memory, the most singular function of the human spirit. I can remember—and I dare say that is the way with everybody—my meetings with people who are quite indifferent to me so exactly that I can specify every minutest detail. Faces that were dear to me have vanished utterly from my mind. No psychological analysis, however thorough, has explained the how and why of this.

During my sleepless nights at Les Milles my memory seemed to me unusually despotic. All of us in camp had a feeling that our memories were failing. We attributed the symptom to the bromides that were mixed into our food.

In earlier and quieter times I had been amused rather than not when my memory failed me on occasion. Now during those terrible nights it drove me into an impotent fury. And my fury only increased at the fact that there were no books, and especially no books of reference, to fill in the gaps in one's balky memory, that one had to depend upon the chance knowledge of one's comrades, especially on the learning of the Austrian polyhistor.

It was amazing how soon we all adapted ourselves to circumstances in the camp. Hard as it was for many to make the shift from their ordinary manner of living to the primitive conditions that prevailed at Les Milles, after a few days they were behaving as though they had been there for years.

The fact is we all "went flat," we were deadened. Discomforts and indignities, our own or others', that would have enraged us a short time before we now accepted resignedly with a shrug of the shoulders. Before long we were not even noticing them.

That had been the case also in the Nazi concentration camps. Many of the men at Les Milles had made compulsory acquaintance with those camps, especially the camps at Dachau and Buchenwald. They all agreed in assuring me that they had so often been forced to attend executions, whippings, and the like, that witnessing such horrors finally ceased to make any impression whatever upon them. With punishments in progress before their eyes they had discussed petty details of their everyday living, or exchanged funny stories. One man told me that a prisoner died under the lash in his presence and that, though nearby, he failed to notice it—he had been bargaining with the man next to him for a piece of chocolate. How that could have been, he now failed to grasp. But so it had been, and they all told the same story.

For my own part I have often experienced sudden changes in fortune of extraordinary moment. When I think them over, I am unfailingly astounded at the speed with which at times I have adapted myself to new surroundings. In the camp at Les Milles I observed again in myself and in others how very quickly the human being becomes acclimated.

Among us were men who had led pampered, fastidious lives, who had gone into a fury if they could not get their customary bath salts on a journey, who had thought it an iniquity of Fate if their favourite vintage of wine gave out. Now at Les Milles they changed overnight. Their hopes and fears narrowed in scope. They came to have the same exigencies, the same enjoyments as the workingman at their side. I believe I have said that individuals probably changed very little in basic character. All the same, a detached observer might well have noted that we, the inhabitants of the camp, all made up a single, unified mass, each of us very like the other. We were each as different as could be, but we were obeying the same laws and these made us more similar. An American physicist has shown that the motion of the electron within the atom obeys laws other than those governing the atom of which it is a part. In other words, the atom as a whole obeys other laws of motion than the electrons of which it is composed. That perhaps gives a picture of the relationship in our case of the individual to the whole of which he had become a part.

Proud or modest as we may have been, coarse or polished, dull or brilliant, broad-minded or narrow-minded, all our thoughts revolved around the same few problems of daily living, the wants and fears of all of us were identical. "What's the supper tonight?" "Is the sifting commission coming to camp tomorrow after all?" "Will the canteen soon be selling mineral water?" "When shall I ever get a newspaper to read again?" "When shall I ever get a letter from my wife?" "No apple, no lettuce—at any price?" "Oh, for a real wash!"

But that was just what one could not have. We grew more ragged and dirty, and however much we may have differed in background or in character, we ended up by being one vast homogeneous mob of ragged, dirty wrecks.

We were not allowed to receive visitors. So far as the members of our families were not French citizens, they could not come to see us anyway, since a special permit to leave one's town of residence was required and could be obtained only in very special cases. We received practically nothing through the post. Letters went by way of Paris for the censor and were weeks on the way. Few of us had any idea at all where our wives and children were. In view of what had taken place in northern France we could only surmise that they too had been placed in internment camps.

For many of those interned, their wives' internment also spelled financial ruin, since they had built up small businesses of one sort or another which their wives were looking after. If they, too, were put under lock and key all was lost. One man owned a fruit orchard. Harvest time was coming on. What would become of the crop? Another ran a rabbit and chicken farm. Who would look after his animals if his wife, too, were shut up? One could take an oath that neither the fruit-grower nor the rabbit-breeder belonged to the Fifth Column. Such cases brought the whole deplorable stupidity of the internment decree into a clear and lamentable light.

Even for the well-to-do preoccupation with the ways and means of keeping up a bare existence became a burning torment. Bank deposits were frozen. Many men had drawn out money at the last moment and given it to their wives for safekeeping. What were the wives to do with it now? If they had been interned it would certainly be taken from them.

And wives who were sick, what about them? Many in fact were ill or else run down through the hardships of exile. Would they be able to stand the strain of detention? And what would become of the children? Soldiers were saying that even the children had been interned at Marseille. They were being quartered with their mothers in a suburban hotel that had been turned over for the purpose by its owner. Later on they would be transferred to the Pyrenees.

One of the men in camp had a child with diabetes. If the child were not treated in a certain way, it would be lost. The man, an apothecary, had a horror of French hospitals and recounted hair-raising stories of filth and inefficiency. If his wife should keep the child's illness secret in order not to be separated from it, she would lose no chance of nursing it properly. Were the child to be sent to a hospital it would be lost, the father was sure. He was virtually insane from worry.

Those among us who were married to Frenchwomen were better off. Such wives were not interned, nor were they subject to the annoying "special regulations," countless in number, which governed the wives of the others. They could travel, they could even try to see their husbands. Husbands of these French wives could not praise their devotion and loyalty highly enough. They counted on their doing everything possible to get in touch with them, and for the most part were not disappointed. These Frenchwomen came to Les Milles, almost all; from near and far they came. But visits were strictly forbidden once and for all, and the orders were sustained by such severe penalties that the guards did not dare to permit meetings between husbands and wives.

So the women would appear, sometimes after long journeys, outside the iron fence and the barbed wire. They would walk up and down the hot, dusty highway hour after hour, day after day, only to catch a glimpse of their husbands' faces, perhaps for half a minute. Sometimes they would be allowed to see one of the camp officers, sometimes they were allowed to send in a message—after it had been carefully censored and adjudged harmless. Often enough, perhaps four or five times a day, one would hear someone call hurriedly, importantly: "Mr. X., your wife is here!" Mr. X. would rush to a window to try to catch a glimpse of her, or he would clamber up on one of the high stacks of brick (it would keep falling down under him), or his friends would shove him up as high as they could so that he could peer over the wall, which was a hundred feet or more distant. If Mr. X. was so fortunate as to recognize his wife and she him, he would be sure to shout something to her that she would fail to understand. So they would go on shouting back and forth till the guards came and shooed the wife away, and Mr. X. would be ordered indoors from the yard. It was always a heart-rending scene.

On one occasion a good-natured guard smuggled a five-year-old boy, the child of one of these French wives, into camp to see his father. The latter had been a prominent resident of Marseille. Here he now went around ragged and unkempt like the rest of us. The little boy, very pretty, the picture of neatness, gazed at his father in astonishment. Wouldn't his father come home now, he begged. Mamma too was waiting out on the road. The father thought up a rather far-fetched story: he was an officer there and had to keep an eye on us. We all joined in and played the game, showing the father all manner of respect. The child was partially comforted.

I have already reported that bodily functions were necessarily performed among us in the most public way without trace of embarrassment. This compulsory lack of physical modesty may have had something to do with the fact that many were not at all shy about baring their souls as well. Even in quiet times many people are tempted to let down the bars in the presence of a writer, thinking of him as a sort of father-confessor. They like to confide to him their secret tribulations and hopes, their hidden prides, private feelings of inferiority that they normally conceal. Such people literally overwhelmed me in the camp at Les Milles with confessions on all sorts of subjects, even the most intimate. They usually coloured their experiences, making themselves out now better, now worse than they had really been. At times these distortions would reach the absurd.

The sojourn in the camp brought out another trait in many people—an abnormal irascibility. We were crowded so close together and for so long a time that friction was continual. The man who was your friend today became your enemy tomorrow. Vanities were ever being ruffled. People were prone to think they were being cheated, or that good turns they had done were being poorly repaid. Quarrels in almost every case had the most trivial causes. One man had borrowed another's share of water one morning on promise to return the favour the day following. He had failed to make good. One man had given a slice of sausage to another, counting vainly on a like courtesy in return. Altercations were loud and shrill; then, twenty-four hours later, both parties would be ashamed at the extravagant waste of words and emotions.

Chief among the causes of dispute were bargains that were concluded in the field of camp business. Every conceivable commodity was bargained for. The daily food rations were bought and sold. Men sold their places in the lines at the canteens or even at the latrines. Each of us could post a letter every two weeks. You could buy that privilege of another and mark your letter with his name once you were sure your correspondent would recognize your handwriting.

Although newspapers were forbidden, a few were smuggled in by bribes to the guards. Commercial talents would get hold of a copy and rent it out ten, twenty, thirty times. So it would happen that for a paper that had cost him a franc or a franc and a half a man could make thirty or forty francs. A little knot of people would gather about a newspaper in a corner, while a number of others would keep watch to give timely warning of the eventual approach of an officer. The paper's owner would watch the clock to be sure his customer did not overstep the two minutes bargained for. The customer would read aloud—probably to the renter's rage.

The wildest altercations were those in which one or more members of the Foreign Legion participated. The Legionnaires were also the wildest traders. There was not a little rabble among them, but when one knew them better many of them were not at all bad fellows. And it must have angered all of them that France should be treating them in that manner. Later on the French guards were replaced with Arab soldiers and indignation over the situation in which France had placed these Legionnaires of hers became general. They had conquered those Moroccans and now had to submit to being guarded by them as prisoners.

Many Legionnaires were coarse of speech. They boasted monstrously in tales of their battles. They were greedy for money. But they were also brave and, after their fashion, honourable. Two Legionnaires made a deal with an elderly gentleman whereby for a consideration of three thousand francs they would help him to escape and to reach a certain place. The man paid a thousand francs down and they gave him loyally the promised aid, sharing the comforts and discomforts of the journey with him. The thing went so far that on stealing a bag of gold coins from a mail car they honestly offered him a third share. A noisy lot of insolent bullies, these Foreign Legionnaires, brave, tough, boastful, predatory—multi-coloured, in a word, like the many medals which the Republic had pinned on their chests.

Noticeable as were the differences between rich and poor in the camp, there was little class snobbery. The groupings into which we automatically divided were formed with reference to other than property criteria. They were made on the basis of special and formally legal considerations, in other words, on the basis of the chances of release an individual had as indicated by his papers. We fell into one category or another according to the claim we had, in the opinion of those among us who were supposed to know, to being set aside in the vaunted sifting.

On the lowest rung of the social ladder were the holders of German passports; on the next lowest, holders of Austrian passports. Better off were such as held German or Austrian passports with visas for overseas. One rung higher stood those of us who had married Frenchwomen, with special distinction for the fathers of French sons who were serving in the French army. Men of the Saar were well thought of because France had promised them protection in very solemn and ceremonious language. The real aristocracy fell into two groups: first, the Foreign Legionnaires and, second, we who were stateless, since we had been recognized by France as political refugees and enemies of Hitler. The various groups eagerly weighed their chances as compared one with the other. In spite of all our disappointments, the rumour would not die down that the next day or the day after the much-talked-of sifting and releasing would begin and that one group or another would be the first to be considered. Members of the privileged groups looked down in scorn on the wretched holders of mere German or Austrian passports.

One who has passed his life as an inhabitant of a country that has never been shattered by domestic revolution, by war, or by foreign military occupation, knows nothing of the role that an identification paper or a rubber stamp can play in a man's life. It is usually a ridiculous scrap of paper and a still more ridiculous rubber stamp apathetically applied by a nondescript clerk. Yet how many thousands, tens of thousands, millions of human beings go chasing after just such scraps of paper, just such rubber stamps. How many thousands of intrigues, how much money, how much nerve, how much life are wasted by thousands and thousands of human beings in getting possession of them. How many swindlers get a living by purveying, now legally, now illegally, just such stamps, just such scraps of paper. How much happiness, how much unhappiness may come from the legitimate or illegitimate possession of them.

In the struggle for papers lawyers play a great role. It is assumed that they are competent guides through the labyrinth of administrative regulations. Lawyers played a prominent role in our camp too. They would explain solemnly that our detention was illegal and contrary to international guarantees that France had given at the Évian Conference. Accordingly, they drew up a document that made formal protest against our internment with reference to that treaty. When it was set before me for my signature I could only comment with a loud laugh. How in those days could a man in his right mind think of appealing to international guarantees? I suppose the human being has to cling to some hope or other.

The urge to be somebody spurred a number of our lawyers to activity. Still other petitions were circulated. Some few individuals were always getting themselves appointed representatives of some category of internees or other, such as the Saarlanders or the fathers of French sons. Then they would stand around importantly in groups, argue the draft, and finally make a ceremonious call on the commandant, who would listen courteously, promise to hand the document on, and, when they had gone, toss it into the wastebasket.

Our relations with the guards were always pleasant. They were bored and liked to talk with us. They would tell us what they had seen in the newspapers or what they had heard over the radio—unfortunately with no great understanding as a rule.

They were sceptical in general, having no faith in their government and regarding the whole war as a swindle designed solely to make a few rich men still richer. They thought of themselves not as soldiers, but as poor devils who like us had been caught in the wheels of a stupid machine. They were peasants, or artisans from small country towns, who had been thrust into uniforms and who wanted nothing more than to go home to their wives, their children, their chickens, their acres. Especially good were the relations between the interned workingmen or peasants and guards drawn from the same classes. One could often see one of our men at the barbed wire chatting with the guard on the other side—two neighbour farmers gossiping across a fence. Without much to-do on the point those Germans and Frenchmen knew very well that they were stewing in the same pot.

Our relationship to the officers was a peculiar one. Many of us at some time or other had had business or social relations with men who were now officers in the camp. There were those who had been friends of the hat manufacturer, now our jailer, and of the silk manufacturer, his lieutenant. The captain had been their guest at dinner or they had dined with the lieutenant in one or another of the good but unpretentious hostelries in Marseille. These French gentlemen adapted themselves admirably to the new situation. They were friendly but they kept their distance. They were less like army officers than government officials whom the ministry had entrusted with an unpleasant duty, and they were now fulfilling it as well or as badly as possible.

I may remark at this point that neither during my first internment at Toulon and Les Milles, nor during my second at Les Milles and Nîmes, did I experience or witness anything that could be described as cruelty or even as mistreatment. There was never a case of beating, of punching, of verbal abuse. The Devil in France was a friendly, polite Devil. The devilishness in his character showed itself solely in his genteel indifference to the sufferings of others, in his *je-m'en-foutisme*, in his inefficiency, his bureaucratic sloth.

More and more clearly as time went on we came to fathom the nature of that Devil. A Devil of that sort was worse than a cruel, wicked Devil. Cruelty and malicious cunning would have been easier to deal with than this red-taped routine, this sloth. A fluid, mollusk-like creature, this Devil in France! Squeeze him and he offered no resistance. He merely contracted, only to ooze out again at some other point. He was the Bøyg, the shapeless, unconquerable creature of *Peer Gynt*.

Few of us may have seen this clearly. We all sensed it. We kept on saying that the sifting commission would be coming, but no one counted on that seriously. Secretly, rather, we assumed that our situation was to last and were making our accommodations accordingly. We accustomed our ears to the grunting and the cursing, our palates to the bromide, our noses to the effluvium of the latrines. Yet our hearts would rebel at times, our hearts would not admit that this dull, senseless existence could go on without end.

Uncertainty as to what they would do with us became more and more of a torture. No letters, no trustworthy news. All we could be sure of was that the political and military situation of France was growing worse from day to day.

We told ourselves that with events piling one upon the other in that fashion the officers responsible for us would certainly have no time to worry about our fate or to come to any decisions regarding it. We had a paralysing feeling that we had been forgotten by the outside world. Many among us wailed that we would rot and die where we were and no one outside would be the wiser.

That was not my feeling. I had an unwavering faith that my friends out in the world of freedom would not forget me.

PART TWO

THE SHIPS OF BAYONNE

Cursed shalt thou be when thou comest in, and cursed shalt thou be when thou goèst out....The Lord shall cause thee to be smitten before thine enemies; thou shalt go out one way against them, and flee seven ways before them....In the morning thou shalt say, Would God it were even! and at even thou shalt say, Would God it were morning!

At the beginning of this book I mentioned the little room on the ground floor in Sanary where I kept my radio. I had most remarkable experiences in front of that receiver. It was my connecting link with Germany, with my homeland, with my hometown Munich. Voices of people, whom I had not seen for a long time but had not forgotten, had a strange sound as they came in over the air—voices of actors who had once had parts in my plays but could now be heard declaiming Nazi oracles, broadcasts from places one knew so well but which were now the scenes of loathsome Nazi mass meetings. There I lay on my sofa, in the security of France, listening with mixed emotions as some minister or other, some Nazi official, stormed senselessly against me.

Out of that radio—shortly before I was forced to exchange my attractive house for the internment camp—news of the collapse in Belgium was blared at me. The Nazis made the announcement barbarously effective. First the usual broadcast of victories, then a request:

"Keep tuned in. In about five minutes we shall bring you a special bulletin of great importance."

We waited uneasily. Then after the five minutes:

"Special dispatch from Army Headquarters. German troops have entered the Belgian city of Louvain." Then came that vulgarly animated tune:

Give me your hand, your little white hand,
For we're sailing, we're sailing 'gin Engeland—

One of the falsest songs in the world, false in its aping of the heroic spirit of the medieval Hansa, false in its use of the far-fetched archaism Engeland for England, false in its mawkish sentimentality—the bomber pilot or the submarine mechanic bidding good-bye to his sweetheart. As the lively, mendacious war song died away, the announcer's voice came again:

"Keep tuned in. In a few moments we shall bring you another special bulletin."

Another five or ten minutes of anxiety slipped by, then the same cheap tune was played again, after which the voice:

"German troops have entered Brussels, the Belgian capital."

"Keep tuned in," we were told for a third time. "We shall soon have another special dispatch for you."

A brief and thoroughly uncomfortable pause followed. Then again: "We're sailing 'gin Engeland…" and: "German forces have taken the fortified coastal city of Antwerp." Then Haydn's noble strains for "Deutschland, Deutschland über Alles" followed by Horst Wessel's vulgar Nazi anthem.

All this was but one of the many baleful foretastes of what we were to hear later on in the internment camp. There we heard of the capture of Amiens and Arras, of the German advance everywhere in the North, of the fall of Boulogne and Calais. There we heard that the King of the Belgians had ordered his soldiers to lay down their arms. There we heard of a speech by the French Prime Minister in which he accused a long list of French generals either of incompetence or of treason and removed them from their commands.

All that we heard but vaguely, in sketchy outline. The newspapers we managed to get hold of were days old, and the censored official reports glossed over real situations. But we listened eagerly for the little we could learn, weighing and debating every word, poring over such maps as we had smuggled in. Not a few of us turned war strategists and told or foretold whats, hows, whys.

One thing was certain: the Nazis were pressing forward, the Nazis were threatening Paris. If they took Paris, what would become of us? It was ghastly to sit there in camp, helpless, imprisoned, unable to take any step against the disaster that was drawing nearer or even to get any definite information about it.

We could measure the growing success of the Nazis by the conduct of their sympathizers among us. These were a small minority and so far they had kept quiet. Now they could scent the way the wind was blowing. They opened their mouths wide and declared triumphantly that Paris could not hold out under any conditions, that France was done for. One of the Nazis kept a little radio hidden in his straw pile and sneeringly shared with us reports of Nazi victories that he received.

Things looked black for us, and the countless rumours made them look still blacker.

I, for my part, was convinced that whatever might happen in France would not decide the war. I was convinced that however great a success Hitler's people might win for the time being they would never come off with the final victory. The Germans had not been able to hold out against the whole world in the first war, neither could they in this one—that seemed to me mathematically certain. So I kept saying to my comrades over and over again. Convinced myself, I convinced others, though the doomsayers would have their innings again the next day and I would have to begin all over again.

Great as the disasters in the North were, people in the South of France—and we along with them—were probably more interested in what Italy was going to do. We were only half an hour by plane from the nearest Italian airfield. If Italy entered the war what would happen to us?

So far, during the full nine months of fighting the districts of the South had seen few traces of war. Now suddenly it began to get under our skins. Our officers were going around the camp with set, anxious faces; the soldiers scowled and looked worried. They did not know how they could deal with this new scourge.

We internees were set to digging bomb shelters to protect us from air attacks. The man in charge of these works was a second lieutenant who had been a town clerk in civilian life. He had not the slightest idea of how a bomb shelter should be constructed. He made us dig deep, zigzag trenches in the camp yard. There was not much room, and the trenches ran in large part close to the main building. Experts among the internees adjudged the work in progress hopelessly amateurish. Anyone taking refuge in the trenches during a bombardment would surely be buried under debris from the falling walls. These criticisms were laid before the town clerk-lieutenant in very deferential language. Gruffly he brushed them aside—he had been ordered to build air-raid shelters, and orders were orders.

The camp command wanted the work done in a hurry, so we began working in shifts. The ground was hard and the trenches had to be deep. It was not easy work, but we enjoyed it, most of us, and the best of order prevailed. We were glad enough to have something to do after the long period of forced inactivity. We turned to with a will. Off came coats and shirts—even the sleek-cheeked priests threw their cassocks aside—and with picks, shovels, wheelbarrows, we began roboting around with naked backs that soon were burned red in the blistering sun.

There seems to have been a French airfield near our camp, not more than two miles away. A first bombing came two days after we had begun work—not from the Italians but from the Germans. The attack was severe and stray bombs fell very close to us. The camp commandant must have shared the views of our experts. He did not send us into the shelters during the bombardment. He had us herded into the building, barring the great door behind us as at night and closing the windows entirely with wooden shutters. There we were, two thousand of us, huddled together helpless in that dark death-trap. We waited with tense nerves, expectant, anguished. Bombs exploded in the far distance, then nearer, then far off again. Those of us who were near the windows peered out through the cracks in the shutters. The yards were empty. We felt that we had been deserted. Some of us had been through bombings before. We could tell from the sounds what sort of bombs they were and how far away they were striking.

We were locked up for more than four hours, the hours that crossed noontime. No midday meal was served. We were alone inside the building; no French guards, only internees. Our anger began to grow and the lawyers among us led the chorus. To shut us up there in close proximity to a military objective, an airfield, was, they explained, in direct contravention of international law.

During these hours only the four toilets inside the building could have been available, but, as I have said, they were kept locked during the day and the Command had forgotten to order them opened. That probably was what angered us most. Finally they were broken open. But then the Foreign Legionnaires intervened. The toilets, they contended, belonged to their domain and they demanded an entrance fee from anyone who wanted to use them.

We all drew a deep breath of relief when at last the great doors were opened again and we could return to the sunny yards.

A second bombing came during the night of the same day, but it did not seem so bad to us. During the attack at noontime the dark building into which we had been locked, helpless, had seemed to us like one vast common grave into which we had been thrown alive. At night it made rather the impression of a dormitory. Most of the men were asleep by that time and were not even awakened by the exploding bombs.

The following day an officer of higher rank came to inspect our air-raid shelters. He ordered them filled in again. The senseless back-breaking labour of scooping out that hard earth and then shoveling it back again was a symbol of the whole inane perilous life that we led at Les Milles. Its sole result was that the ground in the yards was now rough and uneven.

The Nazis in the camp claimed to have heard on their secret radio a German announcement that the High Command knew that some good Germans were confined at Les Milles and had therefore ordered their flyers to spare the brickyard.

More bombings came during the days following. We now knew that all northern France was in the hands of the Nazis. We read of the French Premier's desperate appeal to America to help, to help immediately or France would be lost.

Those were glorious June days, not too hot, not too windy. We stood about in our dusty yards and debated eagerly amid mounds of earth, the remnants of our effort to protect ourselves from the bombs. When would the Germans take Paris? The capital had already been declared an open city, which meant undoubtedly that it could not be defended. The Nazis were seventy miles from Paris, no eighty, no forty-eight. Our guards, good fellows that they were, were suddenly set to drilling. They marched out four abreast, armed. Machine guns were put into position all around our camp. Everyone made sarcastic jests about these moves. Our guards declared angrily that if the Italians came, they intended to go home.

They could well enough go home—but what about us? From the north the Germans were coming, from the east the Italians, and there we were, locked up, helpless. Even if we succeeded in breaking out, we would find ourselves in a land of enemies, driven hither and thither between the armies of still worse enemies.

We made jocular calculations as to our chances of getting out of that ugly fix with our skins whole. We took into account the war reports, the psychological state of the country's inhabitants, and our own physical and technological capacities. We reached the conclusion that at that moment the chances of a fatal outcome for any one of us were sixty percent, the chances of getting free forty. Or rather, no! That ratio was probably optimistic. Perhaps our chances of getting free should not be put at more than thirty percent. Besides, each case was different. The man who had worked openly against the Nazis, who had been attacked by their officials in their newspapers, or been sentenced by their courts, had of course a far smaller chance of getting out safely.

The traffic in newspapers was now flourishing. They were rare and expensive. A group could be seen in every corner going over some much-thumbed paper. The men would pay their francs and then move on to another group where someone chanced to be reading a different paper aloud. An officer would come strolling by and the newspapers would vanish, to be brought out again the moment he had moved on. Even our Nazis were now charging and getting money for passing on the news from their radio.

Italy declared war. The Germans crossed the Seine. France disappeared as a nation.

New shipments of prisoners were arriving every day at our brickyard—for the most part, people who had been interned in northern camps and were now being transferred to camps in the South. But there were not only internees. We were also getting refugees from Holland, Luxembourg, and Belgium. Dead tired, they would squat about the yards for a time and finally be marched off to get something to eat, leaving their luggage scattered about in the dust and the sun, the shabbiest sort of luggage, all they had left in the world.

Strictly speaking, we were not allowed to talk to the newcomers. But discipline, never very severe in the camp, was now less than nothing. We ignored the rule.

What we learned from them was terrifying. Those who came from internment camps in Belgium told how they had been transported across France in sealed cars. No one had paid any attention to the trains and the occupants had been left without food or water. Their Belgian guards had robbed them of everything they possessed. Not a few people had died of exhaustion in the cars and the others had travelled on with the dead bodies beside them. All reported that millions of French people were rushing south in headlong flight. Railway tracks and highways were jammed with them. There was a mad scramble for means of conveyance and no trace of organization anywhere.

The transports of refugees from Holland, Luxembourg, and Belgium did not, as a rule, stay with us very long, those from internment camps in the North somewhat longer. These latter told almost incredible stories of privations. They had been sent off at the last moment. Then came unending journeys with the people now packed together in freight cars, now standing upright in motor trucks, all day long, all night long, without food, without water to drink, in the dust of the roads under a midsummer sun.

They were hardly better off with us. They were quartered on the third floor of the main building, which was even less suited for human habitation than the floor below, being almost wholly occupied by racks for storing finished bricks with practically no free space at all. The newcomers had to get along as best they could. There was hardly any straw left. Many slept on the bare floor in the alleys between racks. The flooring was loosely laid, with wide cracks between the boards. Shafts for brick lifts ran from the ground floor all the way to the top of the building. Holes everywhere therefore, and through them bits of straw and countless small objects kept falling down upon our heads below.

The stairway to the third story was closed off at night. There was only one toilet on that floor and it was without water. As a result, those above provided for themselves wherever they happened to be, causing an uproar on our floor that lasted till the guards interfered.

Our camp was now changing in physiognomy from day to day, hundreds arriving, hundreds going away. Workers in the kitchen cursed. Soup and coffee, well and good—but for two or for three thousand?

Old men and boys were conspicuous among the new internees. From Luxembourg, for instance, came a seventy-nine-year-old man with two grandsons, one fourteen, the other fifteen. They were now sharing the same luck, the same hardships, the same worries. One also noted several midgets from a troupe that had been about to start for South America when French bureaucracy broke it up by detaining male members of it who were of military age. For that matter, as I was told, the midgets were all Nazis and were not a little pleased at the German victories.

We old-timers at Les Milles now came into our own. We enjoyed visible favouritism from the camp authorities. As our officers put it, they at least knew who we were, good enemies of Hitler, devoted to the French and detained on a mere legal technicality, whereas the flood of newcomers brought not a few real spies and an enormous amount of rabble. Nobody liked the new situation: the officers and guards complained because they had much more work to do, we because the new arrivals took up our elbow-room and our food and were always getting in our way. Most absurd of all was the fact that we, the "oldest inhabitants," the permanent residents, considered ourselves the aristocrats of the camp and looked down in utter scorn on this flotsam of strange faces that came drifting in.

The new internees had many stories to tell of rank bureaucracy. A young German of a well-known family of exiles happened to be a Czech citizen. Living in Switzerland, he had taken the advice of the Czech consul and started for France for the purpose of joining the Czech legion in Paris for the war on Hitler. Not only did he have all the necessary papers; he could show a warm letter of recommendation from the French minister in Berne. On presenting his papers at the French border, he was arrested and interned. Since then he had been shipped from one camp to another and had never been allowed to get in touch with anyone outside the camps. A young engineer of some reputation from Yugoslavia was born in a province that had been Austrian before the First World War. A rabid anti-Fascist, he had given up a good position in Yugoslavia in order to volunteer for the French army. He, too, carried a letter of recommendation from a French minister. He, too, was seized at the border, interned, and thereafter shipped from camp to camp.

Many of the prisoners newly delivered wore French uniforms, having been volunteers in the French army. They were "foreign labour soldiers." The initials T.E. (*Travailleurs Étrangers*) were stamped in large black letters on the backs of their tunics. Jauntily on their heads sat the twin-peaked cap of the French soldier.

For that matter, coats and caps of the French army now glutted the market and many of us took advantage of the opportunity to replace our tattered clothing with odd pieces of uniforms. Our comrade Weinberg bought a cap and looked funnier than ever in it. Short, pudgy, pleased, he was still going about the camp in his dirty white pajamas, but now with the grey-green cap cocked on one side of his head and with his little dog barking and yelping around him.

The whole South of France was filled with rumours and panic. Would the French make a stand on the Loire? Had Verdun fallen?

One thing was certain: at Les Milles there was no safety for us. The Nazis had overrun the ramparts of France. In no time at all, they would be in the Rhône Valley, close upon us. If we were to find safety anywhere, it would have to be in the Southwest, in the Pyrenees. The chances of our getting out of our trap with our skins kept dwindling. We were quoting our hopes now at twenty, then fifteen.

Obviously something had to be done about it. We could not simply sit there and wait for the Nazis to seize the camp. The French might well have the best intentions of saving us, but we feared the carelessness of the French authorities, their devilish shiftlessness, their disposition to let things take care of themselves. We had had experiences in plenty. We knew French bureaucracy. The French officials who were directly in charge of us would never dare to take any step on their own responsibility. They would wait for instructions from higher up, the higher-ups would do the same, and in the end the Nazis would be upon us before the French had come to any decision. If we did not help ourselves, no one would help us.

With new contingents steadily streaming in and out of the camp, and with the guards being constantly changed, camp discipline had fallen off appreciably. We did very much what we pleased. We had not been allowed to stand in the part of the yard that led to the commandant's office. We now gathered in just that spot, and in groups of hundreds, by way of showing the commandant our anxiety and our indignation. We shouted, we gesticulated, debated. The guards made feeble efforts to drive us back, but we paid no attention.

We decided to force the issue with the commandant and urge our very serious remonstrances upon him. We could count a number of professional politicians among us, well-known ones, and famous lawyers aplenty. Legalists, formalists as always, they were still bent upon pointing out that what was being done to us was contrary to law. They grew much excited over the fact that our right to be removed from the danger zone was explicitly guaranteed by international treaties—we came under the jurisdiction of the Red Cross or something of the sort. There was more talk about the Évian Conference and the international agreements that had been reached there as to persons recognized as political refugees.

Thereupon several of them sat themselves down on little piles of bricks and brittle laths, scribbled away eagerly, drew up petitions, formed committees, polished up what they had written and decided on. A delegation was to wait on the commandant and present our demands. Even at that moment, when it was a question of life and death, there were those who wanted to seem important. The composition of the delegation and just what demands should be presented were matters of vociferous argument. The Saarlanders, the Austrians, the Czechs, those who had been recognized as political refugees, Germans who had been deprived of their German citizenship, the husbands of French wives, the holders of overseas passports—all wanted to be represented on the delegation, all insisted on being represented on it. Who should represent whom, and what, after all, should we ask for?

In the end an agreement was reached. We should demand of the French military authorities that, with as little delay as possible, they remove such among us as were in danger beyond the reach of Hitler's advancing armies. The delegation would be made up of ten people. I was urged to head it, since mine was the only name that meant anything to the camp authorities. I did not consider myself very well suited to the purpose, yet I found it hard to refuse.

With a noisy crowd assembled in the yard in front of the commandant's windows, we, the delegates, sent in our names to him. He answered that he would see me alone.

I entered the little office. The officers of the camp were there, eight of them, seated. There was no chair for me. In that bare little room, between the eight silent uniforms, I stood in my rags and tatters, ill at ease.

"What can I do for you?" asked the commandant.

I did not like the look of things at all. It did not strike me as very fair that those French gentlemen who held power in their hands should sit there eight strong and leave me standing alone. Two or three thousand of my comrades were waiting outside to hear what would happen. All their hopes rested in me. A good idea came to me suddenly.

"Captain," I said, "I am here to speak for two to three thousand of my comrades in a very important matter. I consider my French inadequate to the situation. I would be very grateful to you if you would allow me to call in one of my comrades."

"Very well," answered the captain. "Whom will you have?"

I thought fast. "Monsieur S.," I answered. Herr S. was an elderly man, cautious. He was sent for.

Some minutes passed before he arrived, unpleasant minutes for me. Nobody spoke. The officers sat there. I stood facing the captain across his ugly little writing desk, uncomfortable, not very representative, I fear.

Herr S. came in.

"What can I do for you?" the captain said again.

Then I spoke, explaining the dangerous situation in which we found ourselves. Many of us were wanted by the Nazis and under prosecution in Germany. Several of us had death sentences hanging over us. In the Nazi newspapers and radio speeches many of us were referred to as the ranking enemies of the regime. We were lost if we fell into the hands of the Nazis. We might have been able to save ourselves or could perhaps still do so were we not obliged to sit helpless in the camp condemned to wait in inactivity. I wasted no words. I spoke plainly, to the point. I suggested that it was the duty of those who had forced us into that situation to get us out of it.

When I finished, the cautious Herr S. began. He qualified. We took it for granted, he said smoothly, that the gentlemen of the General Staff were aware of our whole situation and had doubtless made adequate provision for our protection. But merely to allay the surely understandable anxiety of our comrades we would be grateful to the captain if he could give us some comforting message to take back with us.

"What do you think I should do?" asked the captain, somewhat ruffled.

I answered. We might, I said, be given back our passports and our money. Then, in the extreme case, we would be in a position to look out for ourselves.

"That would suit you, wouldn't it?" the captain retorted. "And me with half the camp running out on me! While more thousands of people would be wandering around loose in the neighbourhood complicating transportation and food problems still further! Well! I can give you the comforting reassurance you ask for. Of course! I do have my instructions in case of any real danger. Tell that to your comrades and try to calm them down."

It was all pretty vague. If we went back with that reply, it would surely have anything but a calming effect. We stood there, hesitating, trying to find the words for our objection. The captain was himself aware of the emptiness of his reply.

"I give you my word of honour as an officer," he said. "Arrangements have been made for your safety. You will be taken somewhere else at the right time. That is not such a simple matter as you may imagine. Our rolling-stock is needed down to the last car. The lines are jammed. Besides, we first have to find out how many of you, after all, are involved in the transfer. We must have a sifting and find out just who is in danger and who not. That takes time."

We stood aghast. The sifting over again! No, we had to call a halt there. With that sifting business, the famous *triage*, we had been made fools of long enough. It was the *triage* that had got us into the fix we were now in. If now we had again to go through a sifting by the French bureaucracy before anything happened, we were lost. All France would be in the hands of the Nazis long before the French authorities had come to an agreement as to the basis for the sifting.

"Excuse me, Captain," I said, "but isn't there a very simple way to find out who is in danger and who not? Anyone who feels safe with the Nazis will scarcely risk the hardships of a transfer into the unknown. We are all well aware that a transfer under the conditions prevailing today will be anything but pleasant. Anyone who feels sure of himself as regards the Nazis will certainly prefer to stay here at Les Milles and await their arrival. I beg of you, Captain, simply ask who wishes to stay and who feels strongly they should be transported away."

The captain hesitated, but my reasoning seemed plausible. "I'll think it over," he promised.

What we said did make an impression on the captain, there could be no doubt about it. Our comrades, alas, were disappointed. What did it mean, the captain had his instructions in case of extreme danger? What would be a case of extreme danger? Our guards claimed to know that Lyon was already in the hands of the Nazis, in fact that they were already thirty miles south of Lyon. Wasn't that your case of extreme danger?

Uneasiness in the camp increased. New groups everywhere, arguing everywhere. Wild schemes for escaping were devised and propounded. There were speeches.

We had a distinguished orator among us, Dr. F., a lawyer and sometime member of the Reichstag, deputy from southwestern Germany. He had been brought in with about two hundred others from a camp in central France. A man of about forty, bearded, he made an impressive appearance, fairly breathing brilliancy and magnetism. On the way to Les Milles he had won not only the confidence of his two hundred associates, but the friendship of the young French officer who was in charge of the transfer. The thing went so far that the young French officer vowed he would rescue the group entrusted to him under any circumstances. He provided himself with identification papers which showed that the bearers had been released from their former camp by official order. The spaces for names were blank, but the papers were stamped and signed. He was going to give them to his charges if worst came to worst.

The brilliant Dr. F., lawyer and ex-deputy to the Reichstag, was not at all pleased with the result of our visit to the captain. He called a meeting of his two hundred companions—they were soon joined by others—and made a magnificent speech. What he said I have forgotten, but I remember that it was a brilliant and an effective oration.

I am sceptical of speeches and speakers. That does not prevent me from being swept off my feet every time by a good speech, but I am swept off my feet, so to say, with reservations. I know how dangerous it is to trust a speaker, and I have made it a principle to wait to see a speech in print before forming a final opinion.

A man may have nothing to say and yet—possibly for that reason—be an excellent speaker. Adolf Hitler is the best of speakers for his particular public, yet he has never in his whole life expressed a thought that was worth the printing. But no, that is perhaps going too far. A few pages in *Mein Kampf* are indeed worth reading, the pages, I mean, that relate to the orator and to the difference between the orator and the writer. The passages on the orator and on propaganda were written by an expert. They are worth reading and will always be. They spring from the innermost being of a man born to nothing but to sway masses of men, and in spite of themselves emphasize the risks that a man runs in listening to a good speaker without taking the necessary precautions.

But here I must resist the temptation to go further into the case of the born writer against the born orator. I must return to my story, to our orator, lawyer, and ex-deputy, Dr. F.

He argued that we must take a very different tone toward the camp authorities, a more vigorous, more threatening tone. We must set them a very brief term, twenty-four hours at the most, and make clear to them that if they do not transfer us by that time we will make our way out forcibly. Should the French soldiers in the latter case fire on us—he did not think they would—well, it were better to die under the bullets of the French than perish under the tortures of the Nazis.

Speeches of this sort naturally increased the unrest among us. Those young Austrians who had come so effectively to my rescue on the day of my admission to the camp called on me again, imploring me to wait no longer, but to make my escape. They would help me to do so. Some ten miles away, they said, in a modest farmhouse lived a farmer and his family. The man was a friend of theirs and shared their political views. They had made all arrangements with him through a soldier. He was ready to take us in. I could hide for weeks in the house in perfect safety.

My two friends also had a plan for escaping from the camp already worked out in detail. A sort of drain or sewer ran under the escarpment out into the open country. For a few yards, but no more, the going would not be very pleasant, they thought. It would be a tight squeeze on all fours through slime and excrement—rather hard on the nose, probably. With their help, however, I could certainly make it. There they stood, young, strong, confident, inspiring confidence. All the same, the thing did not appeal to me. I liked neither the few weeks in the farmhouse nor the few yards in the drain.

Undoubtedly one might bribe the guards and get free in a much pleasanter way. But what was the use? There was no sense in escaping alone and on one's own. Without the energetic and effective help of the French authorities there was no prospect of our evading the advancing Nazis.

It took the guards a long time that evening to get us back into the building, now by friendly persuasion, now by a gentle use of force; and then inside there was no quiet.

When the last signal had been bugled and the lights were out, at least half the camp forgathered in the catacombs. There we exchanged worries and the latest rumours. Two officers appeared. It was of course against the rules to stand around that way in the catacombs at night, but instead of sending us back to our straw piles they joined in the talk. Our situation was perfectly well understood, they said, trying to calm us. But it was altogether apparent that they were not quite at ease themselves.

The whispering, buzzing, arguing went on in the catacombs all night, with frequent outbursts of bitterness against the slackness and irresponsibility of the French. They had no idea even now how quickly the Nazis were moving. We knew! We knew that they might well be upon us within twenty-four hours.

One of our Austrians, a newspaperman, drew the picture with masochistic gusto. The German officers would be all courtesy and correctness toward the French. They would have the camp surrendered and take it over with all due regard to forms. Even in us they would manifest no particular interest at first. They would simply ask for the list of internees, hold a roll-call, and make sure that we were all there. They would not linger long on the names, even on names that they would be tickled to see—Feuchtwanger, for instance. At the most the flitting of a significant grin over their faces—and then they would read the next name.

Among those of us who were in serious danger, not one had the slightest doubt that the best thing he could do in case the Nazis really took over at Les Milles would be to end everything by killing himself. But how was one to manage that? There was no great amount of rope in sight. And even if you got a rope, where could you hang it—undisturbed, that is? We appealed to the Austrian court-barber, the expert smuggler, to lay in a stock of poison. He turned us down.

"Some of my competitors will promise to do it for you," he said. "They will even take your money and hand you any old white powder. Try it, it won't work. Humbug! Toothpowder! Now I'm an honest man. When I promise, I deliver."

Few of us got any sleep that night.

The next morning squad leaders received orders to get the names of men in their squads who wanted to be transferred and to have them in at the office by two that afternoon. Such haste was a good sign, we thought. It gave us confidence.

As soon developed, the preparation of the lists was not such a simple matter after all. Many men could not make up their minds as to what they ought to do, whether to go or to stay. Not that there were so many Nazis among us. It was a question of old people and sick ones who explained that they could not stand the hardships that such a journey would entail. Whatever might happen they preferred to stay where they were and take things as they came. Then there were a lot of poor devils who had never concerned themselves with politics or aspired to anything beyond saving their own lives and the wretched existence they had provided for themselves and their families. They wondered whether the Nazis would really do them any harm. If they were to declare themselves in danger now and so get a transfer, would not the Nazis become suspicious? In that case the Nazis might very well take their relatives at home as hostages and confiscate what was left of their property. What were they to do? It was a pitiable struggle for them. They laid their problems and their doubts before one another—and before me.

Those of us who had everything to fear by remaining at Les Milles waited hopefully for a transfer. We had no other choice. Escape on one's own had shown itself to be a hopeless recourse. Several men had tried during recent nights. In no case had they gone very far. They had been caught at the bridges across the Rhône when not earlier. It was better to wait, we concluded.

In spite of the order for the hasty preparation of lists, our confidence rapidly waned. Some of us were soon wondering whether the order was not a mere feint to put us off and quiet us.

The Nazis in the camp meanwhile were becoming more and more assertive. It was now apparent that there were far more of them among us than we had ever supposed. Hitlerites seemed to sprout more numerously the nearer Hitler's armies came. They were now teasing our French guards and greeting one another publicly in the yard with the Hitler salute.

All that showed, we thought, how great was their confidence, how near they believed their protectors were. Would we be transferred in time, would we be transferred at all? Bad signs increased in number. Stocks of ammunition were being brought into the yards and more machine guns set up. Our soldiers were suddenly reinforced with reservists and gendarmes who stood around aloof and hostile and refused to talk with us. Was this strengthening of our guard a measure of protection? Hardly. Certainly they were there merely to prevent some desperate act on our part.

Our mistrust and excitement grew. Once again we begged the captain to receive us. We had to wait. Finally he let us in.

This time there were five of us. Captain G. assured us he was doing all he could to save us. The General Staff had decided to transfer those of us who were in danger. Actual arrangements for the transfer were now the only matters left. Unfortunately many more desired to be transferred than had been anticipated, and the lists were not yet closed. That made the necessary provisions more difficult.

We listened with the closest and most anxious attention. Our faces must have betrayed no great assurance; in fact, one of my companions rather unfortunately asked whether we could not get our papers and our money back at least. Angered at this manifestation of distrust, the captain turned military and snapped gruffly: "That is my concern!" Just what steps were to be taken in our rescue, he went on, were for the authorities alone to decide. Never had France betrayed the laws of hospitality, he declared pompously.

Our interview had not ended when he was informed that a call from Headquarters was on the wire. He stepped into an adjoining room. One of his officers started to close the door behind him, but he ordered: "Leave it open. These gentlemen are quite at liberty to hear what I have to say"—a human gesture that has erased from my memory much of the evil that the captain allowed to happen to our harm. We listened anxiously. The question seemed to be whether we should be conveyed to Marseille in lorries or whether the railway cars assigned to us could get directly to Les Milles.

So then, one thing was certain. Marseille was actually getting ready to make up a train for us.

That brought us some comfort. But, trustful as they had been some hours before, our comrades were not now to be lifted from their despondency. They had lost faith in any transfer. Not a few went so far as to suspect that the captain's telephone talk in our hearing had been only make-believe.

What were our chances of rescue now? About twelve in a hundred, we agreed; make it ten.

I was walking across the yard a half-hour later when the captain stopped me. Speaking in the manner one would use to an old acquaintance, he told me that he now had the lists, practically all. Some two thousand men wanted to be transferred, twice the number the people in Marseille had been expecting. He thought, however, that we would be able to get away by the next day, or the day after at the latest. Meanwhile he would do everything possible to relieve the nervous tension among the men. Many of the internees, he added, had turned in to his office papers which were designed to prove their loyalty to the French cause. If such papers were found by the Nazis after our transfer they might prove inconvenient and provoke reprisals against members of our families who might be still under German control. He intended therefore to return them to us, leaving it to us what disposition should be made of them. He hoped that I, on my side, would do all I could to calm the people down. With their everlasting questions and delegations they were merely robbing him of valuable time that he could better spend in our interest.

The captain's very sensible and very humane decision was made public forthwith. Lines formed in front of the office. In them we stood waiting to recover papers on which we had once staked such great hopes. In former days we had spent untold efforts to obtain them. Now we were eagerly tearing them up and burning them.

I had formed the impression that Captain G. meant well by us and that he would do everything in his power to put through the transfer. Others were as mistrustful as before. Herr F., the lawyer and ex-deputy, made a new speech. Many level-headed men joined me in making speeches in rebuttal, but he succeeded in having a new delegation appointed to call on the commandant, seven men this time, himself among them. An excuse was devised to justify the dispatch of this new delegation. The night before inmates of the camp, known to be Nazis, had attacked certain of our number. A fight had taken place in the dark and there had been some stabbing. It was feared that the same thing or worse would take place the coming night. The delegation would ask that precautionary measures be taken. Dr. F. of course was not much interested in all that. His idea was that we spoke far too politely, too calmly to the officers. When it was a question of life and death, one should strike a very different tone. Let him come face to face with that captain and he would "touch a match to the seat of his pants."

As things turned out, the commandant was the first to strike the different tone. The Captain G. who received us now was not the Captain G. who had talked with me that morning in the yard.

"What do you want this time?" he roared at us. "Kindly spare me your everlasting cowardice and nervousness. I have already told you— your train leaves tomorrow!"

On that occasion only three or four of the officers were present. We were six or seven, including the ex-deputy Dr. F. The old gentleman Herr S., tactful, propitiatory, was going to explain that this time we had called in connexion with another matter. Dr. F. would not let the old man get a word in. He took the floor himself in firm resolve to speak plainly to the captain. Dr. F. spoke a marvellous French—let us hope he still speaks it, that he did not leave his pelt in France. In his marvellous French he opened for the prosecution with a brilliant arraignment. France, he declared, had made us a most solemn promise of hospitality. He pointed out that he and many others had volunteered for service in the French army.

The application of heat to the seat of the captain's pants did not have all the success that Dr. F. had foreseen. The captain, furious, struck back. We were a lot of neurasthenics, he said; we were not acting like men! Then sounding an emotional note himself, he declaimed: "One must even know how to die if need be." Dr. F., in fine fettle, retorted that we had all demonstrated our readiness to give up our lives in the fight on Hitler. What we did not want to do was to die a senseless death, as victims of a brainless French bureaucracy. We did not want to die because the French government was too incompetent to organize our transfer.

"Be silent! That will do!" thundered the captain, fiery red, imperious. But Orator F. had begun and had no idea at all of halting. Slender, elastic, and imposing to look at in spite of his shabby suit, he towered before the stout, red-faced, pug-faced captain in uniform and fanned the fire.

"It is all very easy for you, Captain," he shouted. "When the Germans come you will salute politely and the German captain will salute politely. You will turn over the camp to him, take off your uniform, and go home. And you ask us to do the dying!"

For a fraction of a second the captain tried to think of a reply. Then he brought his riding-crop down upon the table. Fussy old Herr S. tried to say something that would smooth things over, but before he could open his mouth the captain strode into the adjoining room, slamming the door behind him.

So there we were. Dr. F., the ex-deputy, was a great orator, but he had patently done a very stupid thing. In our situation one could hardly have done a more stupid thing than to alienate the man who held our fate in his hands. Monsieur G. was the one man who had connexions with the offices that could help us. Not only that, all that had been said had already been said many times. The captain was right: negotiations served only to deprive him of precious time. Sending delegations had been nonsense in the first place and now Dr. F.'s fiery oratory had only angered our well-meaning commandant.

All the same I must confess that Dr. F.'s procedure, unwise as it was, delighted me. In the course of his speech I inwardly applauded every word he uttered. So it was with the others. The whole camp was exultant when word of Dr. F.'s "energetic" speech spread abroad. Devoid of sense and purpose, nay, as harmful as it had been, we were all glad that someone at long last had told those Frenchmen what we thought of them.

THE SECOND NIGHT

The night that now followed was torture for most of us.

Even outwardly it was a different night from other nights. The fight that the Nazis had started in the dark the night before was not the first of its kind. An order was issued that thenceforward a few more electric bulbs should be allowed, and French guards were posted inside the building. They were stationed at the stairway and near the big outside door and were relieved every two hours. They yawned and nodded good-night to us as we went up.

That night there was more whispering, more anxiety and excitement in the big room than ever. One had an almost physical sense of those hundreds of men lying there on their straw piles, listening to the whispering around them, of the hopes and anxieties of the day that now in the dark were assuming gigantic stature and of the weighing, weighing, weighing that was going on in every mind: Will we succeed? Will we get out of here alive? Will the Nazis take us by surprise? Will we be rescued?

I would be lying were I to say that I was spared all anxiety that night. At the same time the coolness that I exhibited, quite to the amazement of my comrades, was by no means feigned.

I believe I alluded to my fatalism in the early pages of this book. I must touch on it again here, for my attitude during the happenings that now become part of my story would be hard to understand without taking account of these beliefs or, if you will, superstitions of mine. To the two confessions that I made some pages back I must here add a third.

Most of the things that happen around us are determined by a great multiplicity of causes. We are able to discern only a few of these causes at the time. We see now one link, now another in their chain. We never see their sequence as a whole. We never learn anything about its beginning or its end. It is therefore the wiser part for us not to single out particular causes and think of them as *the* causes, but, however repugnant it may be to our over-presumptuous intelligence, to ascribe to chance the leading role in the lives of all of us. Einstein resignedly acknowledged that the best explanation science can offer for things that happen in the universe is that they happen as in a game of chance.

On the other hand, the human spirit is so constituted that it must absolutely have its explanation of this unfathomable game of Life and Fate. We cannot accept the fact that our lives should be governed by chance, in other words, by laws that we do not know. Finding no explanation that satisfies our reason, we seek one beyond reason, in superstition, mysticism, religion. Unbeknown to himself perhaps every man among us, however level-headed he may consider himself, carries thousands of superstitious notions around with him. And at the decisive moments in our lives more especially we are governed not by our reason but by magical conceptions that we have inherited from our primitive ancestors.

It amuses me to dig deep down into myself and uncover the magical conceptions that may be determining my conduct. I try to catch them by surprise just as they are pressing forward to the threshold of consciousness. I am not ashamed of my superstition, I confess it, and I do not consider myself more stupid on that account than people who refuse to admit their own.

Knowing full well, moreover, that it is all nonsense, and laughing at myself for what I am doing, I nevertheless assume that I have found a line, a secret law that determines the course of my life. I know that I am going to be continually tormented in my daily living by thousands of little annoyances, by a thousand tricks of the world about me, but

I believe that these little irritations are just the compensation that Fate requires of me for the good fortune that I am certain to have in the big things, the decisive things.

All my life long I have been and shall be afflicted with little and not seldom ridiculous troubles. I am a person who loves orderliness and security, yet for long years I have been obliged to live without my proper legal papers. And precisely I, who particularly abhor dealings with government officials, have always been battling with such people for passports, certificates, permits. It has been much the same with my finances. In the course of nearly two decades I have earned quite reputably, by productive activity alone, enough money to have lived very much as I pleased; yet wherever my earnings have been banked they have never failed to be frozen or confiscated. My health has followed similar laws. I have a tough constitution and it has enabled me to survive serious illnesses. But my health is delicate—I am susceptible to colds, my eyesight is poor, I have difficulty in speaking clearly, my digestion is not as good as it might be and has played me unpleasant tricks at important moments.

In a word, in whatever I undertake, in whatever sphere, I encounter absurdly petty difficulties that most of my contemporaries are spared. A publisher of mine failed to copyright one of my most successful books and the greater part of my income from it went by the board. People in my employ have committed offences for which I have had to assume responsibility and pay out considerable sums. I have ever been called upon to squander money, time, nerves, life, on unspeakably silly things. I was always on the look-out for a good lawyer, a good doctor, a good banker, for people who were better versed than I in such matters and could take them off my shoulders. Well, I did find the right doctor, the right lawyer, the right banker. The lawyer worked for me for half a year and then was killed in a railway accident. The doctor took care of me for two years, then committed suicide on account of Hitler. The bank handled my property for nine months, then it was seized by the Nazis.

Over against these little sufferings I can set a number of decidedly fortunate circumstances. I experienced the First World War at an age when I had not yet hardened and was still capable of developing. That enabled me to recast my war impressions in forms of practical knowledge that proved of signal value to my life and my work. I have written the books I wanted to write, and though I may often have cursed the labour they required of me, it gives me a satisfaction that I would not exchange for any other. More than that: society is so organized today that it not only allows me to do what I like to do, to write well, that is; it even pays me for doing it. In short, I have had the extraordinary luck to be successful albeit I am gifted. Add to it all that I have found the women and the friends that I wanted and they have stood by me. All these circumstances, taken together, incline me therefore to imagine that the general line of my destiny is the one I have just described—good luck in the things that matter, bad luck in non-essentials.

An atavistic, fetishistic conception I am well aware, something very like the faiths of those who imagine that they are the special protégés of God or of some saint. But after all I have this superstitious feeling and, to tell the truth, I am rather satisfied that I have it.

That superstitious feeling is reinforced in me by a second superstition which is a strange mixture of meticulousness and pride.

I have some few more books to write. More exactly, of the hundred or so books that I have in my head, I have chosen a certain number that I intend to write whatever else may happen. Fourteen books are haunting me, fourteen books that I have to write, because I assume that only I can write them and that they are highly important. I know of course that they are important only to me, but my self-complacency impels me to assume that they are also important for the world. And I simply cannot imagine that anything serious could happen to me—or even that I should die—before completing those fourteen books. God, or Fate, simply cannot allow it.

This feeling that after all nothing serious could happen to me probably accounted for the stoicism that so astonished my comrades that night, and if I felt less panicky than the others during those sinister hours, it was because the same feeling sustained me.

Let it not be thought that my sense of security remained untroubled the whole night. I remember this night very vividly, I remember many details. There I lay on my straw pile, hearing the men around me, sensing their nearness, thinking many different things, feeling many different things. My worried intellect warned me not to take things lightly. It coldly marshalled facts that justified the greatest alarm. The Nazis really were pretty damn close. And even if the train did come, even if the transfer were effected, the day when all France would be in Nazi hands was only being postponed. Where would that day find us? Really across the border? More than unlikely.

To bolster myself up I thought again of the fourteen books that I was longing to write, that I was sure to write. But that heartening idea was troubled by another, no less superstitious. Certain numerologists in Germany had figured out that the number nine was fateful to German artists. Beethoven, Bruckner, and Mahler each wrote nine symphonies, Wagner nine operas that are still sung, Schiller, Hebbel, and Grillparzer each nine plays that are still produced. Very clever people have discovered that out of Goethe's works only nine were really alive, from which it would follow, in a manner of speaking, that he died not of his eighty-two years but of the completion of *Faust*. Now on finishing the third part of my *Josephus*, I had completed exactly nine works that fulfilled my purpose. The fact troubled me. I toyed in mock-melancholic fashion with the thought of my death. I balanced accounts. What had I really had in life? What had I failed to have? Had I led a full life? Had it been a wise or a foolish, a happy or a wretched life? Had it been worth living?

I came to the conclusion that, after all, my fifty-six years had been good, full, rich years. I would have been as reluctant to have missed the bad they had brought as the good; for both the bad and the good had enriched me. Without the seasoning of the bad I could not have appreciated and enjoyed the good. "Welcome Good! Welcome Evil!" a German poet once wrote, and ever since I was a boy I had repeated an apophthegm from the Talmud in my mind. Of evil it said: "Gam su letovo" (That too is all for the best).

With a certain obstinate meticulousness I tried to determine whether among the various projects that had occupied me all my life I had really executed the right ones. Should I not have written one of the fourteen books I still have to write rather than the ones I actually chose to write? The time I had spent on women and other pleasures, had it been well or badly spent? With the same obstinate meticulousness, but striving for the severest honesty, I tried to determine how much time I had devoted to worthwhile things and how much to things and people that had not been worthwhile.

I was content. It amounted to this: everything had been worthwhile, at bottom even the foolishness. Certain particularly foolish things that I had done drifted through my mind and I rejoiced in the memory of them. Lying on my straw, I smiled.

Day broke. The big doors were opened. There was the greatest excitement. What about the train? The promised train, was it coming?

From one point in the camp one could see a railway embankment and on it a bit of track. Sharp-eyed people thought they could make out railway cars on the bit of track. And cars in fact were there. Only a few—the guards soon made it clear that they were not for us.

Our hopes sank. But then a report spread that out of practical considerations the transfer would be made by squads and, in fact, those of the men in Squads 26 to 50 who put their names on the lists of prospective transferees received an order to form in line in the western yard at two o'clock in the afternoon with their luggage.

Squads 26 to 50 were greatly envied. Some of them still had not made up their minds whether to go or to stay. Two elderly men in particular talked things over with me. They had no idea at all what to do and they were desperately unhappy at being called upon to make so momentous a decision. A little more and they would have said it was all my fault. Was I not the one who had persuaded the captain to leave the decision to individuals? Indeed they would have been better satisfied if the military had disposed of them without asking any questions.

All in all, however, when the four hundred men from Squads 26 to 50 who had asked to go gathered in the yard around two o'clock, a mood of happy excitement prevailed. They formed in line and waited, and we others waited with them, almost as excited as they.

Ten minutes passed, a quarter of an hour, half an hour, another half-hour. Then an order came: the men in line should disband. The train would not go that day.

Disappointment and deepest despair. We were beside ourselves with helpless rage. The French were making fools of us. They were letting us sit there till the Nazis came. They were pretending that something was going on just to dissuade us from escaping. Their idea was to hand us over to the Nazis in order to gain a point of favour with them.

My young Austrians again besought me to join them in the escape through the drain. Perceiving that I did not take to the plan, they went on and explained how in case the camp were seized by the Nazis the coming night, I could jump out of a window and join them outside. A breakneck project all around. I had them go over the scheme twice and, frankly, could not grasp it. The plan certainly would not have succeeded.

What I wanted was to be alone. I had to have a few moments alone. In a corner of the yard was a little storehouse, dark, close, musty, inside. It occurred to me that I might go in there, sit quietly on the stone floor for a while or even close my eyes and meditate.

On the stone steps in front of the little storehouse a small group of men was gathered.

"Come and join us—do," one of them urged me. "Cheer us up a little. We are all quite down. You are always so optimistic."

"Yes, my dear Feuchtwanger," said another of the group—Walter Hasenclever, the author. "We need bucking up today. What percentage do you rate our hopes at now?"

We stood there in the sunlight; a gentle breeze was blowing—not too much and not too little. It was wonderful weather all through those days. But I had been bucking up so many disheartened people of late that it was costing me some effort to keep my own chin up. My talk with the Austrians had told on me. I could still see nothing but that line of men standing there in the yard, full of hope, only to be sent back to their straw piles again. The general depression had infected me.

"Our hopes? Five percent," I answered and my voice must have shown how gloomy, how weary, how empty I felt.

I should not have spoken that way. I should not have said "five percent." It was not my true opinion. It was wrong, objectively and subjectively. I was known as an optimist. To make myself out such a defeatist instead of finding the cheering word was a piece of almost criminal thoughtlessness. Presently I had to perceive that my answer impressed the others.

"As low as five percent?" Hasenclever meditated. "I am afraid you are right," he said, answering his own question.

We again fell to discussing how best one could make an end of things if the Nazis really descended upon us. Hasenclever had thought up something new.

"You go up to one of the Nazi guards," he suggested, "give him all the money you have on hand and say: 'Look here, comrade! I'm going to make a try at escaping. Shoot straight!'"

Meanwhile the Austrian polyhistor had joined us. Listening, he poked a big dirty ear forward and presently began to tell of the death of Socrates, quoting a string of authorities from memory. I only half listened. I regretted that I had said that about the five percent. But instead of blaming myself I turned—for that is human nature—on the crazy, innocent Austrian polyhistor. Everything about the man irritated me, his filth, his unctuous voice.

"Listen here, Dr. P.," I said. "Explain one thing! What, in your opinion, did Socrates mean by that obscure utterance to his friends: 'I owe a cock to Asclepius; do not forget to pay it?'"

Not so long before I had read, among many forced interpretations, one that struck me as plausible, but I had forgotten what it was. Dr. P. had not seen the article. His bafflement afforded me satisfaction.

The afternoon wore on, bringing signs aplenty that our discouragement was baseless, that the transfer would begin after all.

First we got our mail and that was not the usual day for it. (There was no great amount of it. Only a few of the men received definite information as to what had happened to their relatives, but when we pieced together odds and ends of news it began to look as though our wives had been interned, almost all of them, in the great camp at Gurs, in the Pyrenees.)

Then men assigned to work in the kitchen reported that tinned goods, along with cheese, bread, and the like, had arrived in large quantities—provisions obviously intended for the journey.

Furthermore, we were informed that anyone who wished could have his money back, and for the last time an interminable line of waiting men formed in front of the little window where the money was paid out. Ironically enough, we had before our eyes as we stood there a large placard admonishing us to "Give for France" and the same suggestion was made to us orally by the lieutenant in charge.

It developed that many of the people who had been shipped to us from northern France were not to get their money. The commandants of the camps there had deposited the various amounts in local banks and had found it impossible in the headlong haste of their departure to withdraw them. Now the authorities were handing out vouchers to the internees concerned to the effect that "Regiment X owes Bearer Y so and so many francs." What was an internee to do with such a voucher? He tried to sell it to any Frenchman for any price he could get.

And then, finally, something fabulous happened! The commandant announced by a posted notice that the train would leave Les Milles station the following morning, June 22, at eleven o'clock. The notice was affixed to one of the open wings of the main door that led from the yard into the building. We stood there before the yawning black hole and read the poster. We had it in writing, in black and white, in typewritten letters. And there was the commandant's signature, big, in his rounded, flourished handwriting, blue—the colour of hope: "Goruchon."

There was a general rush to look at the poster. We all stood in front of it for a long time. We looked at the poster, we looked at each other. Most of the men were probably thinking that now at last it was true. But they did not dare to express their thought.

When I saw the poster I, for my part, was certain that it meant what it said. Yes, the train was going to go! We were going to escape the Nazis. I was ashamed to have had so little faith for even so short a time.

Just then the theory that I had tried vainly to remember flashed across my mind, the theory as to what Socrates meant when he besought his friends to sacrifice a cock to Asclepius, god of the art of healing, god of pharmacy. Perceiving that the potion was doing its work, so the theory ran, he wanted to thank the gods for making the human mind inventive enough to administer powerful drugs in the doses required for desired effects. I was glad that my memory had not failed me after all, and took it as a good sign.

An order was issued that we should be up at three o'clock the following morning and fall in line at five, ready to march, with luggage limited to the strictly necessary.

The camp hummed with preparations. Many of the internees had brought their last worldly possessions with them. What should they carry along, what leave behind? They would sort out their things, pack up, tie up, change their minds, untie, pack up again, leave different things behind. What was "strictly necessary?" They would have to begin over and over again. Many were giving away what they could not take to friends who were to stay behind. Many were trying to sell them, hawking them about.

Numbers of people came and pressed me with questions. There were those who even now did not know whether they ought to go or stay. Others were doubtful whether they would really be taken along.

Accommodations would be inadequate, that was certain. If there wasn't room for all of us, wouldn't there be another muster? Then wouldn't they be the only ones left behind? The unfortunates turned to me. Was it really enough merely to have one's name on the list? Was it certain that all on the list would be taken along? They could not reach the commandant; I could. Would I not go to him and explain that they in particular were in grave danger? I was obliged to give the same comforting reassurances fifty, a hundred times.

That night, too, most of us got very little sleep. The most confident nursed some faint misgivings, the most sceptical some ray of hope.

For my part I slept well during that short night at Les Milles, and when reveille sounded it snatched me from a deep slumber.

There was an air of bustling animation all around. Everybody was busy. One last review of the things we intended to take with us. Everybody was getting his stuff together, a literal "clearing out."

A strange tension had developed overnight in the relations between those who were leaving and those who were to stay behind. We had been so long together by now, welded to one another by the same hopes and fears, by the same conditions of living. Now our ways were parting, possibly—almost certainly—forever. Many were disappointed that others they had come to consider close comrades, and whom they had certainly expected to have with them, were to remain behind. A strangely mixed feeling this that separated the two groups! The reveille at three in the morning was only for those whose names were on the lists; the others were free to go on sleeping. They did not choose to do so. They rose when we did, picked their way among us, tried to make themselves useful, helped us pack, carried our things down the rickety stairs, gave us well-intentioned gifts to take along. Yet all along they had not the slightest doubt as to what the transferees were thinking: that those who were not leaving assumed that they had nothing to fear from the Nazis, that, in a word, they were "traitors." Few of them, certainly, were traitors. Serious sympathizers with the Nazis were very few in the camp. The man who stayed either felt too old and too feeble to endure the hardships of the transfer, or else was one of those poor devils who did not know which way to turn but had finally decided that by staying he had a better chance to save the lives of himself and his relatives. They were hurt at our mistaken estimate of them. They made every effort to convince us and themselves that they could not have decided otherwise. When we waved them away with an "Of course," or "That's all right," they would not let go but stubbornly began over again with their justifications. They kept doing all manner of little favours for us to show that they felt they belonged with us and not with the others. But the rift was irreparable. Most of us looked down on them with a mixture of scorn and pity. The poor fellows had chosen the worst alternative, of that we were certain. They would face far bitterer sufferings if the Nazis came.

So we squatted around, stood around, ran around, drank our last cup of coffee in Les Milles, got ready to clear out. At the height of all the bustle I was changing the cloth tennis shoes I had worn the whole time in camp for a regular pair when a young Austrian physician, who slept several straw piles from me and was Hasenclever's neighbour, came over to me in the greatest distress.

"Come," he said. "Come with me, quick. I'm afraid something has happened. I can't rouse Hasenclever. He won't wake up."

We went over to him. Four or five men were gathered around him, two of them doctors.

"He has taken some sedative or other," they explained; "that is certain. We must pump out his stomach, and soon."

Walter Hasenclever lay there, stretched out at full length, motionless. Hasenclever had always had something busy, something hurried about him. There had been a nervous twitch, of late years at least, to his pointed, mouselike face that was so intelligent, so animated, so alive. It was hard to imagine him asleep. Now there he lay as heavy as a stone and not to be awakened.

The previous evening, just before the lights went out, he had dropped around to see me. I was deep in conversation with my neighbour, the mechanic.

"May I have a word with you, Feuchtwanger?" he asked.

"Of course," I answered. "Just a moment more." I wanted to finish something I had been saying to the mechanic.

"No, no. Nothing important. Don't let me interrupt. So then, good night."

The thought of our talk the day before on the stone steps, in the sunlight, weighed heavily on me. "Our hopes? Five percent." "As low as five percent?" Hasenclever had asked. And now there he lay and we could not wake him. Had he come to think there would never be a train? Or had he simply decided to have nothing more to do with the everlasting, the revolting torments of this wretched, degrading life?

A stretcher was brought and on it the unconscious writer was carried over to the narrow, dirty wooden stairs. He was to be taken to the infirmary barracks to have his stomach pumped out. The steps were crowded with people who were trying to get down to the yard with their bundles. The stretcher bearers struggled forward. As the gloomy little procession went by, a man was jostled and exclaimed bitterly: "They might let him check out in peace!"

But to have done that would have been against the laws of humanity and of French hospitality.

We assembled in the yard. It was a question of dividing us into new squads. The thing was done with the usual amount of confusion and red tape, but we had plenty of time. The train was not to start till eleven o'clock.

We stood around and waited. Those who were staying gathered about us, stood at the windows, looking out, waited with us, as excited as us, always finding one more thing to say.

Of the old Austrian gentlemen whom I have identified as cultivated, only two had decided to go with us. The others sat on their folding-chairs, courtly, majestic, threadbare, resignedly watching the preparations for our departure. One of them secretly confided to me that he had managed to provide himself with prussic acid—"Real prussic acid," he said.

I went to the infirmary barracks to see Hasenclever. The infirmary was a bare, dismal stone building. The patients lay on much-used camp cots. There was a revolting smell in the place. The dying Hasenclever lay screened off from the rest. His face was deep red, his throat swollen, his tongue protruded, thick, bluish—an effect, I was told, of the stomach-pumping. He was rattling loudly. A German and a French physician were in attendance. Hasenclever was unconscious, they assured me, feeling nothing, hearing nothing. The French doctor still had some hope, the German none at all.

I called on the commandant. He listened impatiently—there was so much to do.

"Yes, yes," he said. "I know, the writer."

"We can't leave him here," I said. "We can't let the Nazis get him. We must take him along."

"That is not for you to decide nor for me," said Captain G. "The doctor must say whether he can be moved."

I went back to my squad. We waited. Then something great happened. The train was there. There it was, all of a sudden. We could see it. From the same place where we had discerned a few cars the day before, we could see something that looked like cars now. But this time it was our train. Our guards had seen it. They had already talked with our new guards, who had come on the train. We looked and looked, our eyes starting out of our heads, to see something that resembled cars. Yes, that was it, the train so long awaited—our train.

We waited some more. But the wait now was not so unpleasant. It was only seven in the morning and therefore certain that we would really be leaving by eleven o'clock, as the commandant had promised in his notice.

Even more than before they now talked at and questioned me. One man kept at me: "Tell me truly now. Don't you really think it is better for me to stay here? Why should the Nazis do anything to me? Just because I have a little lingerie shop in Nice and my name is Gustav Kohn? What interest can Hitler possibly have in me? Don't you think I ought to stay?"

And another implored: "You must go and see the commandant at once and tell him that the train must go fast. They say we are to be four or five days on the road. Then there's no sense in the whole business. Hitler's sure to get us. Go to the commandant at once. Tell him that the train must go fast."

The talk about the four or five days started because of the large quantities of provisions that had been distributed among us: tinned foods, cheese, chocolate, and plenty of bread; enough, surely, for a very long journey.

I went back to the infirmary.

"Could Hasenclever possibly travel?" I asked the French doctor.

"The final decision rests with the staff doctor," he answered, and that officer had not yet come in. For his own part he did not think Hasenclever was in a condition to travel.

Again I called on the commandant. "The doctor thinks he may not be in a condition to travel," I reported despondently.

"I told you as much," the captain answered, striking his riding-crop against his leg.

"Well, then, what is to happen, Captain? We can't just leave him behind this way."

"Just what do you take us for?" asked the commandant.

"I give you my word of honour as a French officer, the man will not fall into the hands of the Nazis. If we can't manage any other way we'll slip the papers of a dead French soldier into his pocket."

Around ten o'clock everything was ready. "Forward-march!" came the order, and the first contingent was off. We proceeded in divisions of two hundred to the station, which was not very far from the camp, and from which it must have been the practice to ship the bricks.

I was in the second division. Karl was again separated from me and I had to carry my luggage myself. A scant quarter of an hour perhaps, but it was hot. I am not much good when it comes to carrying luggage and before long I was the last man in my division. The guards who were escorting us kept hurrying us along. "Allez hop!" they would shout the moment I set down a valise. My straw-fellow, the mechanic from the Saar, noticed my difficulties and tried to help me, but he had a load of his own to carry. The sweat poured down from my forehead and covered my glasses. I could hardly see a thing. It was horribly dusty, besides. I stumbled over the rails, I puffed and panted, I tried to wipe the sweat away with my coat sleeve. The road to safety was a hard road from the very beginning.

Then at last I saw it—the train. There it stood in front of us, close enough to touch. A long train, as I became further aware in lugging my things past one car after another. First passenger cars, a few of them, outmoded ones, antediluvian. Then the freight cars, one, another, a tenth, a twentieth, an I-don't-know-how-manyth. They all bore the inscription: "Eight Horses or Forty Men." They seemed to be terribly ramshackle affairs. All the same, it was a train. It stood on rails and the rails led—they led away off somewhere beyond the reach of the Nazi troops, they led to safety. Puffing, stumbling, sweating, prodded by the soldiers, I hurried along the line of cars and as I passed each one I thought: "This last bit and then you are in a car. Then you are safe."

We reached the car to which we had been assigned.

"All aboard! Allez hop!"

It was easy to say that, but how *aller hop*? The car was terribly high and there were no steps. A few spry ones among us clambered up over the struts. The others pushed one another up. Lifting, shoving, we got the luggage in. Strong hands reached down toward me too, strong arms lifted me from below and behind. I was inside my car!

There were four walls, nothing more. A hole forward in the side wall on the right, a second hole toward the rear on the opposite side. They would probably admit very little light. For the moment the bright sunlight was streaming in through the big, wide sliding doors which were open. Not bad at all, taken as a whole. There were some thirty of us there. The car was bare and much worn, but roomy.

What should we do with the luggage? All together in the middle or in piles along the walls? In any event, the individual pieces of luggage would have to be piled skilfully one on the other or one in the other if we were not to lose precious space. Once a piece was stowed away in the pile, one could get it out only in case of extreme necessity.

Differences of opinion, harsh debates, but once we had our luggage in order, angers cooled. Everybody was animated, in a good mood. We sat or lay down on the floor with the sunlight streaming in over us. A fat young fellow, a Hollander, had smuggled in his folding-chair. So there we were in our train and in a half an hour, an hour at the latest our car would be moving, taking us out of danger, out of the enemy's reach.

There was a drop of bitterness in the cup of our joy—the thought of Hasenclever.

The train was filling up. We observed with some anxiety how very full it was becoming. How many were there in our car? Thirty-five of us, but we would be having guards in addition. Suppose we say forty-two.

Sergeants were already calling in from outside: "How many are you in here?"

"Forty-five," we answered, prudently closing the door. But that shut out the sunlight and our car suddenly became a dark cage.

"How many are you?" came the call again from the outside. "Doors open!" a voice ordered and a sergeant clambered in and counted us. "Ten more in here!" he commanded. We protested desperately, but in vain. The ten were already clambering in upon us, disconcerted, bewildered. We resisted, admitting only seven or eight. We blocked the door, fighting. It was simply impossible, there was no room left for more men.

"Too much luggage in this car," an officer declared, angry, perspiring. "Out with those bundles," he ordered.

We all protested. We had really brought only the "strictly necessary." For many those few bundles were the last remnant of their worldly possessions. They had brought with them everything they still owned, two suits, two pairs of shoes. But there was no help for it. They had to

143

give it up. "Out with that baggage!" the officer shouted again. "Do you want your comrades to stay here and croak so that you can take your rubbish along?"

In an uproar of wailing, shrieking, and cursing, bundles were thrown out, a quarrel developing over every piece of discarded luggage. Then even when we stood pressed together as closely as seemed possible, some few men were still wandering along the train unable to find places. Two Algerian soldiers climbed aboard—Arabs in turbans, our guards— and they took up still more space. And men were still wandering along outside. And once more an officer climbed up over our struts. He could not get in the car and held fast to the struts outside.

"Three more men in here," he ordered.

"No more room," we shouted back in despair.

"There has to be room," he bellowed, and one man was shoved in upon us by main force.

Packed shoulder to shoulder we stood there on our feet, sullen. Sitting down was out of the question. The Algerian guards were friendly. One of them was an oldish man with a beard, the other younger, about thirty, a handsome fellow with the eyes of a gazelle. They spoke very little French, but two of our number could manage Arabic. We offered them cigarettes and we got on well together.

It is amazing how soon the human being adapts himself to every situation, even the worst, and finds a way to make the very best of it. We reorganized the luggage to take up still less space. As for ourselves, we accepted our lot. That was the way our car was, cramped, repulsive, but it would carry us to freedom.

And then—we held our breath—the train started.

Though it was against orders, our Algerian guards allowed us to open the big sliding doors again. A few lucky ones could sit in the wide opening and let their legs hang. I stood toward the rear squeezed in the crowd, but by rising on tiptoe I could look out. We were rattling along—there was our building, there the yard. I could see the men who had stayed behind. At a closed railway-gate stood a couple of soldiers, two officers, and our commandant. He waved toward the train with his gloved hand, pride on his face. He had done it. Probably he was glad to be rid of us too.

The train bumped and rattled along. We were thrown against one another. The luggage that we had packed away so artfully began to totter. One piece came down, then another, finally the whole pile collapsed. But we were happy, all the same—at least for the first half-hour. We were out of Les Milles. We were not obliged to wait for the butchers any longer with hands tied.

I looked at that carload of humanity that chance had jumbled together about me. First of all my helpful straw-fellow, the mechanic from the Saar. A friend of his was there too, a small manufacturer who had a son with him. The father was a shrewd, worldly-wise man, originally from Odessa. Beside them another father and son, also from Odessa. Strange that these fathers and sons should both come from Odessa and meet by chance in just that car. They had never seen each other before and despised each other at first sight.

I have already alluded to our fat, phlegmatic young Hollander and his little folding-chair. Obliged to stand on his feet, he held his little chair clasped tightly to his paunch, indifferent to the curses of a neighbour who kept on being poked in the ribs by the iron legs. Gradually he elbowed a little room for himself and began happily unfolding his chair. The whole car blew up. One of the men in the car was sick and the Hollander had no choice but to be noble, helpful, good, and relinquish his little chair to him, which he did, but with a long face. Further on were two businessmen of capacious circumference. Almost all their luggage had been thrown out of the car, but they had salvaged a rolled-up mattress and they sat down on it proudly when it came their turn to sit down. There was a young man with a boyish face and an air of unassuming self-assurance. Leadership in the organization of the car's company fell automatically to him without his making a move to obtain it. A fairly thankless task it proved to be. It was he who requisitioned the Hollander's chair for the sick man, and the Hollander eyed him with the frankest and bitterest antipathy thenceforward. All those people, whether liking or hating each other at first sight, stood there on their feet in one press of humanity, packed together, tangled together, inseparably tied together for as long as the journey should last.

We rattled on, away from Les Milles, and we racked our brains as to where they could be taking us. To the Pyrenees? To one of the camps in the East Pyrenees? Or farther away toward the West? Maybe to Gurs, where our wives were? Perhaps overseas to one of the colonies. No matter where to, our first goal was the Rhône. Hitler's armies were headed down our side of the river. We would not be out of danger till we had crossed.

We had to get over that bridge. But there were no bridges over the Rhône south of Les Milles. We had to go north. North would mean toward Hitler's armies. We were anything but safe, then. Hitler's armies were nearby, they were fast. Who would get first to the bridge over the Rhône, they or we?

The train was unbearably slow and stopped every other minute. But at last, at long, long last, we came to Arles, and there was the bridge across the Rhône.

But we did not cross the bridge. Our train ran through the Arles station and halted on a siding in the open country.

It was growing late in the afternoon and we were still on our side of the Rhône. The train stopped and showed not the slightest intention of going on.

However, it was a chance for us to get out—we were allowed to.

We clambered down and there was green grass and a flowing brook, and people came up, peasants, and they had something to sell—apricots, sour, half-ripe apricots, bad ones, but we were thirsty and bought them and they tasted good. A gentle slope, green with clumps of bushes and a tall growth of new grass, led down to the brook. We had known nothing but brick dust for so long! Now we sat down in the grass, stretched out in it, breathed in its quickening fragrance and the freshness of the little stream. It was wonderful.

The stop lasted two hours almost. We had risen at three in the morning and had been on our feet all day, tense with expectation and excitement. We were tired out. Most of us fell asleep there in the grass. It was a good rest, but a dangerous one and every minute it lasted increased the danger. Every minute brought Hitler's armies nearer. Yet, after such a long privation, the joy of lying on a greensward without a wall around us, under a bright sky, overshadowed any anxiety we may have had. We were almost sorry when we were ordered aboard again.

The train started and it began to cross the bridge. It was a long bridge. We looked at it intently as we crossed. We could see that preparations had been made to blow it up.

There, across at last. We were across the Rhône and safe—at least for a few days.

We did not enjoy our new sense of safety as much as we had expected. Our anxiety had lasted too long and our relief from it had come too gradually. Night soon fell, besides, and its sufferings were to erase every remnant of our sense of release.

With the coming of dark our Algerian guards were afraid to let the doors stay open in disregard of orders. They pulled them to and our cage snapped shut.

Lying down was not to be thought of, but only a few of us could find room to sit down. The young organizer with the boyish face found a solution. Twenty of us would sit down for two hours and get what sleep we could, then another twenty would take our places. There was something quietly authoritative about his manner, and the telling off and dividing were carried out expeditiously and without friction.

The two Algerian guards stretched out at full length athwart the doors. The first twenty of us sat or at least squatted down along the wall as best we could. Our best was not very good.

The others remained on their feet. The car filled with darkness, cold, and stench. We rattled on, swaying now to one side, now to the other with the jounces of the train.

We closed our eyes, we dozed—but one cannot sleep for any length of time standing on one's feet. It is torture to stand upright in the dark, especially when one is dead tired and has had no sleep. You try one foot, then you try the other. Any move you make disturbs a neighbour. You rest your weight on the man in front of you, then on the man behind you, and they do the same to you. A piece of luggage falls. One of the men standing steps on the toes of a man who is sitting. The unending noise wears down one's nerves: curses, groans, snores, low at first then louder.

Rain had begun to fall and it was growing cooler. The car-boarding was not tight. Water leaked through and wet the floor along the walls. Those of us who were on our feet, packed close together, now swayed *en masse* as the train lurched. The cursing from out of the dark increased as one man now trod on another. One heard pleas, entreaties, bursts of anger: "Get over there, a little, just a little!"

Day broke at last. A grey, foggy light made its way through the openings in front and behind and brought the whole wretchedness of that carload of human freight into view. But the mere fact that it was growing light seemed of itself to alleviate the horror. Yes, after all, in spite of one's exhaustion, in spite of one's agony, one felt one's spirits rise. Comfort and misery are relative things.

It was growing light, and we stopped at a station. The side doors were shoved open and we crept out on stiffened legs. There was nothing in sight except rails and stones, no place to lie down anywhere, and it was cold. But we could relieve ourselves. More than that, there was water, water to wash in, water to drink. Besides, we could stretch our muscles, swing our arms, kick out our legs, and sit down. A bit of sun broke through the rain clouds and with it the hideous night was forgotten in the happy feeling that we were free of Les Milles and that Hitler's armies were far away, on the other side of the Rhône.

We engaged in an exchange of thoughts and feelings, satisfactions and cares. The main question was still unsolved: Whither were we bound? No one could answer. The officers in command of the train declared that they did not know themselves. The engineer knew that he was to take the train as far as Toulouse; there he would be relieved by another man.

It turned out that we were in the seaport town of Cette. We weighed seriously the chances of escape. There might be a ship in the harbour. Guards told us that two large ships were docked there, waiting to take on British subjects who were returning to England after the collapse of France. Perhaps these English ships would take some of us along too.

Yet even as we considered the idea we knew how fantastic such projects were. It would have been madness to give up a conveyance we actually had, our train, in the remote hope that an English ship might take us aboard. For the time being at least we were safe where we were, however wretched our train might be; and nobody tried to escape.

The sun shone warmer. We opened some of our tins and broke leaves of bread. There was water to drink. We could sit down. We were alive and glad of it.

Then, however, we had to climb aboard again and our joy took wing. Now the officers saw to it that the cars were kept closed by day as well. Air and light came in only through the small end windows. Our distress of the day before was revived in every evil detail. However small we made ourselves, we took space and air from our neighbours. We were a torment to one another.

There was a stench in the car. Two men were suffering from dysentery. A bucket was placed in the car for their use. They glared defiantly around and the others glared furiously at them.

The rest of us, of course, could not attend to our needs inside the car. We had to wait until the train stopped somewhere. It almost always stopped in the open country. Then we clambered out or, if one had sufficient practice, leapt out. I have already said that the struts were very high and that there were no steps. Once outside, the men stood or squatted on the tracks and attended to their needs. But we never knew when the train was to start again. Sometimes it started off unexpectedly, after only a few seconds. The squatters would then leap to their feet and race after the train. There were old men among us. They ran, pitiable, ludicrous, holding up their trousers, in great anxiety. They would rush headlong, would try, painfully, to clamber up the high strut on their car. One or the other would happen to get at the wrong car. The occupants would beat his hands to drive him away; for the car was full, there was absolutely no room for one more inside. But he had to get aboard; what would become of him if he were left behind?

There was an orthodox Jew in our car and he held fast to his practices. For all the hellish crowding and the unbearable rattling of the train, he got out his prayer shawl and his phylactery, took his bearings to find the East, and then, facing Jerusalem and the Temple, said his prayers.

So we went on and on. We were all ill from sheer fatigue, bitter and irritable beyond words. Some quarrel was always starting. Just who belonged to the group whose turn to sit down had come? Weren't the sitters oversitting their time, and wasn't the organization of the groups all wrong, anyway? The calm and patient organizer had to interfere time and again. Even the two rotund, peaceable businessmen could not get along together on their rolled-up mattress. And in the midst of all the wrangling, the sick groaned and complained, and the rain beat endlessly down on the train.

We had but one wish now: at least to get there, wherever "there" might be. To be out of that car, to be able to stretch our limbs—the next internment camp would do, just so long as we got there.

I made one observation at this time which I shall not abstain from stating: There were of course exceptions, but on the whole the "intellectuals" among us withstood the hardships of the journey resignedly and patiently. They proved to be tougher, quieter, more uncomplaining than many men from other walks of life who were physically stronger and physically better trained.

And the next night came.

During that night the business with the false teeth happened. The man to whom it all happened must have been some forty years old. He was a slightly built individual with palish eyes. Nothing about his appearance suggested that he had false teeth. He had so far been very gentle and inconspicuous, but now suddenly he began to shriek and yell, and there was no quieting him. It was this way: When it came his turn to sit down he had taken out his false teeth, perhaps with the idea of getting a bit of sleep, and placed them in his coat pocket. It appears that in the dark someone stepped on them and the set was crushed beyond repair. The man wailed and lamented. It was a piteous blubbering, for he mumbled; he could not articulate a word with his teeth gone. Nobody manifested the slightest sympathy.

We were running along the Pyrenees. It rained and rained and was very cold. This time too it was some slight relief when the greying day broke through our two small windows, but all of us were now done in. Many remarked grimly that they could not hold out through another such night.

Several of the men assailed me violently as the one responsible for the whole wretched business. If it had not been for me, if I had not arranged to have the choice left with them as to whether they should stay at Les Milles or be transferred, they would probably still be sitting peacefully in our camp. They cursed me, and they longed to be out of that frightful train and back with the fleshpots of Egypt.

Whenever our train halted at or near a town a number of daredevils would invariably try to get hold of some food. Our guards, French as well as Arabs, were good-natured fellows, easy to strike a bargain with. They did not restrain the daredevils. The region through which we were now travelling, the Southwest of France, was flooded with refugees. Food was scarce and shops were crowded with purchasers. The men from our train did not, of course, tell who they were. Pretending to be Dutch or Belgian refugees, they usually got what they wanted, afterward reselling the victuals to the rest of us at a profit. Those who undertook such excursions were usually of the poorer among our number. We had enough to eat on the journey, but we could never get anything hot. Great was our longing for tea, coffee, soup.

Some in our car were well acquainted with the line we were now following. They would explain to the rest of us where one went in this or that direction, and excitement grew as to our probable destination. Tension and curiosity mounted high whenever we approached localities in or near which there were internment camps. Was this the one for which we were headed?

By this time we were in the West Pyrenees and one by one we passed the famous towns of that mountain country, Tarbes, Lourdes, Pau. Then we drew in to the station at Oloron on the cross-line that leads to Gurs, where many of us had concluded our wives were being detained. In eager expectancy we waited to see whether we would be unloaded there and were disappointed when our train moved on.

After that it was clear: we were on the way to Bayonne, the southernmost seaport of France on the Atlantic.

Undeterred by the ceaseless rain, five or six of us were always sitting in a closely packed line in the doorway of our car, dangling our legs over the edge. We met trains as interminable as our own, and trains as long as our own overtook and passed us. They were all crowded with people—people sitting on the steps, people lying dangerously on the tops of the cars. All France was on the move. All France was in flight, and in all directions, madly, at random. All railway lines and all highways in southern France were crowded with fugitives—Hollanders, Belgians, millions of French from the North. There they were, plodding along the roads in endless throngs, under the torrential rains, toward the Spanish border.

What were they going to do with us? Heated discussions broke out in our train. The once slight possibility now loomed up as a virtual certainty: we were to be shipped overseas, to the colonies, perhaps to Morocco, perhaps farther south, to Dakar. Many liked that prospect, regarding it as the one certain escape from Hitler's armies. They were ready to forgive the French for all the harm they had done us if, in the end, they really brought us such perfect security. Others, instead, rose in their wrath against any such deportation. No, they would not let themselves be sent overseas. They would not be separated from their wives and children for who could say how long, perhaps forever. They would refuse to be shipped off into the utterly uncertain.

Gruelling tales of deportations came from the cars of the Foreign Legionnaires. You were stowed away in the hold of some old tub or other and lay huddled together there in the dark and stench, half under water, with rats and vermin for company. Anyone with the slightest tendency to seasickness was sick at once. In our particular case there was the additional and ever-present element of danger. On such a voyage one had to count on the chance of being sighted and bombed by an Italian warship or plane. What it meant to await such an attack, helplessly locked up in the dark, we knew from our experience during the bombardment at Les Milles. No, such a voyage could not be any joke. Many men declared that never under any circumstances would they let themselves be sent away like that. They would rather try to escape, rather fall into Hitler's hands.

We were now getting very close to Bayonne. Already we could smell the sea, already we noticed the salt air of the Atlantic. And look—there were masts, there were ships.

The train came to a stop outside the station. A highway ran along the track past our train, separated from us by a low railing. I could not tear my eyes or my mind from that road, from the sight of the desolate, hopelessly confused procession moving along it. Vehicles of every sort, from the most ancient pushcarts to the most modern motor cars, all of them monstrously overloaded and jammed full; piles of mattresses on every auto top, perhaps to protect them from attacks from the air; in between the vehicles, crowded in a mad jumble, horses, mules, people with bicycles, people on foot—all streaming toward the Spanish border nearby.

Our stop lasted a long time. Finally the train moved, moved on to the station at the waterfront. Our tension increased. Were they putting us directly aboard ship? Another stop, interminable. We were not unloaded.

Then the train began to travel back towards the Bayonne station.

The train came to a stop at the same spot where it had stopped before. The procession of refugees was still moving along the highway. A violent argument started in our car. Anybody who did not want to be shipped abroad could hardly have a better chance to escape than at that moment.

As we stood there waiting, the quiet organizer with the boyish face walked over to me. "Listen," he said. "You must go at once to the officer in charge of the train. There is a report that Hitler's troops will be here in two hours."

I stared at the man. How could the Nazis suddenly turn up at Bayonne? Could he be possessed by one of the crazy rumours that were now running wild through the country? But he was a well-balanced fellow, immune to hysteria. According to the newspapers, the Germans had gone no farther down the Rhône Valley, but had swung west toward Bordeaux.

"Come along!" he urged.

We hurried forward along the train toward the captain's car. Would there never be an end to that string of cars? Finally we got there. Several men had arrived ahead of us. The commandant was standing on the running-board of his car. Our men were staring up at him, terror-stricken. Catching sight of me, he said: "Listen, Monsieur, tell your comrades we have to go back. The Germans will be in Bayonne two hours from now. Try to prevent a panic."

"Prevent a panic;" that was easily said. I personally was calm. I forced myself to be. But all about me was an uproar of wailing, shouting, angry recriminations. Things had turned out just as we had feared they would. As usual, the French were too late; we were too late. We had said that from the very first. But after all, raving and raging got us nowhere. What were we to do? The Spanish border was close at hand. Might it not be wisest to join the stream of refugees and see whether we could get across? A hundred different suggestions were put forward, a hundred precipitate proposals. Ought we to go to the American consulate and ask for advice, protection, help? To stay there in the train was madness. We would have to get through on our own without the French. The French had failed again and again, failed miserably. To count on them further was folly.

Absurd were the various projects for escaping. That at least was what sane reason indicated, and the judgment was later borne out by the facts when we were in a position to look back and view them calmly. It was true that the Spaniards still had their borders open at that moment, but they required papers and permits and allowed only French citizens to pass. As for the American consulate, there was none in Bayonne.

To cut loose from our cursed train was certainly a temptation. But what was there to gain by doing so? One might get along for two or three days. But if the Nazis began looking for us and ran us down, what then? They could be relied on to make the sifting that the French had never been able to make, and when they wanted a man they found him.

And even from the French, from the civilian population, we could expect only bad treatment if we went wandering about the country without papers. Only a few of us spoke French well enough to pass as Frenchmen. To the French public in general, we were more likely to look like Nazis who had gone astray, like enemies, in a word. The proper papers were absolutely essential. We had to be able to prove to the French that we were anti-Nazis and had a right to protection.

We went back to the captain's car. Many of us, we explained, wanted to make a try at getting through on our own.

"Well, go ahead," answered the captain coolly. "Anyone inclined to go it alone is at liberty to do so. But I advise against it. Separately and on foot you will have a very slim chance of getting beyond the reach of Hitler's troops. For the time being I and my train still have the whole machinery of the military authorities at our disposal. We have a chance of getting you to a region which will not be in German hands when the armistice is concluded."

He spoke very quietly, still standing on the running-board of his car. He appeared to be reliable.

"At least give us back our papers," we begged.

"I have no authorization to do that," he answered, and he went on to observe sensibly enough: "But even if I had, in the short time we have left it would be practically impossible to do so. Anyone who wants to leave us does so at his own risk."

We urged, begged, implored, threatened. He stood there, impassive, on the running-board.

"Quiet now, quiet," he counselled, persuasive. "I really have something better and more important to do in your own interest."

But we would not have it that way. We pleaded, we threatened. Finally he lost his patience.

"No, I won't!" he shouted and disappeared inside his car.

The train stood there and stood there. Another train pulled out, then a second, a fifth, a tenth, all of them packed to the last corner with soldiers and civilians. Still our train did not move. Several of our people made off, and they were followed by others in increasing numbers. They went off without papers, many without money, for better or for worse. The rain was falling in torrents. It was getting late in the afternoon. Everything looked grey, hopeless.

My friends, the two young Austrians, came to see me. They begged me to hesitate no longer, but to strike out with them. The South of France was in utter chaos. One could just duck under and disappear without danger or difficulty. We never would have a chance like that again. The train was conspicuous. Hitler's people would be sure to hear of it.

That was all true enough, but what the captain had said was also true. We argued back and forth and finally came to a decision. We decided that my young friends should postpone their flight. I would move over into their car—several people there had already fled and I would find room. Then, in the course of the next few hours, while our train was on the way, if I decided to leave it and entrust myself to them, they would be there and in readiness.

More trains pulled out. We, the Boches, were obviously being left to the very last. No one now had faith in the idea of rescue. We were all making individual plans for flight. Several tried to slip aboard other trains, but only a few succeeded. The trains were full and people were fighting for places everywhere. Heaven help the Boche who was caught aboard one of those trains.

One story I heard later, but it belongs just here. A few elderly Jews succeeded in slipping into a locked compartment of a military train that was about to start. They sat there, waiting for the train to move, fearing that they might be discovered and kicked out with scant courtesy. Surely enough, the compartment door did open. The old men's hearts stood still. But a voice rang out: "Chocolate, chocolate for the long journey." It was one of our own train companions. Fresh, ever alive, even in the very midst of the general despondency, he wanted to do a little quick business on the side.

Discipline had become a thing of the past in our train. Not only internees but some of the guards had deserted. People were wandering from car to car; friends who had hitherto been separated were getting together again.

Only a brief negotiation was required to enable me to move over into the car with my Austrians. Though three or four men had disappeared from that car, it was still packed full and seating accommodations were out of the question: it was worse than the car I had left. Three men in it had dysentery and were provided with a bucket. A fat man with a crutch was always complaining that someone had jostled or stepped on him. The Austrian polyhistor, the half-cracked scholar, was also there.

The artfully erected luggage pile had been torn to pieces; for whoever wanted to be ready for flight knew that he could take along only what he could carry on his person. Those were the things the men were now selecting. The dirty car floor was littered with articles of every description. One trampled on them. There was no room. Certain of the men would snatch up articles, the most valuable ones, and inquire greedily of the erstwhile owners whether, if these had really decided to flee, they could not safeguard their valuables for them.

During this last review of luggage a strange transformation took place in our car, and it was much the same, as I later heard, in other cars. While entraining at Les Milles people had fought tooth and nail to defend and retain their luggage; now they threw it away without a murmur. Not only did they not spare their belongings, they tossed them aside and trampled them destructively underfoot with almost sensual delight.

My young Austrians became infected with this mania for destruction. They extracted from my luggage the things I was to take with me on our eventual flight, then, quite unnecessarily, flung the discarded articles helter-skelter about the floor and proceeded themselves to trample on them as with deliberate purpose, despite Karl's protests. Up to that moment they had always struck me as lads with a special bent for orderliness and tidiness. The fine leather binding, so light, so flexible, on the beautiful thin-paper Balzac that I had been at special pains to take along was now ruined too. It lay soiled and besmirched on the car floor, ground into the dirt by heavy, filthy shoes. When Karl indignantly recovered it, it was such a piece of foul rubbish that I did not care to touch it.

Our train started at long last, but it proceeded slowly and within a brief half-hour's time came to a halt again.

At that point many gave up hope that rescue was to be found here. Evening had come, it was cold, the rain was still falling in a torrent. But they could endure our death-train no longer. They could be seen, nearly a hundred of them, clambering down from the cars into the rainy, hopeless dusk, old men some of them, men who could hardly get about under the best conditions. It was heart-rending to see these men in their rags and tatters tramping out into the rain-soaked fields, dragging themselves wearily along under the relentless downpour, without luggage, without extra clothes, without money, without papers, heading into the unknown, in a friendless land which on the morrow, perhaps that very evening, would be in the hands of their mortal enemies.

That was my last glimpse of many of the acquaintances I had made in the camp or on the train, dim figures tramping across wet fields into a deepening night, into utter uncertainty. Among those who thus vanished were the artist from Sanary and his young son, the imperturbable organizer with the boyish face, the biologist who had been my straw-fellow at Les Milles and had endured the camp and his asthma so bravely. Those and others too I was seeing for the last time at a half-hour distance from Bayonne and I have heard nothing of them since.

There too my young Austrian friends parted from me. They had dug up a good map by this time.

"The train just stands here and waits," they urged. "The Nazis will surely overtake it. Anything is better than being nabbed here in one of these cars." And they served an ultimatum on me: "Are you coming or are you not? We're going now."

Once more I weighed the pros and cons. The boys were certainly right in that for the following hour, perhaps for the two or three hours following, the danger was greater inside than outside the train. But if one were thinking of safety beyond that space of time, it would be unwise to give up the train. In the long run a person on his own was doomed in Nazi-occupied territory. I thanked the boys, I thanked them from the bottom of my heart—and I stayed.

I have not seen these young Austrians since then either.

The car in which I now was settled was still so crowded that sitting down was out of the question. Greedy hands were constantly reaching out for belongings abandoned by those who had fled, and the close quarters made the scramble for booty still wilder.

The faint dusk darkened into night. It still rained. A damp chill made its way under one's skin. We were dead tired, worn out by the tense excitements of the day. There was the fear, too, that at any moment Hitler's motorized columns might fall upon the train. Misery, anxiety, exhaustion made us ill-natured and irritable. Everybody hated everybody else, disputed with everybody else. Never in my life have I heard such obscene curses as during that night, and the broad Austrian accent, ordinarily relished, made the curses seem even commoner.

The sick moaned, the well cursed, and there were those that snored; and the car was filled with night and fear and appalling stench. We stood, swaying hither and thither; some sobbed and were possessed of one desire: "Oh, for the morning." And as often as the train stopped, our hearts stopped in fright: They're here, the Germans.

Once the train halted in a tunnel. It was pitch-dark and the stop was long. But that time nobody cursed, nobody groaned, not even the sick, and nobody stirred. It was the silence of a tomb, no sound but the beating of our own hearts. For on the top of the hill inside which our train had halted a German motorized column was rumbling.

Then word came that the danger had passed and we moved on. It rained harder and harder and the cold increased. My every muscle, my every hair, ached from fatigue. But when it came my turn to sit down, I could not get to sleep. My tortured, sleep-hungry weariness was pierced by the clang of a voice that wailed monotonously the whole night through: "God of my fathers. God of my fathers." "Shut up," cried one, and: "Shut up, you dirty dog," came from another. But the voice whined on: "God of my fathers. God of my fathers," and I could not sleep.

On we went through the hostile night. Our train moved slowly, and along with it went our misery, the anxiety of our hearts, our malice and our despair.

We had been in such a great hurry the day before to get to Bayonne, within the range of Hitler's armies. Now our train hesitated, wavered, made no progress. It was almost midnight when we were back at Pau again at last.

Pau is an ample, comfortable watering-place. In our car was an oldish man whose behaviour, thus far, had been particularly quiet and sensible. He now suddenly went off the handle.

"I am well known here in Pau," he declared. "I used to spend some months here every year and always in the same hotel. I'm going to get out of this train here and now. I've had enough! I want a sleep in a regular bed. Money will certainly find a bed in Pau. If I do fall into Hitler's hands, I want at least first to have had one more sleep in a real bed." And he got off.

By daybreak we had gone no farther than Lourdes, and there again we had a three- or four-hour stop. On the track next to ours stood two enormously long freight trains, loaded with war materials. On the track beyond them, and guarded by French soldiers, stood a train carrying women internees, German women, our women. Again and again men from our train tried to scramble over the bumpers of the freight cars to reach the women; again and again they would be driven back by the soldiers, who had the strictest orders. All we could do was to shout across to the women from the platform along our train through the spaces between the freight cars, and the women shouted back at us.

Notes and letters were sent back and forth. It developed that the wives of almost all on our train were in camp at Gurs in the Pyrenees.

At Lourdes also we learned that an aged general had taken over the government in France and that he and his Fascist cabinet had issued a statement declaring that they were to cease fighting. They had asked the Germans for an armistice. What would the German terms be? What parts of France would they occupy? And where would we be when the armistice was signed—in occupied or in unoccupied territory? A hundred rumours were about. One could learn nothing definite.

And we moved on, still covering the stretch that we had travelled the day before. My resourceful, helpful young Austrians having gone, there was no sense in my lingering on in their messy car. The passengers of my original German car kindly invited me to come back to them. I did so. There was more room in that car and better manners. It was like getting home.

In the course of the day as we slowly, slowly retraced our way, many of those who had fled rejoined us. They had recognized the hopelessness of trying to get through by themselves. They had explained now to a military official, now to a station master, that they had lost their transport and so had been sent along after us. It was in fact no hard task to overtake us. Most of the trains were being pushed on ahead of ours. Those who had fled our train had had a hard time. They told of long tramps through the night in the heavy rain. Few had found any shelter.

Also with us again was the gentleman who had left at Pau in quest of a bed to sleep in. He had been disappointed. He had found his bed, all right, but months of sleeping on straw and on hard floors had incapacitated him for sleeping on a soft mattress. In the end he stretched out on the bare floor. He was much incensed.

It now turned out that the Germans had not advanced on Bayonne at all and were still not in the town. The fact was that our unhappy train had provoked the most nonsensical rumours all along the line over which we had travelled, until we ourselves had finally fallen victim to a grotesque misunderstanding. We were now able to perceive exactly how everything had fitted together. The territory which we had been crossing was overcrowded with refugees, and food stocks were running low everywhere. If for no other reason than to ensure warm meals for himself and his soldiers the captain in command of our train had to give due notice of our approach. Commissaries everywhere grumbled, so he had been obliged to telephone first to one place then to another.

"I'm arriving with two thousand Boches," he would report. "Have you food for us?"

Rumours of his telephone calls had spread abroad, and in that disorganized, panic-stricken country it had finally been rumoured that the Boches were on the way. The story had been taken seriously. We had been scared into flight by our own shadow.

The sick man in our car had grown worse meanwhile. We called in one of our doctors to have a look at him. The doctor pronounced it a case of typhus and declared that for the man to continue the journey would not only be a danger to himself but would expose us. He should be sent to a hospital at the next stop. He, the doctor, would make that request of the commandant.

But the sick man protested. He did not want to leave us, he did not want to leave the car. Pale, emaciated, unable to help himself, he sat there, with his back bent forward, in a terrible sweat, stubbornly repeating over and over again: "No, I won't leave this car." He thought it would be the end of him if he were ever separated from us. He could not speak a word of French. He did not want to die alone and helpless in a French hospital and, dead, be "shovelled into a hole like a dog" by the Nazis.

French orderlies finally removed him. He protested, plaintively, despairingly. But the Frenchmen did not understand.

We learned definitely the next day that an armistice had been concluded. We halted outside a largish station at the time—I think it was Toulouse. Alongside our train stood a line of empty cars and a charwoman was washing the windows.

"Tell us, Madame," we called across to her, "has the armistice been concluded?"

The woman went on washing her window.

"Yes," she said, "I believe so, yes."

We managed to get a newspaper. It was bordered in black. An armistice had been concluded.

We studied the paper. News items were meagre and their content vague. But there was a map on which the territory to be occupied was shaded, while the unoccupied was left in white. We were in the white zone, that was certain.

I sat down on the running-board of one of the empty cars that the woman had finished cleaning. Some of our men called to me. I paid no attention. Armistice. This war was our war. Had we lost it? We had not lost it. The French Fascists had sold out their country to our enemy. A blow for us undoubtedly, but it by no means signified that the war was lost. It did not prove so very much even as regards the military strength of the enemy. It could hardly be called a military victory. It was only one more symptom of a condition that we had known of all along: the fact, in other words, that when it came to the point the Fascists in every country stood ready without scruple to sacrifice the national interests of their country to their private interests.

Not for a second did I doubt the final victory of our cause. To be sure, I did not dare to conjure up for myself or others the special situations that this war would bring forth. But I had known from the beginning with a certainty that sprang from reason no less than from the heart, with a certainty that nothing that happened in between could ever shake, that at the end of this war National Socialism, Fascism, would be overthrown.

"En voiture, all aboard!" shouted the guards. In our car an animated discussion began. Was the war over? Only a few thought so. The defeat of France in the field had become a fact the moment an inefficient corps of generals, some of them Nazi or Fascist at least in their sympathies, had let the enemy into the country. To a certain extent, therefore, the armistice was merely a recognition of a fact that for a long time no one had questioned. For us, the passengers on our train, the armistice could bring only advantages as regarded the immediate present. We had been forced to live through a war as the shackled, imprisoned, defenceless victims of an unreasoning if not actually malicious military clique. The war was now over, and whatever the outcome it could only be better than the dreadful life we had been leading during those past weeks. Things were still bad and uncertain; but compared with what had been it was comfort itself. Our mood was therefore optimistic rather than not.

And then, too, the sun came out. The Hautes-Pyrenees with their rain lay behind us. We became actually exuberant in our car. We squeezed close together in the wide doorway, dangling our legs over the side, waving to passengers in trains that passed, and they waved back to us. After all, the French refugees aboard those crowded trains felt the way we felt. The newspapers were edged in mourning, but conquered France breathed a sigh of relief. So it is when relatives gather at the bedside of a slowly dying man. He has been given up. They know they are going to lose him, but his dying is a long-drawn-out and painful process. They stand there, dead tired themselves, worn out by the long night vigils and the other torments of a hard battle with death. The patient gasps, rattles, still he does not die. But now he has gone, the doctor says so, and the living draw a deep breath and feel almost relieved, heart-rending to them as his passing may be. So it was with the French in those first days of the armistice. Their France was dead, but the ghastly horrors of the previous weeks were over.

Fighting was over. The sun was shining. Danger had ended. One's life was no longer under threat, one no longer needed to dread a call to rush to a cellar and fear that a bomb would send a house tumbling down upon one's head. Soldiers took it for granted that they would soon be released from service, millions of refugees that they could now return to their homes, mothers and wives that they would now be getting their sons and husbands back again. The newspapers had black borders, but the French people in the overcrowded trains that passed us did not have sorrowful faces. Some were even singing.

We in our car were as pleased as they.

Though when all was said and done we did not know what was really to become of us and certainly not whither we were bound. But this latter question had ceased to be a question of life and death. We were in a part of France that Hitler's men were not to occupy. Indeed, we were moving farther and farther away from Hitler's men and the deeper we went into the Southeast of France the more a feeling grew in us that we were returning home. Internment in a camp in the West? That was foreign exile. Internment in a camp in the East? That was going home.

And there we were once again at the sea. Not the Atlantic this time; that cruel Western Ocean lay behind us with the whole long chain of the Pyrenees in between. The sea we saw before us was our sea, the Eastern Sea, the Mediterranean. It lay in the sunshine, lustrous dark blue with bursts of spray leaping in delicate white lines from the surface. Our spirits rose.

Had we had bitter quarrels over little things, sworn at one another, cursed? How had that been possible? Well, it was past and forgotten. It was not true. We thought kindly thoughts of one another. Some of the men whose turn to sit down had come even started a game of cards. That was not a simple matter. Cards could not be flung down on a table; they had to be carefully balanced on the player's knees and it was hard to keep from seeing other hands. But one laughed at all that, and when there were disputes they were the good-natured twittings of doughty burghers over their glasses of wine or beer.

A long, long way we had put behind us in going from Les Milles to Bayonne. Now we had gone the greater part of the way, almost the whole way, back again. The junction just ahead, the knowing ones declared, would be the last. There it would become clear whither we were being taken, whether to Les Milles or somewhere else.

We amused ourselves imagining the sort of face Captain G. and his officers would wear, and our old comrades too, if they saw us turning up at Les Milles again.

The train ran on. As the junction came into view our strain grew. The train went on—not toward Les Milles, but toward Nîmes. A man in our car lived in Nîmes and had a French wife there and children who were French citizens. He intended to leave the train the moment we got in. Then he would hurry home, see his wife and children, go to sleep in a bed, his own bed at that, eat well, drink well. He was happy, beside himself for joy. He slapped us on the back, flung his arms about us, blustered, sang, invited us all, anyone who wished, to come to his house and celebrate his homecoming.

Evening came on. The sun went down in a blaze of glorious colour. Our train did not pull into the station, but circled the city and came to a stop on a siding, a mile or two beyond the town. That would be our last stop, we were given to understand; we would be disembarked the next day.

So we had made that hideous, torturing journey, stood those terrible nights (literally "stood" them), only to end up in the very locality, almost, from which we had started.

We were standing in a great field strewn with stones. Anyone who so preferred, we were told, might leave the train and sleep in the open.

The day had been hot but, as is frequently the case in southern France, it turned very cold with the coming of night. Many men nevertheless clambered out of the train in defiance of the chilly prospect and found places to sleep in the field. As a result there was more room inside the cars, and one could sit down or even lie down.

It was possible to get water, milk, and even wine at a large farmhouse nearby. So there we were for once stretched out full length, both those inside the cars and those in the field. There stood the train, long, dark, shabby. But this was to be our last night in it or about it. The morrow would see its end.

I had chosen to sleep in the field. I twisted and stretched my weary muscles, wrapping myself tighter in my blanket. Over my head was the starry heaven. I fell asleep, happy.

PART THREE

THE TENTS OF NÎMES

How goodly are thy tents, O Jacob, and thy tabernacles, O Israel!

The next morning we had to rise early and line up in the original groupings, Germans, Austrians, and Foreign Legionnaires.

Then once more we had to wait. It was the usual endless wait and we wondered why they had bugled the rising signal so early. For that matter, the waiting was not so bad this time. We had a lot of sleep to catch up with and many stretched out and slumbered under the good, ascending sun. The rest lolled about and dozed. The sky was light, the air pure and aromatic. Soft blue hills rose in a circle. The train, to be sure, that spectral train that had housed us through all that wretched eternity, was still standing there. But look: it too was rattling away. With a deep sigh of relief we watched it lurch around a curve and disappear. And with it went the bitterness of the most hideous journey of our lives.

We had no idea where we were to be taken. There were two or three places in the environs of Nîmes that could be used for camp purposes. Everything seemed to indicate that we were in for a fairly long march. The march in itself did not frighten us, but what about the luggage? It would be a task to carry it up into those hills.

Several elderly men made their way to the captain. This was a new one, our former guard, officers, and men having departed with the train. The new captain replied harshly that trucks were for the luggage of the sick only; the well would be good enough to carry their bags themselves. The old men grumbled. They had conserved the remnants of their possessions through all the horrors of the journey and did not care to lose them now. They had accepted the torments of the train stoically; now at this trifling contrariety they boiled over. Excited and grim, they declared that they were old men and unable now to lug their duffle up those hills. The officer answered boorishly that in that case they would just have to do without it. And he muttered that at the moment the Army Command had plenty to worry about besides the underwear of a few Boches.

The first group marched off—marched is hardly the word. The men broke ranks there in the field, each one going as he chose or was able. All mixed together, guards, officers, and internees, we walked away along a stony road. It ran through beautiful country: blue hills, much woodland, growths of holm-oak. Valleys with brooks, heath, ravines, no cultivation anywhere, finally a river, and over the whole a bright, light blue sky. The road led uphill, in a gentle grade with wide-sweeping curves. Looking back, I could see our field strewn with pieces of luggage of all sorts. Most of the men had simply left everything behind, and I had done so, too.

None hurried. A sergeant, a couple of guards, would urge us along, but perfunctorily. It was a pleasure to which we were entitled after that wicked journey. It might be that we were heading toward some enclosure such as the brickyard at Les Milles. We therefore savoured to the full this walk under the open sky, stopping now and again to breathe deeply or enjoy the beautiful view.

The road was long; for a hundred yards or so it joined the highway, which was bare; there were only a few cars because of lack of fuel. A crowded motor bus overtook us; it bore the sign: "Nîmes-Uzès."

We had been going uphill for about two hours when I spied a narrow path which at first led down into a hollow and then continued up a steep slope to join our road again. I turned into it. Down in the hollow there was a little brook with many tall yellow flowers. I sat down on a rock. I was alone. For the first time in many weeks I was alone, and not only alone, I was sitting in a spacious meadow under a blue sky, with rolling country all around, misty blue hills, and the purest air.

I had been under lock and key for weeks; now I was basking in beautiful freedom. I saw the hills and the sky and the meadow; the little brook trickled at my feet. Whether I sat there for long or only briefly I do not know. I do know that it was enjoyable.

Slowly I made my way up to our road again. The climb was not hard, yet it required some effort, and when I reached the road, I sat down again on a milestone and rested.

Army lorries passed by. They bore our luggage. The rude officer had not only had the bundles scattered on the field picked up; the trucks also had orders to take on luggage that the men were carrying themselves. Moreover, one of our number had scoured the town and rooted out two or three open vans in which one could sit down. I rode the rest of the way.

We must have gone some fifteen miles in all when we came to an old ornamental gate on which stood the name "San Nicola" in weather-beaten letters. The gate led to a farm that seemed to have been long unoccupied.

This farm and its grounds had obviously been selected for our new living quarters. It comprised a manor-house and a number of smallish outbuildings, all old-fashioned, primitive, but pretty to look at. The officers and guards would probably be lodged in the house and buildings. What was to be done with us?

There was nothing but open fields, a broad meadow planted with mulberry trees, then woodlands all around, broken by more fields, the whole very charmingly situated but hardly suited to housing people in large numbers. We were very thirsty after our long tramp. The available wells provided dubious water for about twenty people, certainly not for two thousand. For the moment we got along with the mulberries.

More and more stragglers arrived. Townspeople were already finding their way up to us. They brought cigarettes, chocolate, bonbons, for sale at prices that were very high because of the toilsome climb, they explained. According to them, the trip from Nîmes was a hard one to make. There was nothing along the road, not even water. You had to bring everything with you from town. The city of Nîmes itself was short of everything; it was swamped with refugees from Holland, Belgium, and northern France. It had tripled in population.

We looked at each other anxiously. The needs of all those refugees would have priority over ours. Who would bother about us? But we shook off our apprehensions. The early summer was beautiful under the open sky; ten times better than the brickyard at Les Milles, a hundred times better than that cursed train.

And here, already, were the first trucks bearing supplies from the army authorities. We crowded excitedly around them to see what they might contain. Water? Provisions? Not water, not provisions, not even boards for barracks, nor picks and shovels for digging trenches for latrines. It was barbed wire.

While I, along with others, was loitering about the field, two young men approached and, with serious expressions, said that they had something to tell me, something that they did not wish to say before the others. Would I not go with them?

We went to a little farmyard that was paved with large cobblestones and separated from the field by a rail fence. On one side was an open shed with a steep-pitched roof. We entered. The floor was covered with straw. There was a manger, a long feeding-trough, an old hay-wagon. I remember the place very well, for, in truth, the two young men had "something" to tell me.

We stood in the shade. Soldiers were strolling or sitting about the sunny little yard, and a number of internees as well. Some of the latter were at a well whose pump refused to work. Catching sight of me, a few strolled up for a talk. But the two who had brought me here asked that they be permitted to speak to me alone. They drew me deeper into a shaded corner in an attempt at privacy.

They handed me a newspaper. "Read this," they said. I did so. It was a newspaper of that morning, from Nîmes, and it reported the terms of the armistice. I remember exactly how I read, I remember the size of the little paper, the order of the sentences in which the text of the armistice conditions was printed. I read, with all my senses strained, slowly yet rapidly, clause for clause. Clause One, Clause Five, Clause Fifteen, finally Clause Nineteen. Clause Nineteen provided that the French were to deliver over to the Nazis all Germans whom they, the Nazis, "wanted."

My knees trembled. I read no further. "All Germans whom the Nazis wanted." For years past the Nazis had been calling me their Enemy Number One in their speeches and newspapers. If they turned in a list of "wanted" persons my name would surely be near the top.

"Thank you," I said and handed back the newspaper. It was the third time within a short period that I had felt death near at hand. The first time was that night when the Nazis came nearer and nearer and our train failed to arrive. The second time was at Bayonne, when it seemed that the Nazis had surrounded me. And now they were making a third lunge for me from close by, and those to whose protection I had committed myself had agreed to give me up.

"What do you think?" my two companions asked. "What should we do?"

"I am Tr—," one of them continued. "Perhaps you remember. Just after that stabbing affair at X— some time ago, the Nazis indicted me for the murder of Party-Member Fischer. I was acquitted. But the

Nazis, of course, regard me as the murderer."

"What should we do?" they repeated. "We are in the same situation, you and we. It is still easy to get away now. Tomorrow it may be too late." They spoke calmly, sensibly.

"Give me an hour to think it over quietly," I requested. "I am always slow in making up my mind. I have to weigh pros and cons all by myself."

"Very well," they said. "We thought we would tell you because you are the one who is in greatest danger. Do you want to keep the newspaper?"

"No," I answered. "I know all I need to know." We separated.

As I left the little farmyard Karl approached, smiling. "Your valise is here," he said, "and I have all your things together. I have something for you to drink," he went on proudly, "and I have found a place where you can lie down and be comfortable. Should I bring you the blanket?"

"Please do," I said. "Thank you, Karl."

He had a little tea for me in a thermos bottle and I drank it. Then he brought the blanket and led me across the field to a little slope that was shaded by trees. As he spread the blanket on the ground, it caught flecks of sunlight and shadow from the foliage above. I lay down and closed my eyes.

Comrades who had had occasion to observe me in the variously wretched and dangerous situations of those months thought that I had shown more courage and equanimity than most of us.

In evaluating courage, physical courage in particular, my views are somewhat at variance with the average. I am a heretic in this matter just as the philosopher Plato was and as Saint-Exupéry, the aviator, is. Plato places courage in the lowest order among the virtues. The aviator, famous for his personal bravery and presumably competent to speak therefore, notes as a fact that courage, physical courage at least, is made up of strivings, impulses, emotions that are of very doubtful moral worth, and specifically of unthinking fury, oftentimes, of vanity, of a commonplace love of sport.

I may contribute to this point an incident from my own experience. I have a brother who volunteered in the First World War at the age of seventeen, went to the front, and performed many feats of heroism there. He won the highest war decoration and was one of the very few privates mentioned by name in a communiqué of the High Command. When I asked him how he came to do such deeds, he answered in some embarrassment and truthfully, one may assume, that "it would have been too much of a bore otherwise."

Physical courage is a fairly common trait in human beings. The other war and this one even more so have shown that there is a far greater quantum of physical courage in the world than has usually been supposed. In both these wars men have been required on countless occasions to perform feats of daring where the chances of succeeding have been far slighter than the probabilities that the men who essayed them would lose their lives. Everywhere and always thousands of volunteers have been ready to carry out such enterprises.

In a great little book that he had the moral courage to publish during the First World War, Sigmund Freud traces physical heroism back to the fact that every man of intelligence knows that he must some day die, but that no man, in his innermost soul, ever believes in his own death. The experimental fact that all men must die has never worked its way deeply enough into our subconscious being to keep that being from revolting with all its might against the conception of a world existing without it.

Though physical courage is a common phenomenon in our day and age, moral courage is a thing that is correspondingly rare. People who have manifested the greatest physical courage, in actual fact, not seldom fail when it comes to showing a little moral courage. I know as a matter of personal observation that men who have held their ground in this war in the face of the greatest dangers, distinguished flyers, are men who, at a cocktail party, would never have the courage to express a conviction of theirs which was against the general trend of opinion among the guests present.

As for myself, physical danger tenses my nerves at the moment when I first perceive it, as when on a lonely road at night a couple of suspicious characters step out of the dark and ask me for a light, or when, for instance, during a period of political unrest, armed men raid my house and threaten to arrest me. At such moments a horrible sensation seems to move upward from the pit of my stomach and sweat breaks out on my upper lip. I never feel quite comfortable when I see a man flourishing a revolver even on the stage. If judging from my demeanour at moments of danger my camp comrades got the impression that I was a man of courage, it could only have been because as a rule my panics last but a very few seconds and are hardly noticeable outwardly. My fatalism, that belief in my destiny to which I have several times alluded, is certain very soon to awaken in me. Perhaps also that superstitious self-confidence of which Freud speaks may be specially active in my case, giving me an assurance at every moment of crisis that nothing can or will happen to me.

I am inclined to think, therefore, that on the whole and to outward appearances my physical courage is not all that it might be. I do believe, on the other hand, that I have on very few occasions failed in what I call moral courage.

The impulse to say what I think is deeply engrained in me. I cannot keep my mouth shut, even when it is dangerous to have it open. If, for example, I hear somebody, even an important and easily irascible Somebody, say that Montaigne was born around the year 1600, I simply have to open my mouth and declare: "You are mistaken, sir,

Montaigne was born in the year 1533."

This lack of talent for keeping my mouth shut at the right time has made me not a few enemies and got me into plenty of hot water. On one occasion somebody said in my presence that the Soviet government had the hands of all Soviet citizens examined every year or so and then sent people whose hands were soft and well manicured to work in the mines. I could not refrain from answering that I knew a number of Soviet Russians who had soft, well-manicured hands but had never worked in any mine, and notably Alexei Tolstoy, the writer, Eisenstein, the film director, and Joseph Stalin, Secretary of the Communist Party. The gentleman in question no longer defended the opinion as to the basis on which the miners of the Soviet Union were recruited, but since then has not been able to endure me.

On another occasion an influential Somebody remarked in my presence that the average American lived in luxury. I could not forgo the rejoinder that, according to authoritative statistics which I had seen, eighty million out of a hundred and thirty million Americans lived on family incomes averaging sixty-nine dollars per family per month. Ever since then that influential Somebody has not been a friend of mine.

For the rest, every human trait is likely to appear under a dual aspect. There are things, for instance, that I think I know. I think I know that two times two makes four. There are things that I consider not at all certain, for example, that two times two makes five. Now, I have a mania for drawing a sharp distinction between those two sorts of things. Call the mania intellectual integrity, call it impertinence if you will. In any event that impertinence, that intellectual integrity, is one of my most conspicuous traits and one that differentiates me from the majority of my contemporaries.

It may be that I have sought to cultivate that trait in myself to such a high degree because I think of myself primarily as a writer. The chief satisfaction in the whole business of writing, it seems to me, comes down to saying what is, or what you think is. Even if I have to pay dearly for the fun of doing that, as I have paid, am paying, and will pay again, I do not regard it as too dearly bought. What is the use of being a writer of some note if one cannot treat oneself to such a luxury?

When on occasion I explain that twice two makes four, it is surprising how often I hear the objection that that is going in for politics, and that politics is no concern of a writer. It is no less astonishing how many subjects—historical, philological, biological, sociological, economic— people regard as politics. Yet the fact is that I, of all men, am not at all interested in politics. I am not a man of action. The pushing, the scrambling, the hustle and bustle apart from which politics is inconceivable, utterly disgust me. My delight is contemplation and delineation.

As a writer I happen to be interested in the interrelations between two domains of intellectual activity, between two sciences, if you prefer; the interrelations between history and philology, to be specific. I am always thinking of that remark of Theodor Lessing, which I quoted earlier in this book, that history is "the art of giving meaning to the meaningless."

This interest in history that I have sometimes lures me into thinking out loud of how a writer of the year 2000 will be likely to express what a journalist of the year 1940 is saying now in this way, now in that; whereas my delight in philology, my insistence on having language clear-cut and exact, impels me, when someone says it is cold and someone else that it is warm, to look at the thermometer and say: "Gentlemen, it is 69 degrees Fahrenheit in this room."

To return to the little hillside where I was lying: Shall I, I reflected, wait here under the protection of the French until the Nazis come and get me? When someone is after you, you run. That is the first counsel of instinct. Those two friends who brought me the news were right: get away. In fact, there's no other course.

"What's the matter?" asked Karl. "Don't you feel well? Has something unpleasant happened?"

"Yes," I answered, "something has happened and it's unpleasant. But don't talk to me now. I'll tell you about it later on."

But one should not trust first impulses. Instinct is not always a safe counsellor by any means. I could get away, of course, right now. But where would I go? If the Nazis demanded my delivery, if they forced the French to make a hunt for me in earnest, I would be lost wherever I might be. In a country that is occupied by the enemy and where all frontiers are closed, a person cannot hide for any length of time. The Germans might comb the country, then they would surely get me.

Why not talk the situation over quite frankly with the French? Wouldn't that be wiser? They may have no intention of handing me over at all. Marshal Pétain says much about honour. Would it be consistent with honour to extradite people to whom one has solemnly promised refuge and hospitality? I would not find it easy to drop out of sight on my own resources alone; but if the French wanted to let me disappear, they would have a thousand ways of doing so.

That's it. The first thing to do is to have a frank talk with the commandant. Getting away from here, just walking out into those woods, that's something I can do any time, even in the final pinch.

I returned to mingle with the others again. It is astonishing how deep a gulf some new thing that changes one's outlook can open between those who know about it and those who don't. Only a little while ago, a short hour at the most, before I had read the news, complete oneness had prevailed between myself and the others. My interests had been their interests: What should be done with the luggage, when would we get water, would the recently promised tents arrive? Now everything was changed. Nothing existed for me now but the danger of imminent extinction. Luggage, water. I despised my comrades for having such petty worries about such petty things.

Word of Clause Nineteen soon got about. Groups formed and discussions started. Many of the men were in serious danger, and I could well understand their anxiety, their worry, their despair. There were also those about whom the Nazis did not care a row of pins, but who thought themselves important and seized on the delivery clause as a pretext for pushing themselves forward before the others. Small shopkeepers who might at some time have given a few francs to some anti-Fascist enterprise were going around conceitedly wondering aloud whether they would be classed as political personages and demanded by the Nazis.

Two or three lawyers explained to me that Clause Nineteen did not apply to us in camp. Most of the internees were non-political. The Nazis would certainly not be interested in them. But according to the language used in the clause the French were not obligated to hand over those of us who were political opponents of the Nazis. For the Nazis had revoked the German citizenship of their political opponents. We were therefore not "Germans" in the meaning of Hitler's words, in the meaning of the terms used in the armistice agreement. If the French were not disposed to yield us up, the wording of Clause Nineteen afforded a convenient handle.

A few young Leftists called that empty prattle. After all, they said, the French Fascists now in power had identical interests with the Germans. *Les loups ne se mangent pas entre eux*—wolf does not eat wolf. Hitler's government and Laval's government were playing into each other's hands. Fascist leaders now in power in France hated the German

Leftists much more than they hated the Nazis. Of course they would hand us over. There was no choice but to escape. A large part of the French population was still on our side. But who could say how much longer such people would enjoy freedom of movement? Thus we dared not hesitate, we had to get away then and there.

Much could be said for that point of view, undoubtedly. But I simply did not want to accept it. Once again my fatalism, my deep-seated laziness, won the upper hand. The arguments of our lawyers found a ready response in me and so did the doubts to which the opinion of our Leftists gave rise.

Meanwhile the promised tents had come. The pegs were driven, the tents pitched, pretty white tents running up to a conical point, the so-called *marabouts* of the French Colonials. On the green fields of that charming countryside the jolly white dots of canvas made a gay and lovely sight.

The tents inside, as we soon discovered, were less attractive. There was not much straw, and damp and cold came up from the ground at night. As the tents ran up to a point in the centre, the occupants had to sleep in circles, with their heads toward the lower edge of the canvas, their bodies running inward at a slant, so that there was great crowding and colliding of feet in the middle. In addition to that, whenever one turned one's head the canvas would brush across one's face. It was always dark inside, and the night was as cold as the midday was oppressively sultry.

Here again sleeping space was inadequate. The tents held sixteen persons each. Up to that time the individual's life had depended upon the group to which he belonged, so at Nîmes tent comradeship became a very important matter.

There were fourteen of us in my tent at first and we had almost all belonged to the same group at Les Milles. Most of the men were co-operative and handy.

The provisions were, on the whole, better in our tent camp than they had been at Les Milles and they were more abundant. The bread they supplied us was very poor, always damp and mouldy, hard to digest. It was the cause of many an illness.

The only thing to remind us that we were prisoners was the barbed wire that surrounded the camp. But before very long we had so stretched the wire in several places that one could get through without any great effort. Still, one had to stoop very low and the barbed wire often tore our coats or shirts or cut into our skin. I have no great sense of personal dignity, but time and again I felt that it was somehow belittling that one should have to crook one's back so often in the course of a day and so senselessly.

I say "senselessly," because no one seemed to have any objection to our crawling through the barbed wire. The guards, who stood at the entrances a few yards away, observed it indifferently. But if one tried to leave camp by a legitimate exit and walking upright, he was halted peremptorily with "No further, there!"

Once when a guard stopped me that way I asked out of my usual curiosity: "What would you do if I didn't stop? Would you shoot?"

"I'm not that crazy," answered the man, "but," he added sensibly, "why not make it easy for yourself and for me and crawl through the wire?"

With so few hindrances placed in the way of departures from the camp attempts to escape were numerous. But not many of those who tried got very far. Roads, railways, and motor buses were being watched as closely as ever. For all the general disorganization, the police were attending to this work stubbornly and dependably. When one of our men fell into their hands he was sent back to camp, usually in handcuffs, after a tiring drive in a police-wagon, and back in camp he would be locked up for twenty-four hours on bread and water in the pigsty, a most uncomfortable structure, too low to stand up in, smelly, and infested with rats.

Nîmes was the farthest point one could reach without serious risk. On the way thither it was better to avoid the automobile road and there were crossings where it was safer not to be seen. If one reached town it was easily possible to drop out of sight in the great throngs of refugees from the North. "Going to town" became a practice with many of us, and in Nîmes we would eat a square meal in a good restaurant and have a sleep in a good bed after treating ourselves to a good warm bath. Very early the next morning we would drive back in a taxi, order it to stop at some point near the camp, crawl in through the barbed wire, creep into our tents, and be nicely on hand for our morning coffee. One man told us with a grin that he had slept wall to wall in his hotel with a member of the German Control Commission.

A considerable number would make the quite exerting walk to Nîmes not to have a night's refreshment from the discomforts of the tent camp, but as a matter of business and a way of earning a living. Along toward evening they would take their knapsacks, slip out into the woods, and follow mountain trails down to the city. There they would buy provisions, carry them back up to camp, and dispose of them at a profit.

There had been no end of trading of this sort in the brickyard at Les Milles and even later on our ghastly train. Here now in the tent camp near Nîmes buying and selling, bargaining and haggling, became epidemic. The café men from Vienna were on hand again and, as it seemed, more flourishing than ever. They were dispensing their tea and coffee in every available place, not secretly as at Les Milles, but openly drumming up trade. "Good hot coffee. Fresh, hot coffee." In active competition with one another, they had rough benches and tables made and soon were offering pastry of every variety.

Our camp rapidly took on the appearance of a country fair. "Business" soon occupied all "Main Street," the road that ran the full length of the rows of tents. There were coffee stands. The owners had obtained some boards and set up counters before which one could stand or sit as at a bar. There were delicacies, hot soups, sausages, and cold meats. Some of them offered music, and the venders praised their wares vociferously. Other booths sold shirts, watches, shoes, leftovers of those who had fled. There was frequent quarrelling as someone claimed for his own an object that was being offered for sale.

It is easy enough to wax indignant at the poor devils who were trying to get hold of a couple of francs by all this petty trafficking and who sometimes stole from their companions in misery. But what could the wretches do? Their clothes were in rags, the food provided by the camp authorities was sufficient barely to sustain life and always left one hungry. Perhaps a hundred among the two thousand inmates of the camp were able to procure available extras and comforts without considering the price. The great majority had to consider costs, and many had nothing, literally nothing, not even a friend or a relative outside to send them a centime. Such people were dependent on the liberality of the well-to-do. And since the well-to-do were few, while the needy were many, nothing was left for them but to resort to trading or to more questionable devices.

All in all, life in the camp of San Nicola was much less harrowing than the life we had led in the brickyard at Les Milles or that on the train. We had those gay lines of tents, we had the bright sky, that lovely landscape. There was no roll-call; the barbed wire was mere show. We were allowed to do exactly what we pleased.

But life in the pretty white tent city had its challenges.

There was the usual trouble about hygiene. We were given shovels and picks to dig a long, deep trench for a latrine in a designated area near the barbed wire. But the trench was public and soon became a revolting thing to use; one slipped, one stood in excrement. Most of the men therefore began to relieve themselves in the woods beyond the barbed wire. Soon, like Sleeping Beauty within her wall, our pretty camp was surrounded by a circle of stench, and the circle grew wider and wider as the men, almost of necessity, kept going farther and farther away. The insufficient water, the bad bread, the overcrowding, the lack of proper hygiene, caused new outbreaks of dysentery and again some few cases of a mild form of typhus.

We had no medicines and no opium.

Day after day as many as a hundred men queued up before the tent where the young French doctor who had been assigned to our camp was functioning.

"What is the trouble?" he would ask.

"Diarrhoea," the sick man would answer. "Dysentery, I think."

The doctor would shrug his shoulders.

"Tant pis pour vous (That's hard luck). Next!"

Virtually all of us suffered from dysentery sooner or later, but there was another great plague—mosquitoes. They increased in numbers as summer advanced. Back at Les Milles many of us had looked as though we were masquerading in the fantastic assortments of clothes that we had thrown together and that had soon become rags and tatters. Now most of the men began protecting their faces from the mosquitoes by wearing veils of red or green gauze. It was a colourful, grotesque sight to look upon. At night big fires were lighted in front of the tents to drive the mosquitoes away with the smoke, while ragged men stood about the fires waving leafy branches to fan the smoke into the tents. Standing atop one of the hillocks that rose around the camp one perceived the spectacle of white tents with countless fires among them and around the fires ragged figures frantically waving green branches within a drapery of smoke.

One became acclimated to life in the camp at Nîmes more rapidly than had been the case at Les Milles. You got used to sleeping in a tent, to the everlasting stench, to the never-ending noise, to never being alone, to the sight of haggard men staggering about, weak from dysentery. As for the dysentery, one assumed fatalistically that one would sooner or later come down with it. But those things were bearable. Worrying about them did not make the food any less good or a substantial discussion less enjoyable.

What one could not get used to, a sting that was not assuaged by time but sharpened, was the unfathomable uncertainty, our anxiety over that clause, Clause Nineteen.

That worry was always with us, that mortal question: Would the French surrender us? It sat beside us as we ate or drank, it brooded over us as we talked, it watched within us as we slept. We acted as though little things about us were important, our meals, our drinks, the country-fair appearance of the camp, the hotels, the restaurants, the girls at Nîmes. But all such interests had their limits: we never forgot how unimportant they really were as compared with the danger in which we were living. The very next day, perhaps, the hand that held us within its grasp might close upon us. Of all the things we went hunting after in Nîmes the most eagerly desired was a dose of prussic acid.

Among the two thousand inmates now in our camp perhaps two or three hundred were in acute danger. Those two or three hundred displayed widely differing traits of character and temperament. There were the gloomy and the gay, the cautious and the reckless, the stupid and

191

LION FEUCHTWANGER

the shrewd, the frivolous and the meditative. But one trait the menaced all had in common: consciously or unconsciously their thoughts kept ever returning to one point. Have the Germans drawn up their list? Will the French give us up? In the midst of a conversation a man under threat would suddenly draw into himself and then abruptly break out with the questions: "Do you think the list is there by now? Do you think we'll be handed over?"

I had, as may be recalled, decided to have a frank talk with the commandant and find out whether the French really intended to surrender us or not. The upshot of that conversation should determine whether I were to stay or to make off.

The commandant received me in the house, in a room that might once have served as the dining-room. Pictures of fruits and birds in a faded fresco peeling from damp ran along the walls. Fairly large, the room was filled with tables at which army clerks were working. The clatter of typewriters disturbed me. The task I had set myself was not an easy one at best. I had to discuss a delicate subject, using cautious circumlocutions in a language that was not my own, and not a little depended on the skill with which I conducted the conversation.

The commandant listened with courteous reserve. I could see from his expression as I talked that he was busy solely with thinking up an answer that would manifest sympathy but not commit him in any way. His answer was ready by the time I had finished. It was one of those yes-and-no answers that bound him to nothing. He explained at great length that, strictly speaking, we were no longer internees. We were assembled in the camp there simply to be disbanded in exactly the same way as French army contingents were now being demobilized. You could not

192

send hundreds of thousands of men home all at once. A thing like that had to be carefully organized, otherwise transportation and commissary services would be thrown into confusion. We too would be sent home in a reasonable time, possibly very soon, but we had to be patient. Men who had disappeared along the way, and those who were now trying to escape, were making a great mistake. Anyone not carrying the proper discharge papers would be unable to get a food card and would encounter all sorts of other difficulties during his whole stay in France. And it would be quite impossible for such a man to leave the country unless in possession of the requisite papers. That our situation was distressing was well understood; our fears, however, were groundless. Marshal Pétain was particularly sensitive in matters touching military honour. He would certainly not allow people to whom France had extended the rights of hospitality to meet disaster.

Was that the commandant's personal opinion, I inquired, or the official view of the French authorities? The commandant replied that he was not a lawyer and that he could not give any official opinion as to how Clause Nineteen was to be construed. Speaking as a French army officer, he could not imagine that the Marshal had signed anything that would not be consistent with French honour.

That was all that came of the interview to which I had looked forward so eagerly. It was not much, but I had nevertheless gained the impression that the French authorities were well disposed toward us rather than not and that they would prefer allowing me to disappear to handing me over to the Germans. However, one could not forget how negligent the French army authorities could be. French honour, French hospitality, well and good; but so far at every critical juncture *je-m'en-foutisme*, the French Devil, had carried the day.

I reviewed the matter back and forth. When the commandant said that it was unwise to try to escape without the proper papers, he was stating the plain truth. It was wiser to stay where I was. I might, of course, get as far as Sanary unchallenged. Considering the general chaos, it was also quite possible that the police in the little village of Ollioules nearby might shut their eyes and pretend not to see me. But what if actual proceedings were opened for my extradition? If I were at Sanary I would probably not be warned in season, whereas in camp the French, if amicably inclined, could easily pass the word along in ample time.

All true enough. But deep down inside me I had a fear that all those pretty reasonings were mere pretexts designed to shirk a decision, to spare me the effort required for an escape. In all probability my sole desire was to go on vegetating comfortably the way I had done at Sanary before the war, when I had shrunk from the problem of leaving France in time. In all probability I was simply too lazy, too easy-going, to incur the dangers and hardships of a flight.

My interview with the commandant took place in the afternoon. I did not sleep well that night. Once more I went over all the pros and cons, and once more came to the conclusion that it was wiser to stay.

As I was strolling about among the tents the following morning, I came across a sturdy-looking young fellow who obviously had been either brought to camp or brought back that very morning. Catching sight of me, he stopped short in the utmost amazement, his mouth actually falling open for a second. Then breaking into the broad, honest dialect of the Vienna suburbs, he exclaimed: "What, you still here? Say, have you gone bats?" (*Ja, bist du denn ganz deppert?*)

The words stirred me more deeply than the young man could have guessed. In a flash I recognized in them the impulsive expression of common sense. All that I had been saying to myself in order to justify my staying was humbug. The man was right. It was criminal folly for me to linger on in camp. The Germans might demand from one day to the next that the lax discipline in our camp be ended and that we be more closely guarded. We had already been hearing that German commissions had inspected certain camps. I made up my mind to get away.

There was a young farmer in camp who struck me as being an unusually capable person. The French have an apt word for a man of that sort, a man who knows how to extricate himself dexterously from all embarrassing situations. They call him a *débrouillard*. I sized up my young farmer as just such a *débrouillard*. I cannot remember at this late day exactly what gave me that impression—it was a mistaken impression in any event.

Some days before, this young farmer had volunteered to help me in any attempt that I might make to escape and I thought he was the man to take with me. He was ready then and there. We ought to start right away, he thought, within a quarter of an hour. It was then about eleven in the morning. The patrolling of the roads was slackest around the noon hour, for to the French police, as to other Frenchmen, mealtime was a sacred hour.

A man from the group of Dr. F., the lawyer-orator, had offered me his pass, one of the passes with which the young French officer had furnished members of that group. The passes, it will be remembered, had been officially stamped and signed, but with names of bearers still to be supplied. I decided to accept the young man's friendly offer now.

We made off, my *débrouillard* and I. At his suggestion I had put on the suit that I had worn to Les Milles, city clothes which, in his opinion, made me look least conspicuous. I carried a briefcase, with a nightshirt, comb, and toothbrush, under my arm. We struck a lively pace from the first. It was a hot day and it soon developed that the outfit I had selected was not the best suited to a tramp through underbrush and over rocky mountain paths. Not only were my clothes uncomfortably warm, in a very short time my suit was covered with burrs, prickly seeds, and everything else that would stick to cloth.

After more than half an hour our path came to a crossroad. My *débrouillard* spoke a vigorous peasant French. He went to a house that stood nearby to ask the way. I sat down on a low wall of loose-laid stones, a hard and uncomfortable seat directly in the sun. But I was tired from the rapid walk and it felt good to sit down. I looked myself over; my shoes were scratched, my brown suit was covered with burrs and brambles, beside me lay my briefcase with my toothbrush, comb, and nightshirt. I was conscious of the absurdity of my situation. I sat in the sunlight and smiled.

Two men came along; they looked at me, then they looked at each other. I did not like that. They walked past me, then one of them came back and asked, in German: "Clearing out? Beating it?"

I hesitated.

The man smiled. "So you're beating it," he said. "Well, you're right. You're in greater danger than we are. We're Foreign Legionnaires. We're just going places. Good luck, Comrade Feuchtwanger."

The *débrouillard* returned with definite information. About a quarter of an hour farther along, and just beyond the point of greatest danger, was a bus stop. How about our taking the bus? It would be a daring thing to do, but perhaps the safest at that. There would be little patrolling around the noon hour.

We decided to try it. The bus was full, with a good number of soldiers aboard. They considerately shoved along to make room for us.

My escort fell into conversation with his neighbours. He had a manner that inspired confidence. Labourers and peasants the world over mix more readily than we others.

We left the bus in the outskirts of Nîmes and continued on foot. Having made such a good start, we thought we would take another bus at once for Avignon. In order to reach the terminal we had to walk the length of the main street. It was very much alive. Just as we had been told, the city was bubbling with refugees. Motor cars everywhere and people sleeping in them. The portals of public buildings stood wide open and one could see that halls and stairs were strewn with layers of straw for refugees to sleep on.

We passed a number of policemen. It was the first time in my life that I walked past a policeman of whom I knew that he had the right and the duty to arrest me. I took a good look at them, more out of curiosity than of fear. Then I grew bolder. The next one I came to I stared at long and critically and he returned my stare, surprised.

Many people were waiting in the square from where the Avignon bus was to start. We overheard talk to the effect that permits were required. We looked at each other. The bus drew in half an hour before the time set for its departure. There was a rush for seats, with people pushing and shoving. It appeared that they were merely staking their claims, and we did likewise.

We stepped into a café. There was no coffee, no liquor. We were served a sweetish drink that suggested the synthetic and, there being no bread, ate something that passed for pastry. My *débrouillard* procured meat and fruit. The bus meanwhile had gone on to a garage and now drove up, this time ready to depart. We took our seats. The driver came aboard, sat down in his seat, looked over the few passengers who were already in their places, noticed us, picked up a newspaper, yawned, laid it aside, then slowly rose, lounged past us, and whispered: "The bus will surely be inspected before it leaves." A shudder ran over me. My companion said: "I think we had better get out." We did. The driver nodded to us.

We entered the café again, sat down, ate another of the poor cakes, drank another of the synthetic drinks. What should we do now?

A friend of mine, a workingman, who had made his escape some time before, had given me the address of a lady to whom I could turn if I were ever in Nîmes and needed advice and help.

We looked her up. She lived in a little hotel on a dreary side street. A clerk told us to wait, showing us into an untidy dining-room. The lady we sought came in before very long—she was a stoutish person with a capable, energetic face. Excitedly she asked: "You bring news from my husband?"

"No," we answered, and I introduced myself, mentioning the name of my friend the workingman.

"You had better come up to my room," she said, disappointed, worried. Her husband had gone on the train with us as far as Bayonne. He had sent her a telegram from Pau. Since then she had had no word of him. She had hoped we would be bringing news.

For the rest, the woman showed herself quite ready to help us; but, contrary to the impression of force that her face gave, she now struck me as a somewhat nervous, timid person, not so very adroit. She referred us to another woman, Madame L., the wife of an internee in our camp, a physician. Madame L., she said, could probably help us. My *débrouillard* set out to call on Madame L., while our timid-energetic friend hurried away to see still another woman who also might have advice and help to give. My *débrouillard* soon returned. He had not found Madame L. Madame Timid-Energetic, however, brought the third woman with her.

She too was eager to help, but equally timid and nervous; in fact, she would burst into tears every five minutes. All the same she had a plan. She knew a wine exporter. Perhaps he could get us to Marseille in an empty hogshead; he had done that twice before. And she hurried off forthwith to see him. But she came back with matters unsettled. It would be three days, she reported, weeping torrentially, before the man could make the attempt, if at all. He would promise nothing definite. Inspections, he declared, had been stiffening of late, and the lady doubted whether he would dare to try the thing again.

Under the circumstances my *débrouillard* thought there was not much sense in his staying on in Nîmes. For the time being I would be taken care of by the three ladies, and it would only make my situation more difficult if the ladies had the problem of looking after still another refugee. In any case he would now know an address at which I could be reached. And with that he left me and went back to the camp.

The two ladies imagined that Madame L., of whom they expected most, must meanwhile have come in. I set out to call on her. Madame Timid-Energetic chose to go with me. She was too timid to appear in public with me, however, and I was allowed to follow her at no closer than twenty paces.

Madame L. lived in the neighbourhood of the Arena, which of all the structures surviving from the Roman Empire is one of the most impressive. I had visited it a number of times. To it I owe a vivid picture of the ways of the Roman circus. Now it was crowded with refugees.

Madame L. was at home. In her I met the first of those selfless persons, ever so ready to help, who were to enable me eventually to escape from the Devil in France and his soft, slatternly hell.

Madame L. lived in a low, narrow-fronted house, the whole

consisting of one small room with a diminutive kitchen adjoining. She had promised to take in a Frenchwoman for the coming night—the woman had come from Nice to visit a friend of hers, a lawyer from Berlin who was an internee in the tent camp. She was also expecting for the night a young German girl who had not been able to find any other shelter. In spite of that, Madame L. would have been willing to take me in too—I would simply have had to sleep on the floor or perhaps in a chair. She was not sure of the young girl, however, and thought it wiser that I should not be seen by Germans of whose political views we were not absolutely certain.

Where could I go, then? The two women racked their brains. The town was flooded with refugees, and no room was to be had anywhere. Madame L. thought she knew someone who might take me in. But in that case Madame Timid-Energetic was apparently the only one who could arrange matters and she was not sure that she dared to do it. After much ardent persuasion on Madame L.'s part, she finally started off, but fearfully and sighing.

With a friendly solicitude for my comfort Madame L. brought out something for me to eat, but then had to hurry away to attend to matters concerning other refugees. We arranged that I should meet her an hour and a half later at the corner of her street to hear what progress had been made in my case.

Carrying my briefcase under my arm I started out on a stroll about the town. It was hot weather and the streets were filled with smells. I thought of entering a café, but there were no seats free; and I had the same luck at a second café that I tried. Suddenly I lost the self-assurance required for walking casually through a crowded public place and feeling people's eyes on me. I gave up the café idea and strolled on through the town. I felt uncomfortable, and the uncertainty about finding lodging for the night seemed to make me still hotter and more uncomfortable. For my own part I would have been perfectly willing to walk the streets all night and occasionally doze on a bench; but according to those who knew that was the surest way to be picked up by the police.

I was glad when the time came to keep my appointment with Madame L. She was late, but finally arrived in a great hurry, breathless, harassed. Kind-hearted, she had the affairs of a hundred different people on her mind. We went off at once toward the outskirts of the town where we were to meet Madame Timid-Energetic. Madame L. noticed how concerned I was over the problem of shelter for the night. Trying to cheer me up, she said that even if Madame Timid-Energetic failed to find a place, not all was lost by any means. There was a certain house outside of town which belonged to a friend of hers. The house was not occupied. All I would have to do would be to scale a garden wall and make my way into the main building through a window in the tool-shed. If that did not work, she added in a tone of finality, why, then, for all the doubt about the uncertain young German girl, I would simply have to sleep in her little room too.

It was a long walk to the place where we were to meet Madame Timid-Energetic. Madame L., who set a brisk pace, asked whether she was walking too fast for me. She had many such walks behind her for that day and was scarcely less tired than I. "But," she added with a laugh, "trying to help a person these days means walking far and fast." She had had her own car and a chauffeur in Berlin. She was a grand person, unassuming, and with the kindest of hearts.

We reached the meeting place, a corner on a broad, tree-lined boulevard. Madame Timid-Energetic shortly appeared. It was not certain, she said, that I could be accommodated, but the prospects were not bad.

The two women walked on with me along the country road, explaining what it was all about. My presumptive host, a retired sergeant-major of police, had bought himself a house and was living in it on his pension. Mentally he was not altogether there, but he had a housekeeper, a Czech woman who had a will of her own. She had taken a former employer of hers into the house, a Levantine banker who had squandered his entire fortune on his wife. Now the resolute Czech woman and the bankrupt Levantine financier were living with and on the senile Frenchman. I could not get the situation altogether straight. What I was interested in was a bed, and whether it belonged to a rich man or a poor man, to a Turk or an Englishman, was a matter of complete indifference to me.

Madame Timid-Energetic impressed upon me that my name must not be mentioned under any circumstances. According to the story she had told the Czech woman, I had not been able to find a room at a hotel in town and would be glad if, out of kindness and for a money consideration, Monsieur S. would take me in. If they wanted to know more about me, I should simply say that I had been discharged from the camp, but had to wait for a travelling permit from the prefecture. I should offer a certain number of francs for my lodging, not too many, but not too few. The Czech housekeeper was agreeable to the arrangement, and if I made a not too bad impression on the old policeman the thing would go through all right.

Madame L. left us just before we reached the policeman's house; she thought it best not to accompany us. Madame L. knew the Czech woman well. She had gone to see her many a time at the policeman's and had gossiped and had cakes and coffee with her. However, Madame L. had a dog and she could leave him at home only with someone to look after him. One day she had been unable to find anyone to stay with the dog and had taken her pet with her to the policeman's. There the dog had frightened the policeman's cat. The cat scratched the policeman, and the policeman had looked at Madame L. with malevolent eyes ever since. No, it was much wiser for her not to come along.

Madame Timid-Energetic was therefore my sole escort when we reached the policeman's house. The Czech housekeeper opened the door.

"So this is Monsieur Feust," she said in a tone of conspiracy. "I have already prepared Monsieur S. Wait here just a moment. Have you any sort of paper to identify you?"

"Yes," I answered proudly, inwardly blessing the foresight that had prompted me to bring along the certificate issued by the young French officer. "But there is no name on it yet."

"That makes no difference," said the Czech woman, "as long as it is stamped. Let me have it." And, taking the paper, she went into the house, followed by Madame Timid-Energetic.

By this time night was approaching, though a red afterglow still illuminated the sky. I sat down wearily on the stone doorstep and waited to see whether the policeman would accord me shelter. I was done in. I was not very keen about climbing over a garden wall and entering an empty villa through the window in a tool-shed. No more attractive to me was the prospect of a long walk back to town with the good-humoured Madame L. and then of spending the night on the floor in her little room under the eyes of the French woman and of the young German girl of dubious political reliability.

A man came out of the house, evidently the Levantine, a Jew, elderly, in fact somewhat shaky on his legs, courteous, curious. His face showed craft, but no lack of spirituality. He might well have been at one time a fine-looking, smartly groomed man. He bowed politely and offered me words of encouragement. "Monsieur Feust, I take it," he said. "It can be arranged, I think. Monsieur S. is always a little fussy at first and inclined to be stubborn, but Madame F."—the Czech woman evidently—"is a determined person and knows how to manage him."

Just then the two women reappeared and with them was the old policeman. He was unsteady on his legs and his voice faltered as of old age. He looked me over. "So you can't find room in town?" he said. "Yes, so many refugees and everybody has to sleep. Your paper has a stamp on it, but only one stamp. You need another, the stamp of police headquarters. I have good connexions at police headquarters. All the inspectors there now have a warm spot for me. You must get the stamp Monday. So there is no room for you in town? Possible, quite possible. So you are willing to pay Madame F. at a fixed rate?"

"Yes," I said. "And if you like, I will pay today and tomorrow in advance. I cannot go to headquarters before Monday."

The old policeman considered acutely. Finally he remarked: "When a man has less than thirty francs in his pocket and no place to sleep, it's vagrancy and we pull him in. In the old days, when a franc was worth something, he could get by with five in his pocket."

"So then," the Czech woman interposed, "I'll show Monsieur Feust to his room."

The Levantine looked at me knowingly. The old policeman muttered something. I thought I caught: "He has more than thirty francs in his pocket. But he'll have to go to headquarters Monday just the same."

Thereupon Madame Timid-Energetic took her leave. She was only Madame Energetic now. "This is far and away the best solution," she said conclusively and obviously much relieved. "Nobody will think of looking for you here at the policeman's. You are safe here. I'll be back tomorrow or Monday. In any event, be at Madame L.'s Monday morning by eleven o'clock."

The Czech woman showed me to my room. The accommodations were rather primitive—the toilet was outside of the house. I had a tiny wash-basin and a diminutive water-pitcher. The room had no door. It was separated from the hall by a mosquito netting. But to me it was heaven itself. It had a bed and a chair, and, outside, what seemed a spacious garden. The Czech woman had a most motherly way toward me and said she would bring me hot water in the morning, and when would I want my breakfast, and of course I could have it in bed, and there was not much butter, to be sure, but honey and eggs and a bit of cake. The next day would be Sunday and I would see what a meal she would give me at noontime—I would be surprised. If I wanted anything, I should just let her know. The money I had paid her covered room, board, and everything. I would find old Monsieur S. a trifle garrulous, but a good soul at heart. Only, I must be patient and show an interest in his long-winded stories.

I went to bed soon. It was not a very good bed, and the next day I noticed that there must have been a good many mosquitoes in the room. But that had not prevented me from sleeping soundly. Now the good, motherly Czech woman brought me an excellent breakfast and the promised hot water. How long it had been since I had had hot water to wash in, how long since I had had breakfast in bed. I could not have felt better.

I dressed and went out into the garden. The Levantine came after me and begged me to wait before going further. The policeman would want to show me the garden himself. He was proud of it, cultivated it himself, and it was really a beautiful garden.

So it proved to be. The pride with which Monsieur S. showed me about was altogether justified. The garden ran up a hillside and here and there offered pretty vistas of the country and the town. Part of it grew wild; then there were trees, walks, vegetable beds, even the ruins of a Roman villa.

There was a table under an arbour and the old policeman, on whose every word I had hung, in accordance with the Czech woman's advice, brought me a sawed-off section of tree-trunk. I now had table and chair, and there I sat down and began to write. I wrote to those closest to me. I wrote to my wife, sending the letter to Léontine, our devoted maid in Sanary, to be forwarded. I wrote to my secretary and to friends in America. I also wrote to the American Ambassador to France and to the American consul at Marseille. I could not be sure, of course, whether any of the letters would arrive. Strangely enough, all the letters that I wrote in that wild-growing garden reached their goals, many, to be sure, only after protracted journeys. My wife, for example, did not receive her letter till five months later in the United States.

It was delightful to sit in that summery bower and write to people who were dear to me. At last I had quiet and composure, at last I was alone, at last I saw distinctly the faces I wanted to see.

Taken all in all, that Sunday in the policeman's house and garden I consider one of the best days in my life. Monsieur S. was garrulous—his household companions were certainly right on that point—and his chatter often lacked logical coherence when it was not downright twaddle. But now and then he would talk sensibly about things worth knowing. He had been stationed in Tunisia in the heyday of the Empire. He had wielded absolute power among the natives, had been their highest court of reference, and had, it seems, conducted himself like an enlightened, benevolent despot. He would tell about his Arabs, then switch to the way he raised vegetables, meanwhile casting a slur upon Madame L. and her dog, which had attacked his cat and made it scratch him. Then, in spite of my protests, he would rise and amble away on his stiffened legs to fetch me certain Arabian sweetmeats that he had on hand.

The Czech woman meanwhile had prepared an excellent midday meal, too plentiful, if anything. We were a good two hours at table. Then, while the others were free to lie down for a nap, I had to listen for another hour to the policeman's tales, and always with an interested expression on my face.

What was left of the long summer afternoon I spent alone in my garden. It was already my garden, and after the noise and the wild hubbub of the camp I drank deeply and deliciously of the silence and the solitude.

The Levantine joined me after supper and for a while we strolled around in the night. He said many clever things, but they belonged to an era that was past. To listen to his subtle comments on events of the present was like listening to a gentleman from the Biedermeier period expressing opinions about a modern airplane factory. He told me stories from his own life, about his wife who was living in the castle near Marseille that he had bought her during his period of prosperity. He had only words of praise for the capable, good-hearted Czech woman who had sent for him, her former employer and lover apparently, and given him shelter in his difficult days.

I took leave of my friendly hosts the next morning. I packed into my briefcase nightshirt, toothbrush, and socks and went into town, ostensibly to get my pass from police headquarters and to return to Sanary, but actually to find out at Madame L.'s, whether the three helpful ladies had meanwhile heard of any chance for me to proceed further.

Madame L.'s little room was crowded with people. I found there not only the nervous lady with the fits of weeping and the French lady, the friend of the interned lawyer from Berlin, but the fat and jovial Herr B., who had struck out from camp with the idea of reaching Montpellier through the help of a wine merchant, a friend of his. He too had landed for the interim in good-natured Madame L.'s little room and had spent the night there.

No opportunity had as yet presented itself for me to go on. On the contrary, Madame L. told me that Madame Timid-Energetic had come to her early that morning and reported that a German commission had now arrived at Nîmes to inspect our tent camp. Madame Timid-Energetic had been more timid than ever; no matter what happened, she declared, I must drop out of sight at once in order not to compromise her and endanger her husband, who was on the road somewhere in flight. Under no circumstances should I return to the policeman's house; otherwise she, Madame Timid-Energetic, might be charged with abetting an unlawful enterprise.

Madame L. did not take Madame Timid-Energetic's communiqué very tragically. If a German commission were really in town, there was all the more reason, she thought, for me to go back to the policeman's and wait there till a chance offered to send me on. But I would have to think up a good excuse for the policeman to explain why I had not obtained the pass. It would be folly to pay any attention to Madame Timid-Energetic's hysteria. For the time being I should stay in town. Two guards from camp were to come to her house at three o'clock with a message from her husband. They might have heard something about the commission. I should therefore be back at her house again by three.

I went out to get something to eat, accompanied by the French lady, the friend of the interned lawyer from Berlin. We chose a good restaurant where we found a plentiful and well-cooked meal at a reasonable price. We were asked to show our food cards as a mere matter of routine. No one cared when we failed to produce them. The table arrangement was attractive, the service attentive. The patrons, mostly French refugees, sat there comfortably eating and drinking in spite of the general chaos.

It had been a long time since I had sat at a prettily decorated table in a roomful of people talking cheerily. My companion was easy to look at and had charming manners, and though my briefcase was a constant reminder of the painful circumstances that detained me in Nîmes, it was a very pleasant dinner.

The lady had been in Nîmes only two days but she had already exchanged letters with her friend in the camp. She was expecting word of him from the two soldiers we were to meet at Madame L.'s at three o'clock. She was counting on going out the next day to some point near the camp and meeting her friend. She spoke of him fondly and with devotion.

Taking the period of our suffering as a whole, there was plenty of evidence to show the surprising strength and permanence of the relations between German émigrés and their French wives or mistresses. Almost all these women came to Nîmes, not shrinking from the hardships of travelling in those evil times. They would spend whole nights, some of them with their children, without shelter in the squares that the municipality of Nîmes had assigned to refugees. They would manage somehow to reach the vicinity of the camp, many of them making the four-hour tramp on foot over the stony paths. They would linger about in the woods or in the fields near the camp, though driven away time and again by the gendarmes. Almost all of them succeeded in seeing their husbands, in talking with them, in getting messages, food, and little necessaries of daily living through to them.

The French lady with whom I was having luncheon had letters of introduction to the prefect at Nîmes. He was reported to be a benevolent individual of some intelligence. The lady told me that many wives of internees kept besieging civil officials and members of the General Staff to obtain one favour or another for their husbands. She herself was amiable, capable, self-confident.

At Madame L.'s we actually met the two soldiers, keen, wide-awake fellows, one of them from the South, the other from Paris. They explained that they were two of a group of four friends. When any of them was on duty he did what he could to alleviate our situation—we could meet our wives as often as we wished, leave the camp, or anything else of the sort. They refused to take any pay for their services.

Everything considered, the majority of the French population was on our side. If the government, by its sloth and criminal irresponsibility, had brought us, guests of France, into the dangerous situation that now faced us, the French people were doing their utmost to help us out of it.

I gave the soldiers a few notes to carry back to friends of mine in the camp, asking the latter to take charge of my mail and keep me posted on everything at Madame L.'s address.

I started back to the policeman's.

Once more, my briefcase under my arm, I strolled slowly along through the hot city that literally swarmed with people. I had very mixed feelings. The report that a German Control Commission was in town—Madame Timid-Energetic vowed that she had actually seen them—was anything but pleasant, and it did not look as though I would reach Marseille very soon. On the other hand, the prospect of spending a few more days in company with the aged policeman, the interesting Levantine, and the good-hearted Czech woman, in that wild-growing, lovely, peaceful garden, was not at all unwelcome.

To be sure, those few days had first to be fought for. How was I to explain to Monsieur S. my failure to procure the pass that I had promised to get at headquarters that very day? So far not even a flimsy excuse had occurred to me. I looked forward to our interview with some misgiving.

In order to postpone the painful moment I stepped into a barber-shop. The barber, who considered it his duty to entertain me, told me that he had his private sources of information and that through them he had learned, among other things, the real purposes of the German Control Commission that had arrived in Nîmes that morning. They had no intention of inspecting flying fields and internment camps. Actually they were working in league with certain internees at the camp, a band of professional spies. With all that, the man gave me a regular hair-cut, and the shampoo he administered was to my entire satisfaction.

But now I could think of no further excuse to defer my having it out with Monsieur S. I made my way slowly up the slope that led to his house. I rang the bell. It was the Levantine Jew who opened the door. He was astonished to see me back and, I thought, a little embarrassed. I concocted a story, not a very good one, I fear: my house in Sanary had been requisitioned and was filled with refugees; I would have to wait till it was vacated. The Levantine replied with a very general remark, something to the effect that nothing was running normally nowadays, that one never knew one day what would be happening the next. While talking thus guardedly, however, he was studying me out of the corners of his sly eyes, and in that shrewd sidelong glance could be read everything that he was thinking: that he did not believe a word of what I was saying, that he knew exactly what was up, that he would be glad to help me, but that he was not sure that my reasons would fool the old man on whom he and the Czech woman were dependent. Nothing of all that did he say aloud; he simply asked me to wait and withdrew into the house to inform Monsieur S. that I was back again.

So there I was once more sitting on the stone step in front of the policeman's house that had so endeared itself to me. But this time it was not a sense of the ludicrousness of my situation that held my attention. There was nothing in me but anxiety, anxiety as to whether I were to find asylum. The Levantine had impressed me as not at all hopeful, and on very good grounds. Old Monsieur S. had his moods. He could be headstrong—that I had already observed. His dislike for Madame L., for instance, over the incident with the dog, was invincible and the Czech woman had had to give up her afternoon coffees with Madame L. on account of it. It was altogether possible that the old man would send me away. And what then? I would have to go back to the noisy, stench-filled camp or else I would have to go back to that steaming city of Nîmes to wander aimlessly about the crowded streets, with terror in my heart at the sight of every policeman and a never-ending worry over a place to sleep.

The Czech woman came to the door. It was as I feared: the sleuth had come to life again in the old policeman. He mistrusted me. But the good-natured Czech woman was eager to help me and volunteered a suggestion. The old man had a son-in-law who was a public prosecutor in Tunis. If now the Italians were to occupy Tunis, the son-in-law would be driven out, the old man feared. Inclined to worry over money matters like most Frenchmen, Monsieur S. was thinking of ways of meeting that contingency and was now playing with the idea of selling the property he owned. How, then, would it be if I were to tell him that I liked the house and the garden and inquire whether he would consider disposing of the property?

Just then the old man came out himself. His face wore a scowl and he was thinking hard. "Show me your paper again," said he, all policeman now. He studied the document a long time. "I don't understand why they don't give you a pass on this," he continued. "I'll go right into town with you myself. I know everybody there. I know Inspector X. I know

Inspector Y. I'd like to see them refuse you a pass if I go with you."

But the offices were closed, I protested feebly. The old man was obdurate. "No matter," he said. "Those men have all been guests in my house. We can go to their homes, and no bones about it. They will be glad to see me."

I managed to put in that my plan was to stay one more night with him. Otherwise I would be unlikely to find accommodations in Sanary, since my house—so I had heard in town—was filled with Alsatian refugees. I liked his property, I liked the city of Nîmes, indeed, I had already thought of asking him whether he might not be willing to sell the property. At first he did not understand, and I had to repeat what I had said. I did so, but with a bad conscience. I hated to be fooling the old man, and so brazenly at that. The Levantine and the Czech woman stood there sly, expectant. One could see how the thing was working in the old man's mind. Finally he said: "Well, then, stay. But tomorrow or the day after I am going with you to police headquarters, and then we'll see whether they refuse to give you the pass. A good piece of property, this," he added; "I've put lots of work into it."

The Czech woman prepared the evening meal. We sat long at table, eating and drinking leisurely. The old man praised the lettuce and the vegetables. He had raised them himself. He drifted on to his son-in-law, the public prosecutor, and then to the city of Tunis and his experiences in Tunisia, and I listened with the usual interested expression. Rising, he took me out to see his hens and rabbits, again emphasized the amount of work he had put into the place, and concluded by saying that if he sold at all he could not sell for less than a set figure. It was a touchingly modest sum, and I was ashamed of myself when I answered that we would have to talk the matter over.

Fatigued by the evening's excitement, the old man retired early. I went out for another walk with the Levantine, this time in the garden that lay shrouded in the silence of the night. The Levantine discoursed on politics. He thought it was quite out of the question that the government of unoccupied France should ever adapt its domestic policies to the principles of the Nazis. "Never," he declared, and the normally indifferent and sceptical gentleman waxed emotional, "never will France pass laws like yours against Jews."

I thought of my Levantine later on when the Vichy government proclaimed laws against Jews that were modelled on those of Nuremberg.

We went to bed. Karl had given me no pajamas, but the Czech woman hunted up a pair from the policeman's wardrobe.

The next morning I read in the local newspaper that a judge named Messia had sentenced three Germans, Messrs. X., Y., and Z., to prison terms because they had been picked up without papers, and that foreigners who could show no papers were now being arrested every day. Apart from that I had a quiet and a beautiful day, a real day of rest. I did not leave the place. I enjoyed my garden. I strolled about in it, made a few notes, and wrote a few letters. The Czech woman still looked after me with the same motherly solicitude. She went into town and bought me underwear, postage stamps, and newspapers.

Then the old policeman came up to see me for a chat. My discharge certificate and the fact that I had been in the camp had apparently roused memories of certain old-time experiences in him. He had been stationed in Tunis, he said, at the outbreak of the First World War. All Germans had been interned at that time too. A number of them managed to take refuge aboard an Italian ship, the *Città da Messina*, which was to sail for Palermo—Italy had not yet entered the war. Now he, the policeman, was ordered to take those Germans off the ship. He knew their stateroom numbers, but the ship was crowded and the Germans kept out of sight. The Italian captain insisted upon sailing on time, and the authorities did not care to anger the Italians. The search therefore could not be continued too long. In that situation he, the policeman, had a bright idea: he ordered the luggage of the Germans for whom he was hunting taken ashore. A number of Germans fell into the trap, went ashore again, claimed their luggage, and were arrested. Others, sly ones, let their luggage go, did not leave the ship, and so escaped.

Such was the policeman's story, and for once it cost me no great effort to listen with my interested expression. I myself was one of the Germans who had been interned in Tunis and had escaped on the *Città da Messina*. I myself was one of the four "sly ones" who had let their luggage go and preferred to stay in their safe hiding place aboard the ship.

If that day passed in blessed calm, the day following bade fair to be correspondingly hectic.

As I was sitting at breakfast early in the morning, Madame Timid-Energetic stormed into the house. She had left a number of compromising papers at the policeman's for safekeeping. Now that a German commission had appeared on the scene, she thought it too dangerous to have them at all and she wanted to get the papers back and destroy them. (They were not in the least compromising.) She was panic-stricken at sight of me. What, was I still there? But the German commission was in town. Hadn't she, Madame Timid-Energetic, urgently bidden me through Madame L. to leave the policeman's house at once and never go back again, so that she, Madame Timid-Energetic, might not be compromised? The angry eyes in her Coleoni-like face glared at me and the moment the policeman turned his back her lips hissed words of rage at me. Perceiving, however, that neither the glare nor the hiss made any great impression, she demanded vehemently that at least I do her a favour. She expected her husband home within the next few days and wanted me to write an urgent letter of recommendation to the American consulate at Marseille, so that matters of his concern pending there might at last be pushed through. I wrote the letter but she continued her growling.

Madame Timid-Energetic had hardly taken her departure when Madame L. came in, receiving a sullen welcome from the policeman even though she was not accompanied by her dog. Ever eager to help, and braving the old codger's displeasure, that helpful soul had made the long, hot uphill climb on foot and walking as fast as she could in order to deliver an urgent note from one of my friends in camp that our soldiers had brought her. Passes were being issued at the camp to those who thought themselves justified in claiming right of asylum in France. Applications had to be signed at once and personally delivered to the camp authorities by the claimant not later than the coming evening. A notice had been posted that anyone failing to comply would lose all title to protection. Knowing of my absence from camp, the commandant had sent for my friend, the writer of the note, and suggested that he get in touch with me if there were any way of doing so and advise me urgently to hurry back and file my application. If I did come back, he, the commandant, would overlook my departure. Such was the message that I received by way of the guards and Madame L.

I considered the matter. How painful to leave the quiet, hospitable home of the friendly policeman. On the other hand, the commandant's suggestion that I return to camp was sensible and well intentioned. If the French were looking for an excuse to evade their obligations to me my flight certainly supplied one.

With a sigh I made up my mind to go back to the camp. I arranged with Madame L. to be at her house at three o'clock, when she would be expecting the two soldiers. I would make the trip back to camp with them.

As soon as Madame L. had gone, the policeman told me the story of the dog and the cat again, showed me the scars of the scratches his cat had given him, and, stroking the cat's back, expressed himself in no favourable terms about Madame L. I said that Madame L. had just brought me word that I was at liberty to return to Sanary, and that I would therefore be leaving after the midday meal. The policeman thought hard. Then he said: "I like you, Monsieur. I should be very glad to be of service to you, but the price I set on my house is really the best that I can do."

It was a very reasonable price, I answered, and I would think the matter over seriously.

The Czech woman had bought a chicken with the idea of frying it in the Austrian style—she was an expert at preparing a *Backhendl*. She had intended to let the fowl hang overnight, considering it still too freshly killed; but, contrary to rule and contrary to her own convictions, she resolved to prepare the dish before my departure, in other words, that very day.

We were all a little glum during the meal. The Czech woman was frankly unhappy both because the fowl was tough and really not a success and because of the uncertainty of my future in general. The policeman sat pondering and unusually taciturn throughout the meal. He finally declared that as a rule the purchaser of a house bore all the costs of a transfer, but that as a special favour and to be agreeable to me he would pay five hundred francs as his share.

I packed my briefcase and took leave of those three good souls with sincere gratitude and affection. For one last time I walked with my briefcase under my arm the length of the hot city, and for one last time climbed the dark, narrow steps that led to Madame L.'s apartment.

The little room was again packed full. Jovial Herr B. was there; he had still found no chance to get on to Montpellier and was still sleeping at Madame L.'s. Then there were the two soldiers, the Frenchwoman who was the friend of the Berlin lawyer, the nervous woman with the weeping spells, Madame L., and myself. We sat in a huddle—the bed, the chairs, the table, the floor were all occupied.

Madame L. dictated to the two soldiers a short list of things that they were to take her husband, in the camp. Dr. L., a physician of some note, had organized the sanitation in a number of prison camps during the First World War. He had asked his wife to send him a certain preventive against the dysentery that was becoming epidemic. Madame L. called out her list from the kitchen, where she was busy preparing a special dish for her husband, who was suffering from the after-effects of a dysentery attack.

The soldiers checked the list, offering also to get a few things for me in case I really intended to go back to camp. They were returning by bus at half-past four and would take me with them. When I suggested that they should order a taxicab and I would take them up with me, they accepted gladly.

They left the house and shortly Herr B. and the nervous woman took their departure. Madame L., the keen-witted Frenchwoman, and I talked my situation over once more. Might not my invitation from the commandant to return to camp be just a trap? A German Control Commission was present in Nîmes—even the newspapers mentioning the fact. There were also well-authenticated reports that such commissions had appeared in internment camps. Was the commandant really a benevolent person? Or was he simply trying to entice quietly back to camp an internee whose return by force would have attracted notice?

The Frenchwoman had called at police headquarters again. She received an impression there that the French authorities were well disposed toward us and intended to protect us from the Germans. They had explained to her that it would be better for us to remain in camp. If we cut loose and began wandering about the country illegally, we would inevitably be picked up by policemen who had no sense of the situation and be sent along to French prisons, which were especially disagreeable at just that time. In prison, moreover, it would be harder to help us make a getaway than it would be in camp in case of an emergency.

All things considered, it seemed best that I should return to San Nicola.

The two soldiers came back. They had attended to everything faithfully. Shrewdly and with friendly thoughtfulness, they had even come to an agreement with the taxi-driver, who was waiting in the street below, on a reasonable price for the journey. As a rule, persons who were evidently internees or strangers in town were charged either an extra or a higher fare. The chauffeur had made the soldiers a price that was twenty francs below the normal.

So I went back to camp with the two soldiers. We talked calmly, reasonably of the war, of the chances of peace, of personal matters, of our prospects and worries for the immediate future. We were great friends by the time we reached the outskirts of the camp.

The taxi halted at a point agreed upon, some twenty minutes' walk from our destination. The soldiers would not allow me to carry a basket containing the purchases they had made for me. They took possession of it, declaring they would get it to me in camp. We were able to walk along together for a part of the way; finally we separated. They continued on along the road that led to the entrance gate, while I veered off into the woods.

I made my way slowly through a growth of saplings, the familiar stench serving as a safe guide. When I came to the barbed wire I crawled through with the usual precautions.

I was back in the camp that I had left with such mingled hopes and fears. I had not gained much by my jaunt, but I had had five days of peace and mental composure, and I had been able for once to take counsel with myself undisturbed by others. All in all, it had been better for me than to have spent the time in camp.

I received a warm welcome and was eagerly questioned. The friend who had sent me the commandant's message urged that I report immediately to the office, obtain an application form, and sign it.

A young lieutenant, a mere boy, received me. "You have given us no end of trouble, Monsieur," he said. "Strictly speaking, the lists are closed. I really ought not to accept your application now."

"But you will accept it, Lieutenant?" I returned.

"Of course," he said.

Then I set out to look for my former tent. During my absence many fugitives had returned, a new division had been necessary, and it was no easy matter to find my old group. While I was hunting about, two men among the older internees invited me to join the company in their tent. By that time, they said, practically every tent was full, my old one too presumably. Theirs happened to have only eleven occupants and they would try to make things as pleasant for me as possible. My man Karl had meanwhile joined me, somewhat depressed at the failure of my excursion, but delighted after all to have me back again. He had visited my tent and found that it was in fact full. I gratefully accepted the offer of the kindly old gentlemen and with Karl's help settled forthwith in their tent.

The "leader" of my new tent community happened to be one of the two gentlemen who had invited me, the noisy, jovial Herr Cohn.

Formerly owner of a factory in Berlin, he was a man of inherited wealth and good breeding, somewhat spoiled by money and good luck. Though nearly sixty, he still made a fine appearance. He was used to giving orders, and enjoyed managing things, "organizing." Loud-voiced, impulsive, good-natured, he could be abrupt, but then always stood ready to retract an inconsiderate word and apologize. He was always quarrelling with everybody, making up with everybody, doing kindnesses and demanding services in return. He suffered deeply because he had no money left, but even in camp he lived as though he had plenty. The fact that his extravagance brought an unending series of difficulties in its train made him none the wiser. In the habit of being waited on, he was always giving orders to my man Karl. But Karl thought of himself as my servant only. He had taken it into his head that he was looking after me and not after any Messrs. Müller, Schulze, or Cohn. As a result there was constant friction between the two, and I was always being called upon to straighten things out.

Another man with whom Herr Cohn lived in a constant state of feud was our tent companion Herr L., a lawyer from Berlin, a shaggy, untidy individual with a huge, fuzzy red beard. Exactly like Herr Cohn, Herr L. was quarrelsome and overbearing. The continual warfare between the two enriched my vocabulary by many a spicy expression from the Berlin dialect that I had never heard before. For Lawyer L. was a witty man and had a gift for turning a phrase. On being asked why he washed so rarely, he answered that he had an iron constitution and that iron rusted in water. And I shall not forget how once during the night, after someone had several times broken wind with great force, his deep, cavernous voice came rhyming out of the dark, with something that might be rendered as: "A fart a day keeps the doctor away." He had an enormous appetite. "He's digging his grave with his teeth," a tent companion remarked of him. Though Lawyer L. liked to eat often and plenty, he happened to have no money. Whenever a trader came along and one of us bought something it became his rule to say: "While you are at it, just get a little something for me too," whereupon he would proceed to consume the greater part of the purchase and then always forget to pay. Herr Cohn, for his part, not seldom did the same, but he was always calling Herr L.'s attention to these oversights. As group leader it was Herr Cohn's privilege to decide who should go for our food allotment at the commissary and he frequently designated Lawyer L. This repeatedly provoked a squabble. Though the lawyer always demanded a large share of the food intended for us all, he refused to carry the pot, offering his advanced age as excuse.

It was no simple matter, really, to apportion the various tasks, which were considerably more numerous than in the days at Les Milles. The tent had to be kept clean, the canvas walls frequently stretched, the pegs driven tighter, the surrounding trenches deepened to keep out rainwater. The food pot had to be cleaned and the water for the cleaning battled for. The rubbish in and around the tent had to be collected and carried away to a safe distance. Wood had to be procured for the fire and mosquito smudges kept going at night in front of the tents. The old men in our company were hardly suited to work of this sort. Herr Cohn and Herr L. might have served. But the lawyer did not mind filth and broke into curses when he was selected for cleaning jobs, and Herr Cohn declared that as group leader he was exempt from working anyhow.

There were a number of men who performed any sort of work for pay, but neither Cohn nor L. would or could pay.

Another shirker was the man who made the remark about the lawyer—that he was digging his grave with his teeth. For that matter he had no small appetite himself. He had been a judge on the highest bench in Berlin. Somewhat moody, squeamishly finical in his ways and habits, not a little spoiled, he could not even in this tent forget his dignity as a member of the highest court. The Lawyer L. and Herr Cohn liked to tease the old man, and mercilessly they would say, for instance, that he had a bad smell. And at times when they were at it, the ex-judge had a way of defending himself with a sort of old-maidish fury that was comical indeed.

"Who smells so bad again today?" Herr Cohn would begin.

"It's not me today," the lawyer would answer. "It must be the judge. I've been smelling it all night long. Listen here"—he would say, looking straight at the poor old man—"this has got to stop. You aren't alone in this tent, you know."

"I don't smell and I haven't smelt," the old judge would retort, sharply but with dignity. "Tell me, Herr V.," he would say, turning to his straw-fellow, an elderly cantor from Berlin, "did you smell anything?"

"I was asleep," the cantor would answer with diplomatic evasiveness.

I liked the old judge immensely. He was an extremely well-educated man, having taken his preparatory studies seriously and lovingly, still retaining everything that he had absorbed as a youth and enjoying a display of it. I was both touched and surprised to learn that he had had the same training in the humanities that I had had, but in his case the liberal education had come to full fruition, encrusting him and cutting him off from the rest of the world. His mind had shaped itself to the exact form his schoolmasters had tried to give it. He had learned what he had been asked to learn and nothing of the chaotic happenings that had overtaken him in after years had added anything to it. He believed in the humanism of the classical era in Germany, in the forms in which it had been laid before him in school; the sort of humanism that is reflected in the poems of Schiller's idealistic period.

I would try sometimes to put myself in the places of the men and women who had been called to answer before such a judge. That he knew the law thoroughly there could be no doubt, but how could he have understood them or they him? There could have been absolutely no point of contact between them and him. There was none even between him and me. To that very cultivated gentleman Sigmund Freud and Karl Marx were mere names. He had never read a book of theirs.

He was passionately fond of quotations. He had been made to learn long passages from German and classical poets. We happened both to have memorized a number of poems that are not so generally known, and what one of us could not remember the other would be able to supply.

All in all, there was a good deal of quoting about the camp and I often wondered what could be the hidden spur to that passion which slowly became a mania. Perhaps having so little, not to say nothing, left in life, we were trying to warm our hearts with a feeling that we were really cultured people. Or it may have been that we were trying to brush up on old attainments in order not to lose them for good, or again it may have been a mere conceit of erudition. We all looked alike, we all lived under exactly the same conditions. We had to find some way of proving to ourselves and to others that in spite of everything we were not altogether as other men were.

I am tempted to go more deeply into the habit of quoting and the passion for it that is so rife among Germans and Jews in general, and which became virtually epidemic among the German Jews in the tent camp at Nîmes. But I will keep to my tent and its occupants.

There were, further, two businessmen among our number, quiet, well-set-up individuals who spent the better part of their day devising ways and means to feed themselves succulently, bountifully, and cheaply. They let themselves go in an orgy of reminiscences about the various regional dishes of Germany. Sometimes they would have differences of opinion as to just how and where a given dish was most tastily prepared.

Unforgettable also were two Jewish cantors from Berlin, excellent cantors and famous ones, with honours from the great synagogues of the German capital. They differed widely in temperament yet could not get along without each other. As a result they quarrelled endlessly, their battles being cunningly fomented by Herr Cohn and the untidy lawyer Herr L.

One of the cantors was a surly fellow, always going around with his head lowered as though about to charge in battle. His bad luck was very much on his mind; he felt like a dethroned prince. The other was an active body always up to something. He by no means considered his life at an end. Even from the camp he was feeling out the synagogues in the South of France for an appointment as cantor, or if not as cantor as an extra to help out on high holy days—though of course such a position would be a long step down from what he had had in Berlin. Nothing could shake his spirit or his self-confidence, not even a piece of downright bad luck which he had just then experienced. He had checked his luggage, all he had left in the world, in the parcel-room at the Nîmes station. He had needed a valise and one of the Foreign Legionnaires had promised to get it to camp for him. He had turned his check over to the man, whereupon, it seems, the Legionnaire got out the luggage, sold it, and calmly pocketed the money. Now he offered the cantor all sorts of tales and excuses, but without producing the luggage. However, the cantor did not give up. He was no fool; he knew that a complaint to the camp authorities or to the police would even his score with the Legionnaire but could not bring the luggage back. So he turned diplomat and was now appeasing the Legionnaire. Never once did he let on that he suspected him. He pretended to believe everything the Legionnaire said, discussed ways and means of getting the luggage out and up to the camp, gave him small sums, ostensibly as bribes to the clerks to release the luggage, but actually as ransom money for the luggage which the Legionnaire had stolen and was withholding. Not once did the cantor doubt of recovering his property in the end.

The two cantors liked to talk about old times in Berlin. They had had good salaries and, what with weddings, funerals, and the like, had made fat incomes on the side. They would boastfully tell how much they had earned on this or that occasion, each improving on the other's story and each doubting the other's statements. Herr Cohn and Herr L. became enthusiastic seconds in such bouts, maliciously egging on their respective principals.

I enjoy lingering on the description of my absurd experiences in the tent camp near Nîmes. Throughout my stay there I fixed my attention rather on the unusual or curious detail than on our distressing situation as a whole. Had I not been thinking always of the ludicrous aspects of my own plight, or of the plight of others, I could not have survived that depressing, degrading experience without spiritual harm.

Gay and charming as it looked, the tent camp was not a pleasant place to be in. It was, I beg my reader to believe me, ghastly.

There was no organization. There was no place where an internee might lodge a complaint or make a request. It was a general dissolution into filth and slovenliness. Bound hand and foot, we were delivered over to excrement and indolence. It was not living, it was vegetation. We longed for death. We endured living there only because we kept telling ourselves that we must not give in, that we had to survive this period. Some day we would get out of the camp, some day we would be able to live again as human beings.

But there were people there—and to see them was perhaps the most distressing thing in the whole distressing experience—who had only one fear, a fear that the tent camp might be abolished and they set free. Yes, there were men among us, and not a few, who shrank in terror before the moment when they would be turned loose again upon life. Wretched as those tents were, they were roofs over their heads. Monotonous and tasteless as the food was at Nîmes, it kept soul and body together, it could be forced down, it could be swallowed. When they lost the camp at Nîmes, they would lose everything, for they had no money, no prospects, nothing. Once driven from that camp, those utterly wretched souls would find themselves standing in the void, with nothing but a few rags on their bodies. They would be strangers, nay, enemies, in a land that had been conquered and was scarcely able to offer its own sons the bare necessities for living.

The reader will, I hope, forgive this outburst. I shall now be coming to a more cheerful subject. I am going to tell you about Bernhard Wolf, the most delightful of the dwellers in our tent.

Though Herr Cohn was the titular group leader, Herr Wolf was the actual leader of our little community. He was a fattish sort of man, perhaps a little over sixty, with a heavy, good-natured Jewish face. He had no great amount of book-learning, but he had a good brain, a kind heart, lots of common sense, and a healthy scepticism. He had an unusual combination of sound judgment, shrewdness, and good-will to men. But why do I say "had?" He still has all those qualities today.

Herr Wolf was the oldest among a large number of brothers and sisters who had worked themselves up from small beginnings to very enviable fortunes. One of his brothers was in our camp. They both came to terms with their situation in sovereign style. They had been in many a bad fix before and had come out all right, and this one too they would get out of, perhaps with scars, but with skins whole.

Herr Wolf owned factories and a country place near Marseille. He had provided work for many people, and a habit of getting on with others had made him a keen judge of human nature. He got attention without raising his voice. Factories, country estate, employees had vanished, but he still had composure, patience, authority.

Herr Wolf and I became good comrades from the very first. He was a more practical man than I and was thereafter to second me in many little matters with sound advice and efficient action, especially in a rather difficult situation of which I shall soon have occasion to speak. Then there were circumstances in which I could be of effective aid to him. I think we both remember each other with pleasure.

Herr Wolf was a master of the art of living. He never essayed the impossible, but got the best possible out of every set of circumstances. For example he was responsible for a number of improvements in our manner of living. He had one of the internees build a rough table under a tree in front of our tent and something that could pass as a bench. There we could sit and eat comfortably, half in the shade, half in the sunlight. In addition to that he got a few tent-poles and had something like bedsteads made for himself and me. They had to be low, otherwise the tent-walls would have come into contact with our faces and rubbed them sore. But they did provide a little air space between our straw and the cold, damp ground. Herr Wolf was marvellously ingenious at procuring provisions and as a result our meals were often appetizing and of considerable variety.

The camp had changed in aspect in the course of the few days that I had spent in Nîmes. It was now a big fair. Cafés, sales booths, one after another in unbroken sequence, lined the streets of the tent city. Hawkers roamed the streets from five in the morning till one in the morning calling their wares: "Condensed milk forbidden. Obtainable nowhere in France except here of me." "Fried chicken with fresh cucumber and tomato salad in ten minutes at Tent 54." "Three fountain-pens, as good as new, at unheard-of bargain prices." "The latest Paris newspapers." "Newspapers smuggled in from Switzerland." "Brown leather shoes, the last pair. Good condition. Will walk all over France and across the borders." "Fine forged passport, Poland, good for gentleman between forty and fifty, only 3000 francs." So it went the whole day long and half the night.

Small restaurants had opened also, good ones, run by experienced Austrian chefs who had improved their art in the outstanding French schools for cooking. Such restaurants were of course against the rules but the officers in charge of the camp began to get their meals in them and even brought up acquaintances from Nîmes, there being better food in our camp than in Nîmes.

Our traders had ingenious ways of obtaining things from secret sources and somehow managed to have on hand anything that a person could really want. One of them in particular, being an orthodox Jew, could transact no business between Friday evening and Saturday night, but he was only the more industrious the other days of the week. He was scrupulously honest, taking a twenty-two percent profit on cost prices, no more and no less. He employed three or four assistant salesmen, and two taxis were always on the road in his service. He offered the finest French wines at astoundingly low prices. Though Paris was cut off, he procured books in the exact editions asked for, to say nothing of suspenders, shoelaces, knapsacks, and similar objects. He had uncanny intuition and understanding of the needs of individual persons, attending to Herr Wolf and me with an assiduity that amounted to a passion.

As organization in France disintegrated, conditions in our camp became more and more fantastic. Had the scenes in our camp been shown on the screen or on the stage the public would have scoffed at them as altogether incredible. Evenings especially, as the sun went down, the tent city presented an ultra-romantic aspect: white pointed tents lying in the midst of a lovely landscape, smoking fires in front of the tents and ragged men poking at them, cabarets, gambling resorts, music and singing from restaurants and cafés, the whole fenced in with barbed wire, hemmed in by a wall of stench, and, with all the rest, now and then a police-van delivering men in handcuffs—fugitives who had been caught again.

As implausible as all this were the life stories, the life destinies, the worries, the hopes of this or that individual. Among us was a man who had been on the police force in Germany and had had the bad luck to shoot a Nazi in dealing with one of the many frays between Nazis and Leftists. Thorough investigation had absolved him of guilt. But the Nazis had marked him for their vengeance, and when they came into power he had thought it wiser to leave the country—and in that he was certainly right. In the camp his chief worry was about his wife, of whom he had had no word since his internment. Now after more than two months he at last received news. Ill, without resources, she had fled before the oncoming Nazis, and like so many others had fallen exhausted by the roadside. The Germans advancing picked her up, treated her well, and left her the option of returning to Germany. After long hesitation she had decided to accept, seeing no other way out for herself. Loyally, frankly, she informed her husband of all this. He carried the letter around for three days, reading it aloud to anyone who would listen and to many who would not. On the fourth day he went out and hanged himself. A trader had sold him the rope for three francs.

There was an art dealer who, on being ordered to camp, took the valuable pictures that belonged to him, carefully concealed them between the linings and the walls of a number of trunks, and deposited the trunks in various places to be held till called for. In this way precious canvases of old masters went travelling about the country to be held in the parcel-rooms now of this station, now of that. The man could not get in touch with his wife and was therefore frantically worried as to what was happening to his priceless pictures, to which he alone had access through the parcel-room checks that he held.

A renowned chemist, professor in a German university, had been of great service to the German army in the First World War through discoveries that he had made. He was a man of perhaps sixty. Short, slender, erect of carriage, he went around for the most part wearing tennis clothes that became more and more soiled, and a monocle. He had the demeanour and manner of expression of a German officer of the Kaiser's day, abrupt, sharp, polished. He spoke in short, crisp, idiomatic sentences that had an almost telegraphic style but showed a remarkable choice of words. He moved in an effluvium of alcohol, and on meeting an acquaintance would unfailingly offer him a whisky or some other sort of drink and clink glasses, looking him intently in the eye and holding his elbow sharply squared, but meanwhile taking it for granted that the treat would be returned. He was subject to depressions and at such times would call out to you: "Don't come near me today—I have le cafard." But as a rule his attacks of despondency had a touch of good humour that evinced his sense of superiority to his situation. On one occasion he confided to me that he carried a dose of cyanide in the pocket of his tennis shirt, genuine cyanide—a French chemist, one of his colleagues, had obtained it for him.

Many men in that Brueghel's hell which was our camp would have given a good deal to have a dose of poison in their pockets.

For in the midst of the motley hurly-burly of that country fair, despair had a way of growing. What wore a man down most was not so much the ever-present and very real menace of the extradition clause, as the forced inactivity, the crushingly patent senselessness of our detention there. It was always the same monotonous round, a stroll, a chat, a chat, a stroll, and, in the offing, first dysentery and then delivery to the Nazis.

One could stand it for a day or two, for a week, for a month. But in the long run a man in full possession of his health and his faculties could not endure it. You were sure at every other turn to meet some acquaintance with a face shrouded in gloom who would wave you violently aside when you asked him what the matter was; there was always someone who was sniffling quietly to himself or someone who was sobbing aloud.

Our *cafard* expressed itself in other and very strange forms. One pitch-black night when I had gone out to the latrines, I heard a voice issue from the dark, unaccented but positive and spiteful: "And to think that my ancestors settled in Rothenburg across the Tauber in the year 1400." That was all, and the man who said that certainly had no idea that anyone would hear him—I never knew who he was.

It was summer and usually very hot at high noon. But mornings and late afternoons it was pleasant to take walks out in the lovely surroundings.

I took such walks frequently in company now with the writer R., now with Herr Wolf, who liked a comfortable pace and a comfortable talk, now with Herr Cohn, who thought a walk was a cross-country run. Before long Herr Cohn knew all the farm people in the neighbourhood and talked in jovial familiarity with them. If you went to walk with Herr Cohn, you were sure to be invited to a glass of wine and to come home with beer, butter, or an occasional chicken, obtained at very reasonable prices.

It was against the rules to take such walks, and one had to look about before crossing a public highway if one would not come afoul of some police patrol. Dignity was hardly the word to describe us as we crouched low in a ditch, then craned our necks to see how the land lay, and finally darted across a road behind a bush or over a hedge in guilty haste, to be gazed at suspiciously by some autoist who chanced to be passing. But the walks more than repaid the humiliation. It was a delightful country of infinitely varied aspects at every turn—old farmhouses, now occupied, now deserted, thickets, broad, flat uplands, blue hills with graceful, magnificently sweeping curves, distant vistas over the towns of Uzès and Nîmes, a swift stream that wound snakelike with many twists through a deep ravine, high bridges, ancient cloisters.

One of our company had acquired great skill in cutting gnarled knotted walking-sticks out of a sort of stout rush. They were useful curios and with them we walked, raced, climbed about, half naked in our tattered shirts and patched trousers, and sandals of cloth and hemp. We would have preferred to wear shorts or even bathing trunks, had not the French sense of propriety forbidden such things.

Quite apart from whiskies, wines, and food one could have all sorts of amusements in camp and for very little money. Partners were available for any imaginable game of cards. Shrewd speculators set up roulette tables, though games of chance had considerable sentiment against them. Gambling dens were certain sooner or later to be raided by crowds of internees, who would rush the tables, smash the equipment, confiscate any loose cash, and beat up the banker and his customers.

Musical enterprises were multiple and varied. Two or three times a week we would be invited, by notices posted on trees, to attend a "big cabaret and floor show." Several hundred men would sometimes gather

233

on such occasions in front of an improvised stage. Offerings were not
exactly bad, though as a rule they were fairly vulgar. Noticeably better
were the occasional performances given in the small cafés or restaurants.

By "restaurant" or "café" or "bar" one must understand a sort of
hut, made of tent-poles or sapling trunks, covered over with a loose layer
of green branches. Under this leafy shelter one would find two or three
improvised tables and benches at which as many as a dozen men might
be accommodated. Fifty or sixty people would gather outside these huts
when there was singing or instrumental music inside.

I have a vivid memory of one "cabaret evening" in particular in one
of the restaurants. The writer R. and Herr Wolf were with me. A man
in the tent next adjoining had gone fishing in the stream and had sold
us his catch. We had had the fish cooked at the restaurant. They turned
out well, especially when supplemented with a bit of local wine. The
cabaret evening began when we had finished our meal. An excellent
violinist played a number with a harmonica accompaniment instead of
an orchestra. Next came a night-club singer who had been famous in
Berlin. The Nazis had first sent him to a concentration camp in northern
Germany and then to Dachau. During his stay in those camps the Nazis
had kept him at hard labour all day and then at night, though quite
exhausted, he had to sing to them for their entertainment. To us now he
recited and sang the witty verses and songs, filled with such a healthy
hate, that had won him fame in the old days in Berlin.

A cabaretist from Vienna, a man of extraordinary talent, next
appeared and we had him sing "Die Moorsoldaten" (The Peat-Bog
Soldiers), that ballad of Germans interned by Nazis, one of the most
agonizing songs in the world, which one never forgets once one has
heard it. As he sang it we joined in, humming or singing the tune with
him. After that he sang a song that he himself had written there in the

camp of San Nicola, a lullaby for a child born of a German mother in France while her husband is a prisoner in a concentration camp. This song, too, of the popular variety, mournful and with savage thrusts at French hospitality, had a catchy refrain, so that at the end of his third stanza we were able to join in and sing it with him.

So through the evening we sat there, listening, singing, drinking. Through the green branches of our shelter we could see a great full moon, round, red, while all about us were stench and haggling and shouting and laughter and sickness and despair. And the week before a man had killed himself and that week another.

Every day fresh rumours about the application of the extradition clause circulated through the camp. The Nazis had handed in their list, a list of two thousand names, or rather, no, only forty names; and then, later, none of the names of men in the camp were on the list—it referred only to renegades from the National Socialist Party. We believed such rumours, for an hour, for a day.

Sometimes a rumour would be embellished with a declaration of its exact source, now the prefecture in Nîmes, now Staff Headquarters at Marseille, and, on occasion, reports actually did emanate from such sources, for there were still anti-Nazis in every office who kept us informed of everything touching our interest that they learned. Unfortunately the things they learned were unreliable or contradictory.

Several of our men who had been lucky enough to get to Marseille had, contrary to rules, received permission from the municipal authorities to stay on there. But the police were paying no attention to such permits and were ruthlessly arresting all Central Europeans whom they came across during their frequent raids. Men so arrested were not well treated. They were not allowed to get their belongings from their places of residence, and as a result they almost always lost everything they had. Certain former members of the Foreign Legion made a business of offering to recover property of this sort that had been left in hotels or private houses. But the owners rarely saw any of it again. If it had not already been stolen in the places where it had been left, it was appropriated by the commissioner.

Most of us nevertheless had our eyes fixed hopefully on Marseille. There the great majority of the populace was friendly toward us. There we would find friends who stood ready to make sacrifices in our behalf. With their help probably we could find ways to drop out of sight, to sink below the surface in that great city of so many nooks and corners. There, too, was a harbour, the sea, the one road of escape to some foreign land or at least to one of the colonies.

Though most of those who got as far as Marseille were arrested again and shipped back to camp, some few did make a success of it, did get away overseas. There was the case of W., for instance, who, on reaching Marseille, met a young Arab with whom he had had a previous acquaintance. The Arab had a job on a ship of the line running to Algeria. He smuggled W. and one other man aboard, and they were now in Casablanca or perhaps even farther along. The story emanated from a man whom W. and the Arab offered to take with them. But he had decided not to risk the venture. Now remorsefully and enviously he talked of the luck of his more courageous comrades, and enviously and longingly we listened to him.

No trace of discipline was now left in camp. Wives and sweethearts of internees boldly appeared just beyond the barbed wire and their men openly went out to join them.

Officers and guard patrols still ordered the women away. "You can't stay here," they would say, and then add jocularly and crassly: "We'd all like to sleep with our wives." And then, finally, in an undertone: "Go a little farther away, or better into the woods where we don't have to see you."

Our old friend Weinberg had had his dog with him even in Les Milles. Now he was having visits regularly from his wife, a Frenchwoman. Dog, wife, and Weinberg, reunited, would go on walks together, he again in tasselled nightcap and dirty pajamas, she prettily and neatly gowned, and the dog capering and yelping delightedly about them.

On the edge of the woods across the field where men and women were now habitually meeting, I saw my helpful Madame L. again and with her the Frenchwoman with whom I had had luncheon in Nîmes, the friend of the Berlin lawyer. The two women were picnicking with their respective men and having a great battle with flies and mosquitoes. Madame L. had meanwhile not relaxed her efforts in my behalf. She had written scores of letters trying to discover the whereabouts of my wife and she had heard that Frau Feuchtwanger had been interned at Gurs, then released, then interned there again. Now, apparently, she had been released a second time and was en route to Sanary. One never could tell about travelling in France in those days, and it might well be weeks before my wife would reach our neighbourhood or Sanary.

At this point I cannot resist setting down a word in praise of our women. They behaved magnificently through all this ghastly experience. They may have complained at times or at times scolded, but there were very few cases of nervous breakdowns or weeping hysterics. Our wives, German women or French women as they may have been, stood loyally by us and wisely, cool-headedly, did what they could to help us all. They were allowed greater freedom of movement than we men. They were less closely watched—even in that desperate emergency the Frenchman remained gallant. With shrewdness, a certain amount of good looks, and a dash of coquetry our women could obtain favours for us in many different directions. Very few shrank from the hardships and dangers of the journey to Nîmes. They came to see us from all parts of France. Now without papers, now with papers obtained by one device or another, they found ways to get through to our tent city.

The erotic played a surprisingly insignificant role in life at our camp. Of course one heard most shocking remarks now and again, and the white canvases of our tents were often defaced with primitive expressions of obscenity; but the prisoners did not suffer from erotic privations to any such degree as I had foreseen.

On the other hand, family ties, the tie between man and wife, held firm in almost all cases. Many a time it would have been possible for husband or wife to escape alone without the corresponding partner, but exceedingly few took advantage of such opportunities.

The sick became more and more numerous in our camp and the general health of all of us progressively deteriorated. The doctors explained that hospitals in the neighbourhood were overcrowded and that opium and other necessary medicines were not to be had; in other words, they simply gave us up.

Many of the guards deserted, refusing to stay on in such a plague spot. Health inspectors came, one after another, shook their heads, declared it was all a crying shame, ordered the latrines sprinkled with chloride of lime, and issued a few dozen commitments to hospitals. That was all. Nothing decisive, effective, was ever done. Some two hundred of us fell sick of dysentery one after another. Those who were not yet afflicted expected, with a kind of fatalistic resignation, to catch the disease any day.

Of the many physicians among the internees some enjoyed Continental renown. Dr. L., Madame L.'s husband, for instance, as I have already noted, had been physician-in-chief to prison camps during the First World War and was regarded as an expert in the sanitary organization of such camps as ours. He pointed out to the authorities in charge of us that the use of a few inexpensive remedies would rid us of most of our troubles. The commandant and the French doctors listened courteously but answered that unfortunately not even those inexpensive remedies could be obtained.

Luckily the malady that was epidemic among us was of a mild form. Very few died of it. A patient generally ran a high temperature for a certain number of days, after which the fever would rapidly abate. Meanwhile he would suffer a constant diarrhoea with loss of blood, which reduced him to utter weakness. A man suffering from dysentery offered a spectacle of the most pitiable debility; he could scarcely get about on his feet.

THE THIRD NIGHT

I fell sick under the following circumstances.

I had eaten a good meal at midday and in the afternoon had taken a walk. The weather was close, sticky. Ordinarily the mosquitoes did not come out till just before evening, but that day they had tormented us from early morning. I had to visit the stench zone several times in the course of the afternoon and became aware of symptoms of weakness and dizziness toward evening. Herr Wolf and I had rooted up a bottle of especially fine wine through the good offices of our supply man, the orthodox Jew, and we had invited the writer R. to dinner, knowing well that he would be able to appreciate the fine quality of our trophy. I did not want to spoil the fun and refused to admit even to myself that I was sick. I sat down with the others but was soon unable to hold out any longer and retired to my tent.

The usual mosquito smudge had been lighted out in front and the smoke that filled the whole tent seemed to trouble me. However, I simply could not keep on my feet and, smoke or no smoke, had to lie down. Karl came to help me with the usual evening chores. He did not like my looks and called one of our physicians, Dr. L., a young Austrian. Dr. L. shook his head and gave me a medicine, but was afraid that it might be too late.

In spite of the smoke and noise I dropped off into a dull half-stupor. I was conscious of my tentmates coming in, undressing, and going to bed. My fever was soaring. Everything swam before my eyes—the mosquito veils of red and green gauze that the men were wearing, the flickering lights, the red moon still not long past the full, the Brueghelesque hubbub all around. The outlines of the two cantors, of the bushy-bearded, gnome-like, red-headed lawyer, of the prissy old judge, of good-natured, plumpish Herr Wolf, all melted one into another. I was suffering miserably from my fever, from weakness, from the noise roundabout.

An attack of cramps came and in spite of my weakness I had to rise and go out into the hot, steaming night. I staggered through the tent city to the latrine. Yes, there was blood. I started back toward the tent, dragging myself along—a painful, endless journey. Would I ever get there? There it was at last. I crept inside and collapsed exhausted upon my pile of straw.

I lay there in great distress. Noises from outside and within, snoring, groaning, wind-breaking, all the sounds of sleeping men. I did not think I would recover. I was deathly weak, fever was clouding my brain. I was going to die, I longed to die.

Figures began to dance before my eyes. No, it was not a "dance." They reeled, they wheeled, they made the vague uncertain flight of bats. They were bats. No, they were not bats, they were not real things, they were figures from Goya.

What did it matter whether they were real or Goyas? They were filth, they were dung. Everything was foul; everything was miserable. Not only my present condition, my helplessness, the flat, degraded existence in the internment camp, the compulsion of being always with people and never alone; not only this, but my whole life till now, all fifty-six years of it—which, when I was well and in my normal frame of mind, seemed so good, so full and worthwhile—now struck me as senseless, empty, vile.

As a little boy I had been taught a bedtime prayer in Hebrew verse against the terrors of the night, and evening after evening was made to repeat it in my childish voice: "Look, there is the camp of Solomon encircled by heroes, three lines of them, heroes of Israel. Swords they hold, all, mighty warriors are they all. On each hip a sword to guard the king from the terrors of the night." I babbled the verses in my fever now.

They came, they went, and then they came back—in German, in verses of Heine:

Wo wird einst des Wandermüden
Letzte Ruhestätte sein?
Unter Palmen in dem Süden,
Unter…an dem Rhein?

What kind of trees on the Rhine—and they had to fit the meter—oaks, birches, beeches? Nothing fitted just right. I was desperate, for if I did not remember the tree, the exact tree, I would die.

I said to myself: If I find the right tree and the right word, I'll pull through. If I don't find them, I will die.

I did not find the tree or the word for it. So I would have to die and I was resigned to dying. Only, it seemed unfair that I should die there in that filthy camp among so many people, that Fate should not allow me to die alone and in peace.

A great longing swept over me for a clean white bedroom to lie in. Other illnesses passed through my mind, operations of mine, and what a comfort it had been in all my anguish to feel myself well cared for, to know that I had skilled physicians in attendance, and my wife's solicitude, and ever-watchful nurses, clad in white. Whiteness, neatness, that was what I longed for so desperately.

I had to get up again. Again I had to make my way out into the hot, steaming night. If only I could stop where I was; but no—it was against the rules. The men in the tents beat you up for doing that, no matter how sick you were. And rightly so, with so much infection about. I had to drag myself on beyond the tents. The road to the latrine was a long road—five minutes long, five hours long, five years long. I went on, swaying, with sagging knees, stopping at every few steps and catching my breath. At last I was there, the end of the camp grounds, but the latrine was still far away. I could not make it. I squatted down. Swarms of mosquitoes immediately attacked my bared thighs, but I was too weak to beat them off. Sweat streaming from every pore, I squatted there, and finally I collapsed, miserably, in blood and excrement.

I dragged myself back. One tent looked like another, with snores and moans coming from every one, and mosquitoes around them all. Here was Tent 67, then Tent 59, but where was Tent 54? Where was my tent?

So there I was on my back again, happy that death was near. What a useless life I had led. Often enough in hours of normal health I had debated the value of writing books. What did one accomplish by writing, what influence did one exert, what improvements did one effect? The nihilist intelligentsia had sustained the thesis that writing was merely a pastime like any other, an empty amusement of the writer like sports or liquor or whoring or what you will. I had never accepted that view. I had declared that a well-turned sentence, written and read at the right moment, could influence the life of a reader, and permanently. My personal experience had shown it to be true in myself and in others. But now in that bitter night I forgot all that and gave grim approval to the contention of the Nihilists that all writing, all living, all great things that were ever thought or done were stuff and nonsense.

I took a sentimental turn. Oh, if only I could see that woman again and that friend, go to the Prado once more, see the Velazquezes and the Goyas. Why should I have to die just then, such a short time before the final overthrow of the barbarians? I wanted to hear *Carmen* once more at the opera in Moscow. German rhymes began running through my head—*Wein, sein, geben, leben*—and I fashioned them into despondent phrases about wine and girls and "nevermore."

Und es wird ein Wein sein,
Und wir werden nimmer sein,
Und es wird schöne Mädel geben,
Und wir werden nimmer leben.

I had to get up again and again and again for the endless journey out into the night toward the centre of the stench.

It was a July night less than seven hours long. To me it was seven years long and more than that.

Karl came to help me dress. Herr Wolf asked how I felt and what I wanted for breakfast. I replied that I felt as wretched as a dog. We could not see each other clearly in the half-light of the tent. The men stooped over to look at me and shrank back in horror.

The young Austrian physician came in, accompanied by another physician. Their faces fell and they stepped aside to confer. They knew what French hospitals were like and did not send patients to them even in normal times, to say nothing of the circumstances then prevailing.

They thought of the camp infirmary more as a place to die in than to recover in. It consisted of a single room, bare and damp, in which the sick lay side by side infecting each other and mutually retarding improvement. To use the latrine a patient had to drag himself up a long, steep flight of stairs. The doctors concluded it would be better for me to stay where I was in the tent. But how was I, exhausted, to make the long journey through the tent city two dozen times a day to the latrines? We would have to have a bucket in the tent. Karl, alternating with a second man, could attend to emptying it from time to time.

Would the other occupants of the tent consent to such an arrangement? Could one even ask that much of them? The doctors put the question to them, and my tent companions without the slightest hesitation expressed themselves as agreeable. Not only that, they placed at my disposal a portion of their water ration, for cleaning the bucket.

I shall never forget my pitiable yet ludicrous plight as, weak and wretched, and supported by Karl, I squatted over the bucket, while the stout Herr Wolf stood guard at the tent entrance like an archangel to keep people away. Herr Wolf was especially magnificent in those dreadful hours. He procured—God knows how—a supply of the necessary opium which the French physicians were unable to obtain anywhere. He forced me to accept his sleeping bag so that I would not be cold at night, though that meant that he would himself be cold. That illness was one of the not many occasions in my life when I was to see myself unselfishly sustained and cared for by others. A mother could not have surrounded me with tenderer care than did plump little Herr Wolf. Karl and the young Austrian doctor too worked over me day and night.

Most of the time I lay in a dull semi-consciousness, dreaming a deal of nonsense and probably talking it aloud. I laboured indefatigably digging up from memory lines, poems, scenes from plays that I had been obliged to learn by heart at one time or another. It irked me that, try as I would, I could never find the name of the tree that Heine mentioned in the poem on the wanderer's rest.

It grew terribly hot in the tent around noon. I scarcely noticed it in the burning fever that beset me day and night. Now and then, with permission from Herr Wolf or the doctor, some friend would look in, stay a minute or two, say a few words, and then withdraw. All were shocked at my appearance.

I took practically no food—my diet was tea, morphine, liquor.

Mixed with so much alcohol, the tea began to disgust me before very long—my brain was already dull enough. The doctors insisted that I continue it, however.

My high fever took a sudden drop on the fourth day. Then, however, I felt exceedingly weak, and I was consumed by a wolfish hunger. But I was not allowed any food. When in the morning and in the evening of the fifth day I was allowed a zwieback with my tea it was thought to be a great concession.

Finally the day came when I could go out in front of the tent for the first time and sit in the sun. Many people came by, stopped for a moment, and expressed their sympathy. Again my ghastly appearance seemed to shock them.

After a brief period of relapse I became definitely better and my allowance of food was increased, first cocoa with zwieback, then wine with an egg.

It has always been a blessed experience with me after an illness to feel that I was recovering. Now again my whole being seemed to become conscious of the strength, the life, the muscular control that was streaming back into my body. When I was able to walk a little, and was no longer bound to the stench zone, my happiness mounted. I took deep breaths of the beautiful free air, eagerly inhaled the fragrance of woods and fields, gazed voluptuously at the hills and the sky. I felt that I was alive.

A day or so after, I received an unexpected summons to go and see the commandant. That was a rare occurrence in the camp; the commandant seldom saw anyone who had not asked for an interview. I set out tense with curiosity. As I was waiting outside the office in the stone-paved yard I asked the interpreter what it was all about. All that he could say was that a telephone call in my regard had come from Staff Headquarters. Hope rose high in me. Perhaps the efforts my friends had been making were bringing results after all. Perhaps I would be sent back to my Sanary provided with a genuine discharge certificate, perhaps across the borders, perhaps overseas.

"You sent for me, Captain?" I said.

"Yes," he answered. "I wanted to make sure you were about. Take my advice, don't leave the camp."

I stood there disheartened. What did he mean? What was it all about? I tried to frame a question so that his answer would give me some hint as to what was really wanted of me.

"C'est ça. That's all. Thank you," he said before I could put my question. I had no choice but to withdraw.

The beautiful day had turned grey for me. What could lie behind the strange admonition? Had the dreaded list come in? Were the Germans demanding my surrender? "Don't leave the camp"—what did that mean? The opposite of what it said? I went over our brief conversation in my mind, studying each sentence, examining each word from all possible angles. I could make no sense of it at all. I asked other men what they thought. They too could make nothing of it. I walked about in the greatest depression.

The following day I was taking a walk in one of the fields near the camp when I heard my name called. I hurried in the direction of the voice and as I drew near the voice called again: "Come, your wife is here."

I broke into a run, reached the first tents, then my own. There she was sitting on the bench under the trees with Herr Wolf, Herr Cohn, and others gathered around her. She saw me coming and leapt to her feet. We had not seen each other for two months. For two months we had had only vague reports of each other. Now we were walking toward each other, alive and well. She stood still, her lips quivering slightly. My wife, Marta, is a good-looking woman of the athletic type. She was wearing a coarse skirt and a coarse blouse, and her hair had turned strikingly grey. My heart went out to her.

We were completely happy all that day, the first of our reunion. We were not prisoners any longer, not hemmed in by a thousand prohibitions; the menacing thought of our surrender to the Nazis faded away, the camp lost its noise and its stench because we were together again. She was over-exhilarated, laughed a great deal, and talked volubly and somewhat incoherently. Much of what she said was hard to understand. She ate avidly of such things as our traders had to offer. During her internment and on the fatiguing journey to San Nicola she had virtually starved. She was terribly hungry and had grown very thin.

Marta's arrival explained what had been at the bottom of my mysterious summons to the camp commandant's. She had not been able to find out definitely where I was. On a chance she had come to Nîmes and called on the military authorities in quest of information about me. A well-intentioned officer had got in touch with the commandant at our camp. My call to his office had been a friendly gesture on his part; he simply wanted to make sure that I would be on hand in view of my wife's expected arrival.

Marta did not complain much. She thought that as a result of her fine physical training the stay in camp had not told on her heavily. But her looks and her nervous incoherence did not bear out that optimism, nor did the inordinate hunger with which she threw herself upon any food that was set before her. All her life she had been noticeably moderate in eating; and my heart was therefore wrung with a double pity as I saw how her eyes remained fixed upon the food in unconscious greed as she talked. She had proudly brought fruit and chocolate along with her and was almost crestfallen when she saw that they made no great contribution to our menu. Things that she had procured in Nîmes with the greatest difficulty, we were obtaining in abundance at the camp.

Marta, as I said, made no great complaint of what she had had to go through, but the factual details that she recounted of the women's camp at Gurs sufficed to grip one's heart. Women were taken there in the last stages of pregnancy and children were brought into the world in the camp. Water was as scarce at Gurs as in most of the French internment camps, and when a child was born there many women went without their coffee for breakfast that their water rations might go to the young mothers.

Hygienic arrangements seem to have been no better than ours. The ground of Gurs, moreover, was mostly clay so that when it rained— and rains are frequent in the Pyrenees—the camp became one unbroken swamp. Women prisoners would often get stuck in the mud on the way to the latrines and would lose their shoes as they were pulled out.

The number of women internees at that particular camp varied, but ran around ten thousand. The French indiscriminately interned any women who had at any time had anything to do with Central Europe. (The department of Nîmes was a solitary and a notable exception.) My secretary was interned though she was of Swiss citizenship, and her sister, though a British subject. Even French mothers of French soldiers were interned if they had been born in Germany or were wives of Germans resident in France. It became clearer and clearer as time went on that no serious military consideration, even at the beginning, had dictated the internment policy. That policy was motivated solely by the hatred of Hitler's French sympathizers for the German anti-Fascists. How shamelessly far the French Fascists ventured to go I could myself see some weeks later from an editorial in an evening paper of Marseille,

Le Soleil. Under the harmless title "Postal Difficulties between Occupied and Unoccupied Zones," the article urged that the Nazis also take over the parts of France that were so far unoccupied.

Marta and I were able to see each other for several hours at a time during the four days she could be with me. Not once during that period did either she or I denounce the French authorities or the criminal folly of the edicts that had placed us in that situation. Both of us had long since learned to take the stupidity and indolence of men for granted and as things of which it was superfluous to speak.

Marta put her stay in Nîmes to good use by trying to help me. She constantly importuned the civil and military officials then in power to release me. She found them courteous and sympathetic. The effects of my recent illness were still visible. Marta was greatly shocked by my appearance and managed to transmit her anxiety to those gentlemen. One of them, an army officer, had an idea. He did not see how I could be released from camp from one day to the next without setting an unwelcome precedent. I could be transferred to a hospital and there, without attracting much notice, I could be granted indefinite leave of absence to convalesce at my own expense.

One day, accordingly, I was called before the camp physician, a new man.

"How do you feel?" he asked.

I had listened to Marta's account of the officer's plan with not more than half an ear, having long since lost all credence in the comforting words of French officials. The whole project had slipped from my mind and I had not the faintest idea of what the doctor was driving at in sending for me. I thought he had heard some criticism because of my bad condition and was thinking of putting me into our ghastly infirmary. I therefore replied: "Pretty well, thank you. Not at all bad."

The doctor told me to open my clothes, palpated my abdomen in a number of places, and asked: "Any pain?"

"No," I answered eagerly.

"So, then," he growled, "everything is all right. Put your clothes in order again. Thanks."

And with that I left his office. Neither he nor I had divined the shrewd manoeuvre of the Staff, and the ruse of the ingenious officer to get me out of camp came to nothing.

The camp authorities had been allowing us to go bathing in the stream nearby, and during those hot days several hundred of us went down there every afternoon. It was a full hour's distance on foot. A sergeant and a couple of soldiers were sent along with us. They paid no attention to us, but went about their own business.

The river—the Gard or the Gardon, I forget which—wound in just that region through a deep ravine that was most varied in character. At one point there would be a strong current, then places where the flow was so imperceptible that one felt one was swimming in a pool. Here the banks would be high rocky cliffs, there gentle slopes covered with grass, farther along wooded. The water, green and clear, would at some points reach depths of fifteen or twenty feet; at other points it would be very shallow.

Anyone who saw those two or three hundred men, men of every age, sporting naked in the water and sunlight, laughing, talking, chasing one another about, swimming, diving, displaying their skills, would scarcely have thought that he was looking upon prisoners, many of whom were in mortal danger and hardly any of whom knew what the future had in store for them.

For Karl especially those bathing expeditions were great events. He was an accomplished swimmer and diver and his passion for the sport was as great as his skill. Throw a coin into the water and he would come back with it every time, from no matter what depth. I enjoyed the hours at the river too. To be sure, the long walk back was often arduous for me. But on the other hand I was glad when I could tire myself out: I slept better at night.

Anarchy reigned in the land. No one knew for certain who had the right to command. When they were not at once replaced by others, the prefects expected to be dismissed before very long and hesitated to take any drastic measures. Only the vaguest instructions emanated from the central government, so called, and that government itself, being Fascist, was hated by the majority of the population and of the officials. The main responsibility for the defeat of France was laid at its door and it was thought to be intriguing with the Nazis. Enemies of the new government had desks in every office and were sabotaging its decrees while new appointees were prevented from getting the run of things. Continuity in the conduct of official business was ensured by the fact that the new men were as poorly paid as the old and therefore accepted bribes just as readily.

The newspapers published strict admonitions to soldiers that they should not demobilize themselves, and they were told that a man without his discharge papers would find it hard to get work. Many soldiers simply packed up and went home for all that, and those who stayed with their regiments did exactly as they pleased. So it was with the guards at our camp. A detachment of gendarmes from the Mobile Guard, the most reliable troops the country had left, were sent to reinforce them. But when the new arrivals saw that no beds had been provided for them at San Nicola and that they were exposed to the dysentery infection, they too deserted without more ado.

Our officers were at no pains to conceal a feeling that the task of watching us was a burdensome duty hardly less humiliating to them than to us. They thought of themselves as plain citizens and of their uniforms as mere window-dressing. One of them was a banker. He went around from tent to tent, trying to locate American dollars. He offered my Karl a commission if he would bring him people who had American currency to sell.

The barbed wire was still there of course, with sentries patrolling just inside it, but no one paid any attention. Our wives and children were now coming to the tents to see us. The days when they had to keep at a distance from the camp, anxiously hunting for places where they would not be caught by the gendarmes and guards, were long past. Now they walked boldly into the camp and stayed there all day long, sometimes all night long.

In that situation it would have been easy to leave the camp and take up residence somewhere in unoccupied France under much pleasanter conditions. But we had to think further ahead than that: our problem was to get out of the land, out of France. For the whole land of France had become one great prison, and its jailers were our fiercest enemies, the Nazis. The current prerequisite to an attempt to escape from France was the possession of papers in proper form. If it was inadvisable for soldiers to quit their regiments without discharge certificates, it was still more inadvisable for us to quit our camp illegally. A man whose situation was not "entirely regular" might manage to live comfortably for some days or even some weeks, but he would thereby be ruining his chances of ever leaving hostile Europe behind him. Without papers it was simply impossible to move from a hostile France across a hostile Spain and a not exactly sympathetic Portugal and thence reach an overseas country that was itself fussily bureaucratic.

So once more we began pestering the authorities to set us free at long, long last. We sent telegram after telegram to anybody who, we thought, might help us, especially to all the great American relief agencies. Whenever we heard that a Red Cross Commission or a delegation of Unitarians or of Quakers had arrived in France, our hearts would leap up and we would try in no end of ways to get in touch with them.

There had been an internment camp for Italians not far from San Nicola, so close at hand indeed that many of the men there had been in the habit of visiting us—they liked our concert evenings especially. This camp was now discontinued and the occupants set free with properly drawn certificates. That increased the unrest among us. When, oh, when, would they let us go?

French officials tried to comfort us—it would be a matter of days, at the most of a few weeks. A rumour began to circulate that the government had decided to order a first release of permanent residents in France who were in a position to be self-supporting. We had another attack of list-making and we began writing and telegraphing in order to marshal proofs that we had money or regular sources of income and permanent homes in France.

Cases were now becoming frequent where one or another of our number, usually manufacturers or businessmen, were being given leaves of absence for three or four days to attend to their private affairs. On one occasion one of these men came back to camp filled with happy excitement. He had had a talk with a government minister, and the minister had assured him that we would all be free in two weeks. We believed the story, yet did not believe it, and the man who had had the conversation with the high official began placing bets. There was a full moon, and the man wagered five to one that by the next full moon we would no longer be in the camp—and ten to one that we would no longer be there for the following full moon. He lost money on both bets.

One afternoon a rumour started that a final and conclusive order had at last come from the government at Vichy. Within the ensuing fortnight every last man among us would be free. The Foreign Legionnaires were to go the following day. The report emanated from the camp office and bore all the marks of genuineness.

The Legionnaires believed it. They packed up and in the evening gave a big party in celebration of the eve of their farewell. They drank themselves delirious, made more noise than ever, and sang their songs, which were a mixture of French obscenity and French patriotism. The Saarlanders thought that they were going to be released immediately after the Legionnaires, so they had their party too. They had made up a song in camp and composed the music for it, a sort of anthem full of sentimentality, love of the homeland, and smut. The Legionnaires and the Saarlanders tried to outdo each other in the fervour and volume of their singing. Then they passed to brawling and fisticuffs—it turned into a wild night.

Whether Legionnaire or Saarlander, nobody was released.

If a man did not mind a long walk he could find a little country restaurant in the best French tradition near a charming swimming pool some seven miles distant. By sending notice a day in advance you could be sure of getting a delicious, carefully prepared meal.

Herr Wolf and I decided to take one more excursion thither toward the end of July. A brother and a nephew of his, the writer R. and another of our friends, agreed to come with us. We had planned to start about nine in the morning, take our time on the beautiful two-hour walk, have a swim in the river, lunch at the excellent inn, then take a nap somewhere in the meadow behind it, and come back at our convenience.

It was a hot day and the road to the inn was mostly uphill and steep. In order to be as comfortable as possible I put on nothing but a thin, short-sleeved shirt, somewhat the worse for wear, an old pair of light-coloured trousers, and a pair of sandals with thick rubber soles. The trousers really had too many holes to be serviceable, but a tailor in the tent adjoining hastily patched them up.

We set out, first making the top of a long hill and following the crest high above the river. Then we took a stony path that traversed a wild stand of scrub oak, went down into a pretty valley, then climbed up again to a second hilltop, whence, within view of a high bridge, sharp-cut against the sky, and a beautiful convent, we clambered down a steep pitch straight to the river-bank.

We had a swim, lay about a bit on the grass, and then walked straight on to our restaurant. The host, attentive, solicitous, laid before us the menu that he had planned in advance. It met with our approval: a rich assortment of hors d'oeuvre, an excellent fish course with a light Alsatian wine, guinea-hen, potatoes and a lettuce salad, and a very decent Burgundy, then a dessert with a heavy Algerian wine, finally fruits, assorted cheeses, and coffee topped off with an old cognac. At table we talked politics, literature, and French cuisine. Our host expressed a number of political opinions considerably keener than the views the average professional politician in France had been delivering during all that period. The cognac, he insisted, should be on the house.

After the meal we felt full and somewhat tired, so we went on into the meadow behind the tavern, as we had planned, and stretched out on the ground. It proved to be a fairly hard bed, but the expanse of green was beautiful and there was no stench. We lay in a bit of shade that was flecked with sunlight.

I did not get a good nap. For the first time in a long while I had eaten beyond the craving of hunger and had consumed a good deal of wine. It gave me a headache and I soon woke up. I stared up at the sky from where I lay. It looked hazy and hot through the thin foliage overhead. Then I looked around at the other men. They were still asleep. My eye lingered long and closely upon the writer R. What a head, a heavy head, with a purplish, intelligent, muse-inspired face, somewhat puffy perhaps from drinking. It was the last time I was to see that face.

Herr Wolf awoke shortly after I did. He motioned to me and we rose quietly in order not to disturb the others. Herr Wolf's nephew had not slept at all. He joined us. He felt like exercising after our heavy meal. We went into the tavern, had another round of coffee, and set out on the way home, leaving word with our host for the others.

We decided to take the country road. It was longer, but not so hilly and made easier going. There was little motor traffic left by now and hardly any dust, and the road lay partly in the shade. We walked slowly. For a time I chatted with Herr Wolf, then we both fell silent. My headache was worse, I was tired. The way still to go seemed endless. I longed to be back "at home" at the camp and stretch out on my straw. How far away were we? Just ahead the path to the swimming hole near the camp branched off. That meant that we had gone almost two-thirds of the whole distance.

There, perhaps fifty yards on my side of the turn to the swimming hole, I suddenly saw Madame L. She had evidently been waiting to intercept me.

"They told me that you had gone bathing," she began hurriedly. "I have been waiting for you here. I have news for you from your wife." She handed me a letter. I stood looking at her completely dumbfounded. I did not know what to make of her sudden appearance.

"Thank you," I said, taking the letter.

"But read it," she urged. "Read it at once."

I tore the envelope open. "Do exactly as you are told," Marta had written to me in French. "Do not stop to consider. It is all straightforward and perfectly trustworthy." I read the note a second time, and then looked questioningly at Madame L.

She pointed in the direction of a nice car that was standing not far away on the roadside. Someone was getting out of the car, a young man, in fact I knew him well. It was astonishing to see him on that road, at that hour of the day! He was smartly dressed, and I remember every detail of his white summer suit, his knitted gloves.

"Don't stop to ask questions," he said to me, speaking in English. "Just get in. Don't delay. I will explain everything on the way."

I looked at him. Then I looked down at myself, my ragged short-sleeved shirt, my patched trousers, my sandals with thick rubber soles.

"Get in, please," he repeated, urgent. "There is a coat in the car."

Herr Wolf stood off to one side, waiting. One could see from the expression on his clever, good-natured face how hard he was trying to guess the meaning of all those strange proceedings. I shook his hand for one last time.

"Good-bye," I said. "Thanks again for everything. Please give Karl a few hundred francs and send what I have left in camp to Sanary."

Then I got into the car, followed by Madame L. There was in fact a coat in the car. It was a woman's coat, of light weight, with an English badge on the lapel. I pulled it around me. In a pocket I found a pair of dark glasses and a coloured shawl.

"Put them on, and the shawl too," said the smartly dressed gentleman as the motor started.

I did so. They made me look like an aged Englishwoman. So we drove off, at high speed, in that very good car, off out of the reach of the Devil in France.

PART FOUR

THE GARDENS OF MARSEILLE

And they heard the voice of the Lord God walking in the garden in the cool of the day.

I have written the fourth part of this book, but I cannot publish it as yet.* Some people who would have to be mentioned in its pages are in the midst of events still in progress, and the outcome of those events might be unfavourably affected if what they did in my case were to become known.

I am sorry I cannot publish the ending to my book. I have so far had to talk of many quailings, of much that was cowardly, weak, or petty. My last part would have far more to tell of courage, kindness, and readiness for self-sacrifice.

To five men I am particularly indebted. Had it not been for them, I could scarcely have surmounted the hardships and dangers that I had to face in the vile hell into which our lovely France has been transformed. Of the five, I can mention the names of only two: B. W. Huebsch and Waitstill Hastings Sharp.

I stand on the threshold of old age. My rages are losing their fury, my ill humour its teeth, my enthusiasm its buoyancy. I have met God in many forms, but the Devil also in quite as many. My delight in God has not lessened, but my fear of the Devil has. I have had to learn that the stupidity and the wickedness of men are as wild and as deep as the Seven Seas. But it has also been vouchsafed me to discover that the dike, which the minority of the good and the wise are erecting to contain them, is rising higher and stronger with every passing day.

*In an August 20, 1981, letter to Aufbau Verlag, Marta Feuchtwanger informed the editors at the publishing house that her husband had never written the fourth section of his memoir. "Lion Feuchtwanger intended to write the conclusion of *The Devil in France* after those left behind in Europe were safe from danger," she wrote. "However, this danger remained longer than expected, and in the meantime L.F. had long since become occupied with other projects." [Note appears courtesy of Aufbau Verlag.]

THE ESCAPE

Marta Feuchtwanger

I write this postscript only reluctantly, from a sense of duty that has complex underlying causes.

Readers who have reached this point in the documentary account deserve to find out how the episode—which represents a small fragment of the period's history—turns out. So I will resume the tale at the place where, for various significant reasons, Lion Feuchtwanger had to stop. Large numbers of hunted refugees were still on the hostile soil of Vichy France, which was teeming with Nazi henchmen. Later, I was also at risk of abduction while waiting in the port of Lisbon. I would not have been the only one to suffer that fate.

Partly sabotaged by consular officials hostile to the exiles, American aid organizations were trying to liberate as many as possible of those bound for the safety of America's shores from the grasp of the Third Reich's impending forces. In the boulevard cafés, there were already rumors of abductions of the parliamentarians Severing and Breitscheid, and of the chief editor of the *Berliner Tageblatt* Theodor Wolff.* For a time we felt safe (we were on American soil at the consulate, after all), in ignorance of the fact that the private villa of the consul Hiram Bingham was actually not part of the consulate itself. I was aware that his Swiss housekeeper, who was loyal to the family, was the sister of a Nazi, as the Czech maid had warned me of this. I tried to buy the housekeeper's goodwill with gifts. Perhaps more importantly, I stepped in for her in the kitchen on numerous evenings, allowing her to pay regular visits to her brother, a hotel chef. Bizarre situations of this kind were not uncommon, and I will try to recount all of these memories. Often I had to go into town to obtain entrance or transit visas at the various consulates. I always took the tram, which was a rattling old relic but allowed me to remain inconspicuous. On one occasion the only space available was on the small platform on the outside of the tram. I was perched there

*They died miserable deaths in the Nazi camps.

when someone tapped on my shoulder. My heart stopped; I thought I was being arrested, but it was only the conductor asking for the fare. On the steps of the consulate—if you were lucky, there was still somewhere to sit down—you were liable to meet acquaintances and friends who had turned up in Marseille from all over France. Among them was the well-known Heidelberg mathematician Emil Gumbel, who as a pacifist after World War I had coined the phrase "died on the field of dishonor." In return for this he was beaten up by students and dismissed from his academic post. Leo Lania also showed up, along with Leonhard Frank. Walter Mehring was arrested on the street in Marseille, dragged in chains from one camp to the next along with common criminals until, exhausted and sick, he was released thanks to Lion and Bingham's intervention. Mehring's clever girlfriend Hertha Pauli then took responsibility for getting him out of France. The long waits in the heat and dust were interminable but forgotten once you had the life-saving documents in your hands.

Lion, whom Bingham only permitted outside the house to take a few steps after sunset, was engrossed in the third novel of his Josephus trilogy, oblivious to the present and the world around him. Or if he was aware, he refused to let it show. Only Bingham was disheartened, often in despair over his own powerlessness. The State Department had forbidden him from providing the necessary visas to the swarms of people who besieged the consulate.

I remembered encountering long lines of people in the hot sun after my flight from the Gurs internment camp. The young, the old, and the very old told me that it was like this every day, and at five in the afternoon everyone would be sent home. I then did something which weighs on my mind to this day. I walked along the endless lines of people, who merely stared at me in silence, until I reached the consulate door. I handed over a note with my name on it and was soon let in. One of the consuls, who had visited us once in Sanary, did not recognize me, as I was so scruffy and emaciated. And then something remarkable happened. During internment I had kept my composure no matter what happened, as I had to keep everyone else's spirits up. But now that I was in safety for the first time, I thought of Lion and burst into tears.

Americans can't stand the sight of a woman crying. Something must be done, they said. And so Miles Standish, the younger of the two consuls, paid a visit to the mafia in the notorious harbor district and made inquiries. "Sure," he was told. "You want us to kill your mother-in-law....We do anything for money," but they didn't want to deal with the Nazis.

Standish said, "If no one else will, I'll have to do it myself." He explained he was planning to abduct Lion. He asked me for details about the San Nicola camp near Nîmes. I had been there myself, having managed to sneak into Lion's part of the camp with the help of a Russian taxi driver, who had brought me along in the guise of a black marketeer. The first person I had encountered there was the painter Max Ernst, thin as a skeleton, who took me to Lion.

I told Vice-Consul Standish it would be best to approach the camp in the afternoon. Some of the inmates were allowed to leave the camp and bathe in the river, where they were only lightly guarded. Who would dare escape in only their trousers? I also gave Standish a piece of paper to hold in the palm of his hand. I had written on it: "Don't ask any questions. Don't say anything. Just go with him." I didn't sign it, since I knew Lion would recognize my handwriting. And so it happened. Standish left the car parked behind bushes. He gave Lion a long coat and headscarf. When the car was stopped and Standish, with his American diplomatic pass, was asked who was sitting in the back, he replied, "This is my mother-in-law."

Lion stepped out of the car in Marseille, still in disguise, and found me waiting for him in front of the consul's house. Standish himself disappeared, and we never saw him again. After our safe arrival in America, we were determined to thank him, but no one knew his address. All I could ascertain was that he had left the consulate. Were his actions too bold or not in accordance with the regulations? Hardly a day passes without my thinking about him with profound gratitude. (What happens to our thoughts about others? Can they tell when we are thinking about them?)

Soon visitors arrived, unusual visitors sent by aid organizations, the Quakers, and Mrs. Roosevelt. When I broke down in tears at the consulate, Bingham said he already knew about Lion's case, and that both the consulate and the embassy were now under instructions to locate him and do their utmost to get him out. We later discovered what had been the first stone in the avalanche that led to the rescue of Hitler's personal enemy and the author of *Success*.

Without Lion's knowledge, someone had taken a photo of him behind the barbed wire at the Les Milles camp. This unknown person had sent the photo to Ben Huebsch, Lion's publisher at the Viking Press in New York. Huebsch, deeply shocked, had immediately driven to Washington to contact Mrs. Roosevelt. She showed the picture to the President, and the machinery of his rescue was set in motion. First a trade unionist appeared, a Dr. Frank Bohn. He had been informed by Mrs. Roosevelt that Lion was in jeopardy in France. Bohn, an energetic Irishman with a rich sense of humor, managed to find out that we were hiding out at consul Bingham's residence. Bohn was confident, saying, "I'll get them out whatever it takes." He rented an Italian boat, moored in a harbor some distance away, in which we were supposed to sail to Africa.

Lion then had an extraordinary conversation with Bingham. He said, "We need to fetch Thomas Mann's brother Heinrich from Nice. One of Thomas Mann's sons, Golo, is there as well, and he too needs to be rescued." Bingham replied: "I don't think a group as large as that was foreseen. We'll probably have to make a decision about which one we can take. Do you think we should take the younger one, Golo, or Heinrich? He's the more important of the two; on the other hand he has already lived his life…."

Lion said, "I can't compromise. We need to rescue them both." Bingham was persuaded. Golo arrived, and he too took refuge at Bingham's residence.

At that stage we were unaware that the Werfels were also in Marseille.

It was decided we should walk the 30 kilometers to the harbor where the boat was anchored. Heinrich Mann said to Lion, "Since you're advising me to come, I'll do so." Heinrich Mann was already quite old by then and not in good health.

Suddenly Dr. Bohn appeared and said, "All is lost." The boat had been seized by the Italians, who had spotted provisions being loaded onto it. We were quite lucky that we were not on board.

Then Varian Fry—a Quaker and a professor at Columbia University—turned up. He was working with the Red Cross, and was also under instructions to rescue us. He knew all about Lion and said that, come what may, he could bring Lion and me and Golo and Heinrich Mann and the Werfels to America. Having already rescued the Nobel Prize winner Otto Meyerhof and ensured that he reached America, Fry was well prepared. We would have to drive to Cerbère on the Spanish border and then pass through a tunnel beneath the Pyrenees into Spain.

The next time Fry appeared he was in a state of agitation. He said, "The regulations have been tightened very suddenly. You can only take the tunnel if you have an exit permit." The only option was to cross the Pyrenees on foot. Everyone else was in a stronger position than we: Werfel was Czech, Heinrich Mann had Czech papers, and so did Golo Mann.

Varian Fry drew Lion aside to tell him that everything was in order, but that he, Lion, would endanger the others. The entire rescue mission might be in jeopardy because of us. Lion understood this very well.

In the first edition of his book *Surrender on Demand*, Fry wrote: "Feuchtwanger sat immobile at his table as we told him what had happened. Feuchtwanger took the news very well. He had waited for weeks for the boat to take him to safety, and now his hopes of rescue were gone. All through dinner he talked and joked as if nothing more serious had happened than the last-minute postponement of a long-planned vacation."

Lion said nothing to me. He sat down at his desk in our attic room and continued writing the last part of the Josephus trilogy. He was asleep when I got up in the middle of the night to wake Golo and bring him his breakfast. But Golo was groggy and unaware of anything around him. I made myself scarce without saying goodbye.

At this point, the avalanche gained momentum. To be able to leave France, you needed an entrance visa to the U.S. The name Feuchtwanger was too dangerous, so Bingham came up with an idea. He asked Lion whether he had ever written under a pseudonym. Lion told a story: inspired by Sinclair Lewis's *Babbitt*, he had once published satirical ballads about America in the *Berliner Tageblatt* under the pseudonym J.L. Wetcheek, the quasi-literal English translation of his name.

The American consulate then proceeded to issue papers bearing the unremarkable name Wetcheek. Bingham made various preparations. But how would we actually make our escape?

Finally there was a breakthrough. A Mr. Sharp arrived from

America. Dr. Fritchman, a Unitarian minister in Los Angeles with ties to Mrs. Roosevelt, had been asked by her to do everything humanly possible to intercede on Lion's behalf. Fritchman had arranged for Waitstill Sharp, a minister of the Unitarian church in Boston, to travel to Marseille immediately. Here was Sharp, standing in the garden, seemingly brimming with confidence, telling Lion, "I've been sent for you." His wife, who had recently arrived from Czechoslovakia where she had rescued hundreds of Jewish children, was also in Marseille.

First of all, how would we get to the station? Marseille was full of manned roadblocks, and to travel you needed a pass. Mrs. Sharp had cleverly circumvented this problem. She found out that the city's station hotel was built right into the train station. She rented a room for herself and noticed by coincidence that inside the hotel, guests' luggage travelled along a narrow underground passageway to be loaded onto trains via the platform. The passengers meanwhile had to negotiate a manned roadblock outside the hotel.

During the night we made our way to the hotel, up to Mrs. Sharp's room, thence down into the cellar, and through the tunnel to the platform. Once on board the train, we felt a major obstacle fall away behind us. We reached Narbonne, where we changed trains and caught a glimpse of the beautiful old town. Sharp was somewhat nervous but he remained brave. We continued to Cerbère at the foot of the Pyrenees; beyond the mountains lay Spain. Sharp made various enquiries and came back in dismay, having confirmed that, as anticipated, without an exit permit we could not take the train and would have to go on foot.

Sharp at first thought he could bribe the border guards to let us take the road, as some of them were allegedly receptive to the idea and willing to help emigrants. But not all of the guards appeared trustworthy, and they were constantly being changed. There was too much uncertainty.

Sharp then reappeared with a young American named Ball, who had also been instructed by Varian Fry to help us. Ball showed me the route on the map but dared not come himself. Go as far and high as you can and avoid the roads, he advised. We were both good climbers, and as a skier I was accustomed to difficult terrain. I committed everything to memory, as we did not wish to be caught in possession of a map.

Initially we made our way through vineyards, but thereafter we found only rocky terrain. The main objective was to find the customs house or be summarily shot as smugglers. After a lengthy climb we heard voices below, and there we saw the customs house. We could not go in together because, although Lion had his American immigrant visa with the pseudonym Wetcheek, I had no visa or papers under an assumed name.

Lion went on ahead; I hid and watched him enter. He soon re-emerged and marched briskly down the mountain.

It was my turn. Once again, Bingham proved his worth. As he stuffed my rucksack and pockets full of cigarette packs, he had said you could get a lot done in Spain with Camel cigarettes. I went into the customs house and told the officers I wanted to bring the cigarettes but had heard there was an expensive duty on them, so perhaps I should simply abandon them. I tossed handfuls of packs onto the table. They all pounced, and one of them hastily stamped my papers without even a glance at my name or me. I have never run down a mountain so fast in my life.

We had agreed with Sharp to meet at the Cook travel office in Portbou. It was on the first floor of an unassuming building and was a well-known meeting point. Lion was not there when I arrived—only Sharp. I was shocked. Hunting through the town's restaurants, of which there many, all full of people, I finally found myself in the best one, and there was Lion, munching away with a satisfied look on his face. "Sit down and have something," he said. He had completely forgotten about our arranged meeting place.

The next morning we headed on to Barcelona, where further difficulties awaited. We needed to get to Lisbon but could not go by air, since it was a German Lufthansa plane. Moreover, it was Sunday and we needed money, which we could only get at the American consulate—which was closed. The energetic Reverend Sharp came to our aid once again, tracking down the consul at his private residence and rustling up enough money to allow us to take the train.

Before we left, Sharp had one request. He wanted us to accompany him to the Protestant parish outside the city, home to a small university. Protestants had been persecuted mercilessly in Franco's Catholic Spain, their schools shut down and the teachers imprisoned. According to Sharp, it would be tremendously supportive to the church if Lion were to visit. And perhaps he could be persuaded to do something for them in America. So we visited the Protestants, which proved a successful day for all concerned.

Sharp had determined that it was only possible to travel safely in the sleeping cars, which the police would not monitor closely. Since our funds only stretched to two tickets, I travelled third class, allowing Sharp to keep a close eye on Lion. Sharp gave Lion his briefcase bearing a highly visible Red Cross insignia, urging him to keep it with him at all times on the train. And this proved to be a good thing. When Lion adjourned to the sleeping car's bathroom, the door opposite promptly opened to reveal a Nazi officer in full uniform. The officer greeted Lion in traditional military manner and said in English, "Ah, the Red Cross." Lion concurred. The Nazi officer's English was tinged with Prussian, Lion's with Bavarian.

Third class was completely full and I had to stand. Still suffering from my spell in the internment camp, my legs were apt to swell whenever I stood for long periods. As I stood there in discomfort, I was greeted by an elderly man. "What's going on with this young lady? She needs a seat," he said and moved off up the train to look for one. On his return, he said in French, "Listen, I've found you a seat, come." I was reluctant, as I did not want to attract attention, but I accompanied him to an empty compartment nonetheless. Within moments of our sitting down the police appeared, snarling, "This is our compartment. You need to get out." The elderly man burst into a torrent of German profanity, which made the two policemen very pale. The sound of the German language, the language of the Nazis, scared them away. The old man was actually Swiss and a speaker of both French and German. He was also very cunning. I was now able to lie down and stretch out tolerably on the wooden seats.

At the Portuguese border everyone had to alight. We changed trains and were told to produce our papers. Lion and I stood at opposite ends of the platform, pretending not to know one other. My papers were the risky ones, bearing the name Feuchtwanger.

I was standing on my own on the platform in this way when a woman approached me. She asked in loud English, "Is it true that Lion Feuchtwanger is on board?" "Who's that?" I replied. "That's pretty philistine, not to know who Lion Feuchtwanger is," she answered. From some way off, Sharp had seen that something was amiss. He advanced. "What do you want from her?" he rasped. "I'm a journalist and hoping for a scoop," she said. "I'd heard Feuchtwanger was on board and wanted to let my newspaper know." Sharp told her in no uncertain terms to shut up. Didn't she realize idle chatter put people at risk? he asked. She became embarrassed, murmuring, "All I wanted was a scoop." All at once, everything went back to normal. The train arrived, and our papers were returned to us. Nothing could ever be easy or straightforward.

At Lisbon, Sharp took us straight to the American aid point for refugees. A friendly gentleman named Joy told us Lion could not stay in Lisbon and must board a ship as soon as possible. The city was full of Nazi spies, the so-called Fifth Column, he warned, and there had been numerous abductions already. The Portuguese government refused to take sides, cared little, and would not intervene in abductions, he said.

At the offices of the shipping company we learned there were no available berths for a fortnight. I do not know how Sharp managed it; at any rate, suddenly there were two tickets, and Lion was able to depart with Sharp, who had to return quickly.

I accompanied Lion and Sharp to the steamer to watch them board. Yellow, sulfurous dust lay everywhere, dotted with depressing pools of dirty seawater. A few ragged-looking figures could be seen here or there, but not many. Far too few, in fact.

That was the end of Europe. Lion was on board, alone, without me. It was hard for him, but I felt everything was fine. He was safe.

Two eventful weeks later, I too departed the inhospitable continent, secure in the knowledge that Lion was expecting me in the harbor of New York.

TIMELINE

MICHAELA ULLMANN

JANUARY 30, 1933

Adolf Hitler is appointed chancellor of Germany. At the time, Lion Feuchtwanger is on a reading tour in the United States. The German ambassador in Washington warns him not to return to Germany. Later that year, Nazi propaganda minister Joseph Goebbels calls Feuchtwanger "Enemy Number One of the German people" in a radio speech.

MARCH 1933

Following the ambassador's advice, Lion meets his wife Marta in Austria, where she had been vacationing. Together, they move to southern France. They soon learn that their house in Berlin has been plundered, and their library and possessions have been confiscated.

MAY 10, 1933

Led by the Nazi-affiliated German Student Association, university students burn more than 25,000 "un-German" books—including the works of Feuchtwanger—during the following weeks.

AUGUST 23, 1933

Lion Feuchtwanger's German citizenship is revoked for "disloyalty to the German Reich and the German people."

1934

The Feuchtwangers purchase Villa Valmer in Sanary-sur-Mer, France, where they join a growing community of German-speaking émigrés.

MARCH 12, 1938

Austria is annexed to the German Reich.

SEPTEMBER 1939

Lion Feuchtwanger is interned for the first time in the camp at Les Milles near Aix-en-Provence. He is released after 10 days.

1939 or 1940

Feuchtwanger's American publisher Ben Huebsch receives a photograph from an unknown source showing Lion Feuchtwanger behind barbed wire during his first internment at Les Milles. Huebsch contacts Eleanor Roosevelt, who helps to initiate plans for Feuchtwanger's rescue.

MAY 10, 1940

Germany invades Luxembourg, Belgium, the Netherlands, and France.

MAY 15, 1940

The Dutch army surrenders to Nazi forces.

MAY 19, 1940

German troops besiege Amiens, France, while Rommel's forces surround Arras, and other German units reach Noyelles.

MAY 21, 1940

Feuchtwanger is interned for the second time at the camp near Les Milles.

MAY 25, 1940

The French troops at Boulogne-sur-Mer surrender to German forces.

MAY 26, 1940

The troops defending Calais surrender to German forces.

MAY 28, 1940

Belgium surrenders to Germany; King Leopold III is interned.

JUNE 3, 1940

The German Luftwaffe bombs Paris.

JUNE 10, 1940

Italy declares war on France and the United Kingdom.

JUNE 11, 1940

The French government relocates to Tours.

JUNE 14, 1940

German troops occupy Paris, and the French government moves again—this time to Bordeaux. The same day, Feuchtwanger reports the news of Paris' occupation in his diary.

JUNE 16, 1940

After Paul Reynaud steps down, Philippe Pétain becomes prime minister of the French government. One day later, Feuchtwanger reports hearing rumors of an armistice.

JUNE 21, 1940

The Franco-German armistice negotiations begin at Compiègne. The Italian army invades France through the Alps and along the Mediterranean coast towards Nice.

JUNE 22, 1940

France and Germany sign an armistice agreement. Feuchtwanger and other Les Milles internees are transported by train towards Marseille. On June 23, the train continues from Cette in the direction of the Pyrenees.

JUNE 24, 1940

The Franco-Italian armistice is signed. Feuchtwanger and the other internees continue from Toulouse to Bayonne.

JUNE 25, 1940

France officially surrenders to Germany at 12:35 in the morning. Because of a false report that the Germans were just two hours away from Bayonne, the train with the Les Milles internees turns back towards Lourdes. The next day, it arrives in Nîmes. Feuchtwanger and his fellow internees continue on foot to the camp at San Nicola.

JUNE 27, 1940

Feuchtwanger learns of the armistice and the news that prisoners can be surrendered on demand to German officials.

JUNE 28, 1940

General Charles de Gaulle is recognized by the British as the leader of the *Forces Françaises Libres* (or Free French Forces).

JULY 1, 1940

The French government moves to Vichy, from which it administers the "free zone" of southern France, while the German army occupies northern France.

JULY 18, 1940

Marta Feuchtwanger visits Lion in the camp at San Nicola.

JULY 21, 1940

Nanette Lekisch hands Lion a note from Marta while he is bathing in a river near the camp. Following its instructions, Lion steps into a waiting car with U.S. Vice Consul Miles Standish. He arrives at the home of U.S. Consul Hiram Bingham in Marseille and is reunited with Marta. Known as the "Angel of Nîmes," Lekisch provided refuge to countless German émigrés during the Vichy period.

AUGUST 2, 1940

Charles de Gaulle is sentenced to death in absentia by a French military court.

AUGUST 11, 1940

The Feuchtwangers make plans to escape to North Africa in a smuggler's boat anchored in a harbor near Marseille. They are joined in Marseille by Heinrich, Nelly, and Golo Mann, as well as Franz and Alma Mahler-Werfel.

AUGUST 13, 1940

On *Adler Tag* (or Eagle Day), Luftwaffe Commander Hermann Goering starts a two-week assault on British airfields in preparation for the German invasion of Great Britain.

AUGUST 18, 1940

Bingham issues Feuchtwanger a U.S. entrance visa under the pseudonym of Wetcheek.

AUGUST 29, 1940

After their boat is discovered by Italian authorities, the Feuchtwangers abandon the plan to leave France by sea. Instead, they make plans to cross the southern border into Spain.

SEPTEMBER 1, 1940

Germany's Jewish population is ordered to wear yellow stars for identification.

SEPTEMBER 11, 1940

Feuchtwanger reports that the Manns and the Werfels plan to cross the Pyrenees with help from Varian Fry of the U.S. Emergency Rescue Committee. The Feuchtwangers cannot join them without endangering the others.

SEPTEMBER 14, 1940

Feuchtwanger receives a telegram confirming that his friends have made it safely across the Spanish border.

SEPTEMBER 18-19, 1940

With the help of Reverend Waitstill Sharp and his wife Martha of the Unitarian Service Committee, the Feuchtwangers travel by train from Marseille to Cerbère. From there, they must climb the Pyrenees to enter Spain illegally. After arriving in the Spanish city of Portbou, they meet up with the Sharps again. They proceed by train to Barcelona, where they board another train to Lisbon, Portugal.

OCTOBER 1940

The German forces in Warsaw begin plans to confine the Jewish population to the Warsaw Ghetto. In November, they wall it off from the rest of the city and post armed guards.

OCTOBER 2, 1940

The bombing of London continues throughout the month.

OCTOBER 4, 1940

Adolf Hitler and Benito Mussolini meet at the Brenner Pass to discuss war plans.

OCTOBER 5, 1940

Lion Feuchtwanger and Reverend Sharp arrive in New York on the *S.S. Excalibur.*

OCTOBER 18, 1940

Marta Feuchtwanger arrives in New York on the *S.S. Exeter.*

JANUARY 28, 1941

The Feuchtwangers leave New York for Los Angeles.

FEBRUARY 9, 1941

The Feuchtwangers officially enter the United States from Mexico by walking across the border at Nogales, Arizona. They live in Los Angeles with friends and in apartments while searching for a new home.

JUNE 22, 1941

During Operation Barbarossa, Germany and other European Axis nations—joined by Finland—invade the Soviet Union.

NOVEMBER 1941

Viking Press of New York publishes *The Devil in France*, Feuchtwanger's autobiographical account of his internment. In 1942, El Libro Libre of Mexico publishes the first German edition under the title *Unholdes Frankreich*.

DECEMBER 7, 1941

The Japanese navy attacks Pearl Harbor.

JANUARY 26, 1942

The first U.S. forces arrive in Europe.

OCTOBER 25, 1943

The Feuchtwangers move into their home at 520 Paseo Miramar in Pacific Palisades. The house, later called Villa Aurora, becomes a meeting place for European writers and artists during the war.

JUNE 6, 1944

On D-Day, the Allies invade northern France and later push south, leading to the defeat of the German Army in France. Paris is liberated by the French resistance.

APRIL 4, 1945

The U.S. 89th Infantry Division overruns Ohrdruf, a subcamp within the larger Buchenwald concentration camp. It is the first camp liberated by U.S. troops.

MAY 8, 1945

V-E Day marks the official end of World War II in Europe.

DECEMBER 21, 1958

Lion Feuchtwanger dies at Mount Sinai Hospital at the age of 74. He is buried at Woodlawn Cemetery in Santa Monica. Shortly afterwards, Marta bequeaths the Feuchtwanger estate to USC and is appointed the first curator of the newly established Feuchtwanger Memorial Library at their home in Pacific Palisades. She devotes the remainder of her life to promoting the work of her husband.

JUNE 5, 1980

Marta receives an honorary doctorate from USC.

OCTOBER 25, 1987

Marta dies at the age of 96 in Santa Monica. She is buried next to her husband at Woodlawn Cemetery.

AUGUST 31, 1995

A new space is dedicated for the Feuchtwanger Memorial Library inside Doheny Memorial Library on the USC campus, preserving the rare books from Feuchtwanger's collection. It endures as a testament to the Feuchtwangers and Lion's literary legacy.

DECEMBER 1, 1995

The Feuchtwangers' former home opens as an international artists' residence operated by the Friends and Supporters of the Villa Aurora in Berlin, which purchased the home in 1990 and oversaw its historic preservation. Villa Aurora displays rare books and artwork on loan from the USC Libraries, and the two organizations collaborate on a variety of cultural programs related to Feuchtwanger and writers in exile.

ACKNOWLEDGEMENTS

Special thanks to Marcos Carrillo, Martin Engelmann, Adrian Feuchtwanger, Alex Hagentorn, Lillian Lin, Martin Lorentz, Robert de Neufville, Lee Olvera, Tiffany Quon, Nicholas Tedesco, and Kevin Yan.